**W9-DHT-884**

# THE ECONOMICS OF IMPERFECT KNOWLEDGE

ECONOMISTS OF THE TWENTIETH CENTURY

**General Editors:** David Colander, *Christian A. Johnson Distinguished Professor of Economics, Middlebury College, Vermont, USA* and Mark Blaug, *Professor Emeritus, University of London, Professor Emeritus, University of Buckingham and Visiting Professor, University of Exeter*

This innovative series comprises specially invited collections of articles and papers by economists whose work has made an important contribution to economics in the late twentieth century.

The proliferation of new journals and the ever-increasing number of new articles make it difficult for even the most assiduous economist to keep track of all the important recent advances. By focusing on those economists whose work is generally recognized to be at the forefront of the discipline, the series will be an essential reference point for the different specialisms included. Wherever possible, the articles in these volumes have been reproduced as originally published using facsimile reproduction, inclusive of footnotes and pagination to facilitate ease of reference.

A list of published and future titles in this series is printed at the end of this volume.

# The Economics of Imperfect Knowledge

## Collected Papers of G. B. Richardson

G. B. Richardson

*Formerly Chief Executive of Oxford University Press and Warden of Keble College, Oxford, UK*

ECONOMISTS OF THE TWENTIETH CENTURY

**Edward Elgar**

Cheltenham, UK • Northampton, MA, USA

Published by
Edward Elgar Publishing Limited
8 Lansdown Place
Cheltenham
Glos GL50 2HU
UK

Edward Elgar Publishing, Inc.
6 Market Street
Northampton
Massachusetts 01060
USA

*HB*
*103*
*.R53*
*A25*
*1998*

A catalogue record for this book is available from the British Library

**Library of Congress Cataloguing in Publication Data**

Richardson, G.B.
    The economics of imperfect knowledge : collected papers of G.B.
Richardson / G. B. Richardson.
    (Economists of the twentieth century)
    Includes index.
    1. Economics.   I. Title.   II. Series.
HB 103.R53A25   1998
330—dc21
                                                                98–21067
                                                                     CIP

ISBN 1 85898 849 7

Printed and bound in Great Britain by
Biddles Ltd, Guildford and King's Lynn

# Contents

# Acknowledgements

The publishers wish to thank the following who have kindly given permission for the use of copyright material.

Blackwell Publishers for articles: 'Equilibrium, Expectations and Information', *Economic Journal*, **LXIX** (274), June 1959, 223–37; 'The Pricing of Heavy Electrical Equipment: Competition or Agreement?', *Bulletin of the Oxford University Institute of Economics & Statistics*, **28** (2), 1966, 73–92; 'The Organisation of Industry', *Economic Journal*, **82** (327), September 1972, 883–96.

Carfax Publishing Limited for article: 'Planning Versus Competition', *Soviet Studies*, **XXII** (3), January 1971, 433–47.

Oxford University Press for articles and excerpt: 'Imperfect Knowledge and Economic Efficiency', *Oxford Economic Papers,* **5** (2), June 1953, 136–56; 'Schumpeter's *History of Economic Analysis*', *Oxford Economic Papers*, **7** (2), June 1955, 136–50; 'Demand and Supply Reconsidered', *Oxford Economic Papers*, **8** (2), June 1956, 113–26; 'The Limits to a Firm's Rate of Growth', *Oxford Economic Papers*, **16** (1), March 1964, 9–23; 'The Theory of Restrictive Trade Practices', *Oxford Economic Papers*, **17** (3), November 1965, 432–49; 'Price Notification Schemes', *Oxford Economic Papers*, **19** (3), November 1967, 359–69; 'Adam Smith on Competition and Increasing Returns', in A. S. Skinner and T. Wilson (eds), *Essays on Adam Smith*, Oxford: Clarendon Press, 1975, 350–60.

Every effort has been made to trace all the copyright holders but if any have been inadvertently overlooked the publishers will be pleased to make the necessary arrangements at the first opportunity.

# Introduction

Mr Elgar has requested me to write an autobiographical introduction which, in his words, would trace my intellectual development and the influences on my work throughout my career. I have done my best, but find that I cannot answer the question which most interests me: what was it that led me, from the beginning, to take up the very particular theme, which I continued to develop, with variations, throughout my career as an economist?

I happened to learn, after his death, that Sir John Hicks, in writing about me for a particular purpose, remarked that my academic work became, at an early stage, very specialized. All I can plead, in extenuation, is that the issue which from the beginning claimed my almost exclusive, even obsessional, attention seemed to me fundamental to economic theory generally. Perhaps the focus was narrow, but the aim was ambitious. I set myself to enquire how the working of an economy was affected by the obvious fact that decisions are taken within it on the basis of knowledge that is imperfect, in the sense that it is both uncertain and fragmented. In the process of this enquiry, I came to reject some accepted doctrine. Scarcely anyone paid attention, at the time, to what I was writing, and although there has now been some awakening of interest, my ideas, for good reasons or bad, have not entered the mainstream of economic thought.

But this is to anticipate. Let me start at the beginning, with an account of why I first took up economics. My first degree was a BSc in what, at the University of Aberdeen, was called 'Pure Science', essentially mathematics and physics but, because of the war, shortened to two years and skewed towards what was relevant to radar. After three years in naval (and later, political) intelligence, I went up to Oxford and read PPE (Philosophy, Politics and Economics), this course also having been temporarily shortened to two years.

I was fortunate in having Sir John (then Mr) Hicks as a tutor, but for reasons that reflect no credit on myself, I happened, at a university theory seminar, to present a paper on Keynes's *General Theory*, and chose to give a highly mathematical account of it. The paper had no merit, being contrived chiefly to show off my knowledge of mathematics, a qualification rarer in those days than it is now. Frank Burchardt, who presided at the seminar and who had originally agreed to be my tutor, decided that Hicks, being better able to cope with mathematics, be asked to take me on. My term with Hicks went well and he encouraged me to take up economics as a career. I had, however, already decided that I wanted to join the diplomatic service and, having passed the necessary examinations, this is what I did.

Many of us are not closely programmed to do one thing or another. Such was my case and, although Foreign Office work was congenial, I came to think, after not much more than a year, that I might after all prefer to be a don rather than a diplomat. I wrote to Hicks accordingly and he helped me to get a Studentship at Nuffield (then his own) College; shortly afterwards, in 1951, I was elected to a Fellowship at St John's.

The terms on which, in those days, one could get a Fellowship affected, both for good and ill, the work I did. The custom then, at Oxford and Cambridge, was to offer tenured appointments to the young, on the basis of promise rather than performance. Those elected to Fellowships could then take the long view, without pressure to publish other than that exerted by the desire for recognition and self-fulfilment. On the other hand, they were likely to lack the width and depth of knowledge, within economics, that those obtaining permanent positions would now normally have. In my own case, having studied the subject for only two years, and only part of PPE, this disability was acute.

There were other circumstances then prevailing at Oxford which may have encouraged me to follow an independent line of thought. I had originally applied to read for a doctorate, for which I should have had supervision, but was persuaded by St John's to withdraw, the argument being that those elected to a Fellowship did not need this further qualification. There were then fewer economists in Oxford than there are now. I was the first Fellow in economics at my own college and, as I had to work also for another one, my teaching load, by modern standards, was very high. There was no departmental structure, no hierarchy and no building where I regularly met other economists on a daily basis. In the event, discussion played scarcely any part in the development of my ideas. In those days, joint articles were rarer than now and the total volume of publication much less. The current practice of citing all the relevant literature had not yet been adopted. These several circumstances may have influenced the path I chose, but I cannot say whether I might not have chosen it, sooner or later, in any case.

The articles which I published in *Oxford Economic Papers* in 1953 ('Imperfect Knowledge and Economic Efficiency') and 1956 ('Demand and Supply Reconsidered') pre-figure most of the ideas which I developed later in my book, *Information and Investment*. Where then did these ideas, right or wrong, come from? 'Expectations' were much under discussion at the time, but in a way that left me with misgivings. In Part 3 of *Value and Capital*, entitled *The Foundations of Dynamic Economics,* Hicks postulated so-called 'certain expectations', of which producers' supply plans were a function. He was well aware that expectations would in fact be uncertain, but thought it acceptable, for the purposes of his model, to deal in certainty equivalents, where a certainty equivalent was defined as 'the most probable price plus or minus an allowance for the uncertainty of the expectation, that is to say, an allowance for risk'.

In 'Imperfect Knowledge and Economic Efficiency', I consider some of those forms of business behaviour which cannot be explained on the basis of certainty equivalents, it being necessary to take the uncertainty of expectations into explicit account. In 'Demand and Supply Reconsidered', I go on to argue that it is wrong to represent the traditional supply curve for a commodity as relating 'planned supply' to 'expected price', as was done by Hicks in *Value in Capital* and, of course, by economists very generally. It never occurred to me at the time that Hicks, who had invested so much in the ideas I was attacking, might at some level, resent my subversion. Our personal relationship remained untroubled, but on the basis of a tacit agreement to disagree.

The ideas which I introduced in these early articles arose by way of negative reaction to the way in which expectations were at that time being discussed. But there was one article which influenced me very positively: Hayek's 'Economics and Knowledge', published in *Economica* in 1937. Here I found some of the notions that were beginning to form in my own mind. Hayek provided an analysis of the imperfection of knowlege more profound than any other I had read. Most economists seemed to believe that they had taken this imperfection into account merely by assuming that expectations were uncertain, nothing being said as to whether these expectations were held by some or by all entrepreneurs, were conflicting or were consistent. For Hayek, on the other hand, the imperfection of knowledge implied its dispersion, in fragmented form, among a multitude of minds and in the form of beliefs that were partial, uncertain and sometimes conflicting. The great achievement of prices and markets was to arrange, through the continuous interactive mutual adjustment of individual plans, that resources were rationally allocated throughout the whole economy, despite being based on plans and decisions made by people, each of whom could only see a tiny part of the total picture. Hayek's vision was essentially the same as that which inspired *The Wealth of Nations*, but so formulated that I saw it freshly. I became more than ever convinced that it was absurd to try to explain the working of the market economy in terms of models which postulated 'perfect knowledge' (whatever that might mean), when it was precisely the uncertainty and fragmentation of knowledge that gave to the system its essential rationale.

I imagine that writers chiefly influence those whose own nascent ideas render them susceptible; thinking, as constrasted with just being logical, takes place somewhere between the conscious and the unconscious mind, and Hayek's message came through to me clearly because I was on the right wavelength. When I published *Information and Investment*, I sent him a copy saying how much I owed to his work, but got no reply; perhaps he did not receive the book, or did not read it, or disapproved of the way in which my own thinking had by that time diverged from his. But this is to anticipate, so let me return to the narrative.

My 1953 article dealt with features of real-world economies that have to be explained in terms of the imperfection of knowledge. But, although it had this organizing theme, I allowed myself (as Sir Roy Harrod said to me) to 'ramble rather', failing to realize that in order to catch the reader's attention one should make one or two points clearly and not take him on a wandering *tour d'horizon*. The article's treatment of probability was much influenced by Keynes, whose *Treatise on Probability* I read about that time, and my discussion of liquidity was inspired by Menger, whom I read, while an undergraduate, on the wise advice of John Hicks. These are themes which I took up again in *Information and Investment*, but thereafter abandoned.

In any event, this first article attracted no interest whatever, either inside Oxford or elsewhere. My next publication was the review article, published in 1955, on Schumpeter's *History of Economic Analysis*. It was highly presumptuous of me to have taken this on, given how little of this history I myself knew, but I doubt if other Oxford economists at that time knew much more, with the notable exception of John Hicks. I had read Schumpeter's *Capitalism, Socialism and Democracy* while an undergraduate, and had been drawn to his analysis of the process of competition.

His *History* impressed me greatly, even though his prejudices (which gave the book such wonderful vitality) were not all congenial to me. I thought that he seriously underrated Smith, and doubted his claim (without having the knowledge to refute it) that 'the *Wealth of Nations* does not contain a single analytical idea, principle or method that was entirely new in 1776'. I tried to do justice to Smith, in relation to one neglected strand of his thinking, in the article 'Adam Smith on Competition and Increasing Returns', which I wrote twenty years later. Schumpeter's underrating of Smith, it seemed to me, was matched by his overrating of Walras, whose system, he claimed, 'is the only work by an economist which will stand comparison with the achievements of theoretical physics'. For me, Walras was no Newton; despite the comparisons that he explicitly makes between the economic and the astronomic universes, I knew enough economics and enough physics to know the difference; we do not study the movement of the celestial bodies in terms of intention, expectation or knowledge; with economic phenomena, which are about what people do, we cannot do otherwise.

Schumpeter's position is curiously paradoxical. He put Walras on a pinnacle in the belief that he was 'the discoverer of the fundamental economic problem', which he took to be the question of whether analysis of the interdependence of all economic phenomena 'will yield relations sufficient to determine – if possible uniquely – all the prices and quantities of products and productive services that constitute the economic "system"'. It was for this reason that he regarded Walras's 'system of equations' as the Magna Carta of economic theory and why he thought that 'the history of economic analysis ... might be written in terms of this conception's gradual emergence into the light of consciousness'. How difficult it is to reconcile this statement, which seems to me now almost absurd, with the account that Schumpeter himself gives of the competitive process in his *Capitalism, Socialism and Democracy*! Perhaps he most respected contributions of the kind that he himself could not make and, for that reason, properly judge.

Hicks, like Schumpeter, thought highly of Walras and, unlike Schumpeter, was clearly influenced by his work. Although he and Schumpeter could scarcely have had more different personalities, both had high hopes for the elaborate, mathematical structures which some practitioners have come to believe are alone entitled to be called 'theory'. It is paradoxical that Hicks encouraged me to take up economics partly because he liked the way in which, as an undergraduate, I made use of mathematics, for on my return to Oxford, I ceased to do so. I had embarked on analysis which did not lend itself to mathematical formulation and which challenged the logical foundations of the theory of general equilibrium, which conspicuously did.

In 1956, I published the article 'Demand and Supply Reconsidered', which was followed, in 1959, by 'Equilibrium, Expectations and Information'. These clearly mark a new development in my own thinking, which was later to be carried forward in *Information and Investment*. Previously, I had sought to show how some features of our economic system could be explained only on the basis that knowledge was imperfect, in the sense that each of us could form only uncertain expectations about a limited number of things. I turned now to consider how these expectations could be formed, and to relate the possibility of forming them to the circumstances, and in particular the market structures, in which investment decisions were taken. I maintained that *firms' expectations depended upon information, the availability of which was a function of the market structure within which they operated.* I convinced myself that perfect competition represented a market structure which would make it impossible for firms to have the needed information, the availability of which depended on the presence of circumstances which we had come to regard as 'imperfections'. Given the assumptions that they had made, it was therefore inevitable that Walras and others were unable to provide a plausible account of how equilibrium could be attained.

This, then, was the central idea put forward in the two articles, and the book, to which I have referred. If I am to fulfil my autobiographical obligations honestly, I have to admit that I was excited by it. It seemed to me important, for reasons both theoretical and practical, and it seemed to me new. I can think of nothing that I had read, including the famous Hayek article, which had led me to think of it. The idea had come to me, it seemed, as a result of a kind of prolonged introspection carried out in my room in St John's and in repeated walks around its beautiful garden.

On re-reading my review article on Schumpeter, I came across the following passage:

> One is led to reflect that in economics, as elsewhere, any original improvement in our knowledge of reality is only made possible by withdrawing from it. Under the immediate pressure of reality, in its particular or everyday aspects, we cannot hope to escape from the tyranny of the conventional categories through which we view it. To see problems in the obvious and to find the familiar strange is an indispensable, if unnatural, step to take.

It must surely have been my own state of mind, rather than the history of economic thought, that I was then reflecting upon. There is another passage in the article, in which Schumpeter is quoted as saying that 'new ideas, unless carefully elaborated, painstakingly defended and pushed, simply will not tell'. In my own case, the idea which I considered new did not tell, despite all the elaboration, defence and push that I could muster. Incomprehension, rather than disagreement, was the all but universal response. Some thought I was merely confused but were too polite to say so; others that I was lost in a methodological maze, into which they declined to follow me; and yet others that I lacked the sophistication to appreciate that models have to make unrealistic assumptions. For the most part, however, what I had written drew no response, because it was not read. John Hicks, however, had read the whole of *Information and Investment* and, as a delegate of the Oxford University Press, had the decisive say in whether it should be published. I believe that he liked parts of the book, such as its analysis of liquidity, but probably disliked its principal argument, which, although he and I saw a great deal of each other, both professionally and socially, we never discussed. In any event, he recommended publication, provided that the title I had chosen (*The Economics of Imperfect Knowledge*) was changed. I was sorry to have to abandon the title and never expected that, many years later, I would be given another opportunity to use it.

Not long after finishing *Information and Investment*, I was asked by Sir Roy Harrod to write a book for the Hutchinson University Library series of which he was the economics editor. It came out in 1964 under the title *Economic Theory*. In the preface I said that 'My intention has been to write an introduction to economic theory which, although unusually short, is not unduly superficial. Inevitably, therefore, the presentation has had to be concise and the style terse. Although I have tried very hard to write clearly and simply, the reader's active attention will be required throughout.'

It is clear to me now that I wrote this book with little or no idea about who might read it. I was influenced by the example of two books which I greatly enjoyed reading while a student at Aberdeen: Bertrand Russell's *The Problems of Philosophy* and G. E. Moore's *Ethics*, both of them in the Home University Library. Neither of these provided a compendious treatment of the subject, but sought to introduce it by means of a continuous argument. This is what I tried to do. Both these books expressed the personal opinions of their authors; my text was doctrinally more orthodox, although it took over some of the ideas from *Information and Investment*. In presentation, however, the book was idiosyncratic. It started by introducing the reader to the idea of optimal resource allocation by postulating an omnipotent and omniscient authority, and then proceeded to show how the imperfection of knowledge made necessary the decentralization of decisions. I was influenced here by Lerner's *Economics of Control*, which I had read enthusiastically as an undergraduate.

It is easy to see why the book never became an established text. It was too abstract and too strenuous for most undergraduates. Successful texts, such as Samuelson's *Economics*, which were longer, led the reader more gently along and could be used in teaching a course, particular chapters being prescribed as appropriate. In retrospect, I am taken aback by the extent to which I appear, through ignorance or through arrogance or through both, to have taken no account of the student preference and teaching practice of the time. In any event, I paid for this error, for although the book sold tolerably and was translated into Spanish and Portuguese, the time and effort I put into its preparation were out of proportion to this modest success.

I have a more serious reason for looking back on *Economic Theory* with regret and, indeed, sadness. Some time after its publication, an economist in Czechoslovakia wrote asking for permission to write a translation. At this time, Alexander Dubcek had come to power and there were high hopes of moving away from centralized economic planning. I had structured my book in terms of a movement from a command economy, through stages of decentralization, towards a market system. This for me was merely an expository device and it never occurred to me that the book might interest those seeking a practical programme. It had, however, done so, and I was invited to Prague and Bratislava to meet economists who sought reform.

Only a few weeks after returning, I learned that Soviet tanks had entered Prague. Nothing came of the translation of my book and I feared for those who had proposed it. I heard nothing from them and decided not to seek contact, which might have put them at greater risk. Only when the communist government fell, many years later, did I write to the lady who had taken the original initiative; she told me, in a letter written from hospital, that it had indeed been very hard for her, as no doubt also for the other courageous and enterprising young economists for whom, during my visit, I had acquired affection and respect.

In *Information and Investment* I discussed some so-called 'imperfections' of competition which, by increasing the stability of a firm's environment, made it easier to predict and plan. This effect could be produced by 'natural' imperfections, such as transport costs, but also by contrived imperfections such as price or market-sharing agreements, at one end of the spectrum, and, at the other, the general unwillingness of firms, faced with a temporary fall in demand, to 'spoil the market'. I could not logically maintain that natural imperfections, by providing predictability, could further the successful adaptation of supply to demand, while maintaining that contrived imperfections could not do so. I fully recognized that the stability, and hence predictability, provided by either sort of imperfection could be bought at too high a price, the gains being offset by the losses associated with weaker competitive pressures; nevertheless, there was no reason to believe *a priori* that the balance of advantage would always go one way. The logic of my own theoretical argument made it impossible for me to accept that the restraint of trade need always be against the public interest.

This view was inconsistent with the legislation obtaining in the United States, where agreements in restraint of trade were illegal *per se*, but not with that in Britain and Europe generally, which allowed that they could be justified in special circumstances. Most economists on either side of the Atlantic, however, were vehemently anti-trust, and my argument was regarded with great suspicion. Roy Harrod once encouraged me by observing that the presence of some 'friction' was necessary for the working of a market economy, but James Meade, at a meeting of economists, passionately, and indeed disdainfully, rejected my argument as apologetics not worth reasoned rejoinder. In vain did I point out that price or output agreements were particularly common in precisely those markets (such as the commodity markets) characterized by the large numbers and product homogeneity definitive of perfect competition. In vain also did I argue that the short-term price stability characteristic of oligopolistic markets could facilitate production planning and prevent wide and dysfunctional swings in profitability. These and other similar arguments cut no ice; for many, if not most, economists, the inevitably detrimental effects of the restraint of trade had become an article of faith and my own qualified position was dangerous heresy.

I came to believe, at that time, that economists' views on this matter were, in part, the product of prejudice. What then, I must now ask myself, of my own prejudice? What had led me, consciously or unconsciously, to the position I adopted? Was I in fact merely following the logic of my own theoretical analysis, which had been embarked upon, not in order to defend 'monopoly capitalism', but to criticize the theory of perfect competition? And, if so, were not my views on competition policy free from political or ideological taint? At the time, I may have thought as much, and my work later as a member of the Monopolies Commission seemed to confirm my belief that a balance of considerations had to be taken into account. I dare say, however, that some prejudice entered into my thinking at the pre-analytical stage, in the form of a weak presumption, of the Burkean, conservative kind, in favour of existing arrangements. I was aware that competition in reality had always been in some degree restricted, by both natural circumstance and established practice, and I was less than fully confident, on the basis of what we knew of the working of market economies, that it would be better if all restrictions were swept away. I was as unsympathetic to radicalism of that kind as I was towards centralized socialist planning. I suppose that I thought of the economy, like the human body, as a natural system; when, in either case, malfunction occurred, intervention was called for, but respectful intervention appropriate to the state of our knowledge – less advanced in economics than in medicine – of how things worked.

Although my interest in competition policy arose out of theoretical work, it led me into applied economics. I happened to mention to a prominent industrialist, my neighbour at dinner in a Cambridge college, that I had been writing about competition and its restraint; he invited me to visit him and I became a consultant to his firm. This led to a report I wrote for the firms making heavy electrical equipment for the nationalized electricity industry, which led in turn to the article I published in the *Bulletin of the Oxford University Institute of Economics & Statistics*. During the 1960s I became involved in consultancy work for a number of companies in the private sector, as well as for the UK Atomic Energy Authority, but I gave up almost of all of it when, in 1969, I decided to accept an invitation to become a Member of the UK Monopolies and Mergers Commission.

Sometimes firms seek the advice of economists on what to do, but usually they have already decided what to do and want an economist to justify their plans in terms acceptable to the relevant public authorities. Was I right to do work of this kind? The danger is that analysis may shade into advocacy, but I learned more from the experience than I could have done merely by asking firms for information to help in a research project. I had already been dealing with businessmen as a member of an Oxford research group which interviewed them in a relaxed after dinner context; my 1964 paper on the limits to a firm's rate of growth had come out of such meetings. I found these interviews worthwhile, but working for firms is more rewarding, as managers, feeling that you are on their side, are less on their guard. Schumpeter says, in an eloquent tribute to Marshall, that he 'sensed the intimate organic necessities of economic life even more intensively than he formulated them, and he spoke therefore as one who has power and not like the scribes – or like the theorists who are nothing but theorists'. No amount of working for firms will give us Marshall's power of insight but, if we are lucky, some greater sense of the realities may sometimes be gained.

Membership of the Monopolies Commission gave me another perspective; in this case, the firms before us did not see us as on their side, but we could require them to provide information. My work on the Commission helped me with the article 'The Organisation of Industry' which I published in 1972, chiefly by furnishing illustrative examples, but the ideas I put forward had more distant origins. They came to mind not through looking outwards at new empirical material, but through turning inwards to brood yet again on the theoretical issues which had for so long engaged my mind.

Hayek focuses on how market transactions can produce the spontaneous coordination of individual plans, but has little to say about the contrived coordination brought about within firms or through cooperation between them.

Spontaneous coordination is certainly the more in need of explanation, for the working of the invisible hand, even after over two centuries of exposition, remains difficult even for an intelligent layman to understand and accept. In market economies, moreover, contrived coordination is limited in scope, the subordinate orderings which it produces being themselves fitted together into an overarching order by market transactions. Nevertheless, as different modes of coordination obviously do coexist in market economies, I thought it the proper concern of economists to explain their respective roles. My 1972 article begins by drawing attention to the complex networks of cooperation and affiliation that proliferate in market economies, and then tries to explain them in terms of the need to coordinate activities which are (in senses which I define) *complementary* but *dissimilar*. I refer also to coordination through *direction*, which takes place within rather than between firms, but without saying much about it. Direction seems to me now a less than satisfactory way of describing intra-firm coordination, but I had not properly understood, in 1972, that management is less to do with giving orders than with establishing the rôles and rules according to which those working for a firm cooperate.

The issue which I discussed in 'The Organisation of Industry' was also addressed in a famous article by Ronald Coase; he deserves credit for drawing attention to it, but I was not persuaded that the division of labour between the two modes of coordination is to be explained in terms of transaction costs. Nor did I believe, as Coase claimed, that 'the distinguishing mark of the firm is the supercession of the price mechanism'. When I came to work at Oxford University Press, and was concerned with the terms on which transactions were to take place between component profit centres, I was left in no doubt that where prices did not exist they sometimes had to be invented.

Whereas the work of Coase did not influence my own thinking, that of Edith Penrose certainly did. Her *The Theory of the Growth of the Firm* came out at about the same time as my *Information and Investment*, and although the notion of a firm as embodying particular *capabilities* was present in my own book, I was able to give it much more substance after reading hers. The nature of the bundle of activities undertaken by any particular firm is to be explained partly by the need to coordinate *complementary* activities (those that need to be put together in a process of production) and partly by the gains to be made by combining *similar* activities (those that depend upon, and exploit, a firm's specific capabilities). A firm, Mrs Penrose reminded us, is both an organization for achieving the planned coordination of complementary activities and the embodiment of valuable knowledge, experience and connections.

I was prompted to write the 1972 article partly to draw the attention of economists to those networks of cooperation and affiliation which seemed to me to be an important, but neglected, feature of actual market economies. At the same time, however, and perhaps more essentially, the article represented a further stage in the particular line of theoretical enquiry to which I had been so long and, in the view of my old tutor, too exclusively committed. I thought at the time that it was indeed for me the last stage, for I was about to give up economics and embark on a new career. I had been invited to apply for the post, which was soon to become vacant, of chief executive at Oxford University Press. At first I declined, then changed my mind, applied and was appointed.

I am not sure what moved me to make this change; in my case, at any rate, large decisions of this kind (leaving the Foreign Office being another) are arrived at rather than taken, and by a process to which rational calculation is not central. OUP was a large, international publishing house, owning also – which was exceptional – a printing business and a paper mill. Established to further the increase and spread of learning, it had diversified over the years into almost every field of publishing, save contemporary fiction. Although making money was not its *raison d'être*, it had to make enough to secure its survival, something which, at that time, it was failing to do. I was therefore presented with a challenging opportunity at a time when, discouraged by the lack of response to what I had written, my interest in academic economics was falling away. I had enjoyed teaching, but twenty years of it felt enough. These, then, are the reasons, positive and negative, why I took the plunge.

My experiences at OUP, in so far as they might interest economists, were related in a paper I gave to the Oxford Political Economy Club after my retirement. It may have given the impression that what I carried over from my old job to my new one was greater than it in fact was. The rôle of a chief executive (as it was, at any rate in my case) being to set up structures and to form, lead and manage a team, neither academic economics, nor even business consultancy, were of much help. I had to learn, to some extent, on the job, drawing as best I could on what I had learned during the war, in the Foreign Office and from my general experience of life. The fourteen years I spent at OUP, although difficult, were rewarding, and not only in terms of my own personal development; the business itself, after many vicissitudes, entered into a period of sustained prosperity.

Shortly after retiring from OUP, I was invited to become Warden of Keble College, where I remained for five years. By this time, attention had been drawn to my writing, thanks mainly to Brian Loasby; *Information and Investment* was re-published, with two of my articles as appendices; I wrote a new introduction and David Teece a foreword. At about this time, Nicolai Foss also took an interest in my work and wrote perceptively about it. Not long after going to Keble, I resumed consultancy work. The Microsoft Corporation asked me to study the working of competition in the software industry, which eventually led to the paper entitled 'Economic Analysis, Public Policy and the Software Industry'. It led, more indirectly, to a further paper, 'Competition, Innovation and Increasing Returns', which offers an analysis applicable to all industries characterized by low marginal costs and rapid innovation. But it would be wrong to conclude that this article, any more than my 1972 article on cooperation, resulted straightforwardly from empirical study. Picasso is supposed to have observed '*il faut trouver et puis chercher*' and my perception of the process of competition within the industries dealt with in these two papers was shaped by conceptions, preconceptions or misconceptions already pre-figured in my first articles and fully formed by the time I wrote *Information and Investment*. I had for long wanted to provide a comprehensive explanation of the fact, obvious to all those willing to see, that competition was compatible with increasing returns to scale. And I had been long convinced that we should take more explicit account of the fact, also obvious, that changes in wealth and welfare depend as much, or more, on qualitative rather than quantitative changes in the goods available.

Product development may have been relatively neglected, in formal theory, because of the perceived difficulty of measuring qualitative, rather than quantitative, change. In these papers I do not mention an early experience which caused me to doubt whether quantitative change, or rather what we often regard as quantitative change, is in fact easier to measure. At the cost of a diversion, I shall mention it now. During the term I spent at Nuffield before going to St John's, I worked on index numbers, the aim being to decide upon the best way of comparing differences between gross national product per head in different countries. It was John Hicks who suggested that I should take up this research project, but I found that it was not for me and soon dropped it. Almost half a century later, however, in writing the article on innovation, the subject came back to mind. I recalled a conversation I had had with Sir Henry Clay, a retired, and distinctly pre-Keynesian, Warden of Nuffield; when being told what I was working on, he observed that as gross domestic product was a heterogeneous mixture, one could not measure changes of it in real terms. And whatever one may think of this discouraging opinion, it reminds us of what measuring economic aggregates really amounts to. The index numbers which we use to measure changes in gross national product use prices to weight the component products, so that it is with value or utility, rather than physical quantities, that we are in fact dealing. And the same applies to measuring changes in the output of particular goods, such as books or cars, where qualitative differences within the category are such that mere physical enumeration would be pointless. Where such aggregates are concerned, we have to bring in prices (as a measure of relative value of the qualitatively different components) in order to measure what superficially looks like merely quantitative change. My brief encounter with the theory of index numbers left me with little more than a keen awareness of the difficulty of attaching a precise meaning or interpretation to the measurement of heterogeneous aggregates, such as gross domestic product, which we now regard as analytically indispensable.

In 'Competition, Innovation and Increasing Returns', I drew back from these depths. In writing it, I hoped to cast some light on the process of competition in industries subject to increasing returns and rapid innovation, but am conscious, to the point of uneasiness, that I was sometimes skating on very thin ice. I should be very content if the article were to induce others to re-examine the issues I raised, which are surely important, and in due course to develop an analysis of them more systematic, substantial and secure than my own.

## References

Hicks, J.R. (1946), *Value and Capital*, Oxford: Clarendon Press.

Keynes, J.M. (1921), *Treatise on Probability*, London: Macmillan.

Lerner, A.P. (1944), *The Economics of Control*, New York, Macmillan.

Moore, G.E. (1912), *Ethics*, London: Home University Library.

Penrose, Edith (1959 and 1995), *The Theory of the Growth of the Firm*, Oxford: Oxford University Press.

Richardson, G.B. (1960 and 1990), *Information and Investment*, Oxford: Clarendon Press.

Richardson, G.B. (1964), *Economic Theory*, London: Hutchinson.

Russell, Bertrand (1912), *The Problems of Philosophy*, London: Home University Library.

Samuelson, P.A. (1948, First Edition), *Economics*, New York: McGraw Hill.
Schumpeter, J.A. (1943), *Capitalism, Socialism and Democracy*, London: Allen and Unwin.
Schumpeter, J.A. (1954), *History of Economic Analysis*, New York: Oxford University Press.
Smith, Adam (1776), *Wealth of Nations*.

# [1] ·

## IMPERFECT KNOWLEDGE AND ECONOMIC EFFICIENCY

### By G. B. RICHARDSON

## I. Introductory

I AM concerned in this paper with the imperfection of our knowledge as economic agents, with its influence on the nature of the economic system, and with its relevance to the way in which the system should be appraised.

In saying that our knowledge is imperfect I mean that it is fragmented and that it is uncertain. It is fragmented in that each of us knows only a very small part of all that is to be known, though individual fields of vision may overlap; and it is uncertain in that much of what, in this paper, I shall loosely term 'knowledge', is of the form of personal estimates or opinions which may differ and which cannot be shown at the time to be certainly true or false.

The economic problem is concerned with the adaptation of means to ends. In our theoretical representations of it we normally take the means —factors of production and techniques—and the ends—consumers' preferences, the 'social welfare function', and the like—to be known or 'given', and proceed from there to deduce what the general conditions for optimum allocation will be. Now there is a danger that this purely logical problem of drawing appropriate conclusions from given premises may be regarded, perhaps implicitly, as an adequate description of the actual problem with which our economic system is concerned and from which it derives its rationale. This is, however, very far from the case.[1] The practical problem which our theoretical system would most closely represent would be that facing a single mind to which all the relevant knowledge regarding means and ends were known with certainty and as a whole; that which confronts us is entirely different. Knowledge, in the world as we know it, is neither centralized nor certain, but is dispersed, frequently in the form of subjective and even conflicting estimates, among many minds. In consequence, the actual economic problem is more fundamental and more complex than the theoretical problems of formal welfare economics; its essence is not the allocation of 'given' resources among 'given' ends, but the integration and improvement of our knowledge regarding them; it is concerned, in other words, to ensure that the fullest use will be made of the relevant knowledge which is dispersed among many minds and that the estimates

---

[1] *Vide* Professor Hayek's most stimulating article, ' Economics and Knowledge' (*Economica*, 1937), which has greatly influenced the views advanced here.

### G. B. RICHARDSON

according to which allocative decisions are taken will tend in the long run to be the best available.

The principles of welfare economics are sometimes regarded as applicable directly to economic policy, in that they afford to the government and to the entrepreneur a body of rules to which their decisions ought to conform. This is an entirely mistaken conception, responsible for much of the misunderstanding and misapplication of welfare economics. The optimum conditions of production and exchange do not represent injunctions on how a certain outcome can be attained, but criteria by which the realized outcome can be appraised. They are conditions which an efficient economic system will have to realize to the greatest possible extent *ex post*, but imply nothing whatever regarding the nature of the economic decisions which the component individuals must take in order to bring this about.[1]

There is, however, one circumstance which would justify us in regarding the appropriate rules for the conduct of economic activity and the appropriate criteria for appraising its outcome as identical; that is the existence of perfect knowledge. In a world where expectations never erred, optimum allocation would be reached if entrepreneurs were to implement the welfare principles as if they were rules relating to *ex ante* magnitudes; that is to say, if we take Lerner's Rule as representative, provided they produced at an output such as would equate expected price with expected marginal cost. Whenever we relax the assumption of certain expectations, there remains no logical presumption that the universal implementation of the Rule is the best way of obtaining the required outcome. To prescribe as if there were such a presumption is to assume that individual estimates of the future values of economic variables are objectively correct or at least the best available and that the distribution of productive resources among those who dispose of them must be regarded as optimal; it is to assume, in fact, that a crucial part of the economic problem has already been solved. For there is the question not only of how to allocate but of who is to allocate, or, in other words, of how the system is to allocate capital between entrepreneurs. The economic system, we might say, has a selective as well as an allocative function; both are relevant to its efficiency, although addiction to models assuming certainty has perhaps led some of us to devote to the former very scant attention.

There is, of course, a variety of ways in which the economic units which are to have command over resources may be selected, but I shall confine myself to one broad distinction: to that between selection which is planned and selection which is automatic. The classification is rough but, I hope, serviceable; selection is planned when one man or authority deliberately

[1]   *Vide* Hicks, 'The Foundations of Welfare Economics' (*Economic Journal*, 1939).

chooses another to exercise command over resources; it is automatic where an economic unit gains or loses command over resources according to its success in making profits and to the facility in borrowing which reputation, created by success, engenders.

In this paper I shall endeavour to analyse some of the ways in which our economic system secures, to a greater or less extent, the integration and improvement of our knowledge. Some features of the system which, in over-simplified models, might appear as imperfections will, I hope, be shown to fulfil an indispensable function: either, by providing a form of communication, of overcoming the division of our knowledge; or, by constituting an environment favourable to efficient selection, of securing its improvement.

A warning is perhaps appropriate at this stage. I shall later be maintaining that free enterprise works rather better, in certain respects, than judgement of it based on a superficial understanding, and consequent misapplication, of the welfare principles, would suggest. I am at pains to emphasize the limitation 'in certain respects'. No opinion on the general efficiency of free enterprise can legitimately be formed without thorough study of important issues entirely excluded from discussion here; the dangers of oscillation and of harmful speculation, oligopoly, and the divergences between private and social cost of the type discussed by Professor Pigou, are among the most important. The ethical value of particular income distributions is likewise outside my scope, although I shall have something to say on their indirect influence on the structure of the economic system.

## II. The nature of probability estimates

I now wish, at the risk of breaking the continuity of my argument, to interpolate some observations on the nature of the estimates or opinions which form a large part of our imperfect knowledge. A full discussion of the nature of estimates of probability would be both beyond my competence and unnecessary to the purpose at hand; but it is perhaps desirable to refer at the outset to the well-known distinction, drawn by Knight, between 'measurable' and 'unmeasurable' uncertainty, or, to employ his other terms, between risk and uncertainty, or between objective and subjective estimates of uncertainty.

Knight used the word 'risk' to denote statistical estimates of probability, that is estimates based 'on empirical valuation of the frequency of the association between predicates'. 'Uncertainty' was used in connexion with estimates of probability which were made, he argued, 'without there being a valid basis of any kind for classifying instances', the future event considered being for practical purposes unique. When dealing with risks

G. B. RICHARDSON

proper, according to Knight, it would be possible, by grouping sufficient instances, to approach complete certainty. This was not possible with true uncertainties, although there was 'some tendency for fluctuations to cancel out in some degree'.

Now many writers have argued that the difference between risk and uncertainty is one not of kind but only of degree, depending on the homogeneity of the classification into which we fit the instances in question. No future event is ever wholly unique, neither is it ever identical with a past event. Where we can obtain relatively homogeneous classes without reducing overmuch the number in the class, fairly good estimates of the parameters of the probability distribution can be obtained and, for that reason, grouping as in insurance may be possible. Where the instances can be fitted only into the roughest of classes, only very approximate estimates are obtainable. If the future event is not known to resemble a past event in any way, nothing can be said.

Now, while it may be true that the results of probability estimates of all kinds are different not in kind but in degree, there is an important difference in the ways in which they are made, a difference which is of definite significance for social organization and which represents the essence of the distinction which Knight, I believe rightly, thought so important. Certain things can be done by following exactly a fixed set of rules, whereas others require a specific skill, innate or acquired, and more or less particular to the performance in question. Given a map and good directions most people could find an address in a city, but the fullest instructions will not enable us, without acquired skill, to drive a car or to play tennis. We may, indeed, in these cases suggest a few precepts, but they will far from suffice to ensure success; while a person may possess the skill without being able to formulate the precept.[1] There is clearly something of this kind in the distinction between Knight's two forms of probability estimates. Some estimates are made by applying those known rules which constitute the body of statistical knowledge; others are not so made but require a flair or specific skill. Estimates of this latter type are by far the commonest; they are continually being made and are no more mysterious than any other skilled performances which cannot be done merely by following a set of rules.

Now what is important in this distinction from our point of view is that the first type of estimates, statistical or objective estimates as we may call them, are demonstrable: the procedure by which they are reached can be written down and codified. They can be made quite objectively, in the sense that the calculation is in no way private to the calculator. Thus if I am informed by someone that a statistical probability is of a certain

[1] *Vide* Ryle in 'Knowledge How and Knowledge That' in *The Concept of Mind.*

order, I should believe him, provided he knows how to apply the rules to the material, can do arithmetic, and is not telling lies. It may be that because the past estimates are few in number the figure is exceedingly rough, but it is objective in the sense that, given the same information and the same rules, everyone should get the same result. Estimates of the second and more numerous class, subjective estimates as we may call them, are not like this. There is no way in which the rationale of their calculation can be fully demonstrated or communicated; one cannot accept the validity of another's estimates with only those reservations which were made in the case of objective estimates, but must have formed an estimate of the person's foresight in this direction, either on the basis of his past performance or on experience of men similar to him. The estimate is private to the estimator and in this sense subjective.

This distinction between subjective and objective estimates has, as I hope to explain later, an important bearing on the nature of the social organization which has grown up as a means of overcoming the obstacles to economic efficiency created by the imperfections of our knowledge.

## III. The organization of the capital market

Let is now return to the main course of the argument. I have said that it is characteristic of knowledge in this world that it is dispersed among many minds and that much of it is in the form of subjective and uncertain estimates. Yet society exists; the fragments of knowledge are so integrated and utilized that ends of great complexity are achieved. The mechanisms or processes which make this possible form perhaps the main object of the study of the social sciences in general: we are concerned with the economic aspects, and in particular with the means by which resources are allocated in the free economy, given imperfect knowledge.

Let us first suppose that knowledge, though fragmented, is certain. In this case it is the price mechanism, as ordinarily conceived, which secures integration. The invisible hand of the classical economists is normally regarded as harnessing the forces of self-interest in the service of the general good; by virtue of the division of labour and of exchange, ends are achieved which, though socially desirable, form no part of the intention of the participating agents. In fact, however, the invisible hand, or the homoeostatic controls of society, as it might nowadays less picturesquely be termed, fulfils a yet more fundamental function: it acts as a method of communication, and by integrating the knowledge which is dispersed in many minds, enables society to work as a whole.

The way in which this is done is widely familiar; if, for example, a factor becomes more useful in a particular employment, its price will be bid up, its use in other employments thereby curtailed, and an incentive created for the use of substitutes. The allocation effected by the perfect competition model does not therefore require that the information of economic agents should be complete; indeed, the essential point of the system is that it overcomes these individual limitations in knowledge. For example, if we consider the allocation of a factor with a given price between uses $A$, $B$, and $C$, there being two agents $X$ and $Y$, it is necessary that each agent knows two uses only, provided they know one in common. For then, assuming knowledge to be certain, $X$ will ensure that the marginal products of the factor will be equal, in value terms, in $A$ and $B$, and $Y$ that they are equal in $B$ and $C$. Thus the marginal product of the factor will be equal in all three lines. The number of products may be extended indefinitely; each person need only know a limited part of all that is to be known, provided that their individual fields of knowledge overlap. It ought to be possible to prescribe the minimum knowledge which each individual must possess, in order that rational allocation throughout the economy may be achieved or approximated to, but I shall not allow this rather difficult question to detain me here.[1]

If we allow our economic agents to be endowed with perfect honesty as well as perfect foresight, the optimum allocation of capital among borrowers likewise presents no difficulty; provided lenders' fields of knowledge overlap appropriately, the marginal yield of capital will, in equilibrium, be equal in all directions. But whenever we relax our assumptions and allow knowledge to be uncertain as well as fragmented, in the form of subjective estimates, the situation radically alters. Both the commodity market and the capital market will assume a character different from that of the model based on certainty, but it is the capital market, related as it is to estimates of an essentially uncertain future, which suffers the greatest change. The marginal yields or efficiencies of capital are now, in their relevant sense, merely opinions and should not be considered independent of the mind or minds by which they are entertained; they will tend to equality in the mind of each investor who is able to form the relevant estimates, but not in any more general or objective sense.

The question therefore arises as to how, and with what degree of rationality, capital is allocated under these conditions. Let us first consider the relationships which would obtain if there existed only entrepreneurs, with or without capital of their own, and persons who lend directly to them. If there were no borrowing, the amount which an entrepreneur would invest in any line would depend on his expectation of the profit rate in it relative to that of other lines with which he was familiar; it would be limited ultimately by the quantity of capital in his possession, but more immediately by considerations of risk, that is by the desirability of diversifying

[1] *Vide* Hayek, op. cit.

his assets and of avoiding excessive illiquidity. (The relationship between liquidity and the imperfections of our knowledge will be more fully discussed below.) In other words, investment in any line is limited by the fact that the entrepreneur's estimates of its profitability are uncertain, and by the fact that others cannot be assumed to share his estimates, so that, if it happened that he were forced to sell his assets, he would probably do so at a loss.

The possibility of borrowing does not radically alter the situation. An entrepreneur can obtain funds to a limited extent on the security of his own capital, and also in such measure as lenders hold, or can be persuaded to hold, views about the profitability of the venture not much less confident than his own subjective estimate. One may expect that the wider the circle of borrowers an entrepreneur approaches the less will be the knowledge of his ability and projects, and the greater will be the incentive necessary to induce lending. Nor will the borrower always be able to satisfy his demands within the narrower circle of those who can form good estimates of his projects, for the amount which any single investor will be prepared to lend to any one borrower will also be limited by the needs of diversification and liquidity. Thus risk will increase with investment for a variety of reasons. The well-known Law of Increasing Risk enunciated by Kalecki is a corollary of the fact of the imperfection of our knowledge, of both its uncertainty and its division.[1]

For any firm, therefore, there will be a gap between the marginal efficiency (by which I mean the mathematical expectation or best estimate of the yield) of the capital invested and the rate of interest at which it borrows. This gap will increase with the scale of the investment, depending, *inter alia*, on the uncertainty of the expectation—as measured, for example, by the dispersion of the probability distribution of expected profits, the liquidity of the assets, and the proportion which they bear to the capital borrowed. There will also be a gap between the rate at which the firm borrows and that on approximately riskless securities, such as treasury bills, the size of which will depend of the lender's liquidity preference in the Keynesian sense, that is on expectations regarding future rates and on the needs of convenience and safety, as well as on the lender's estimate

---

[1] It is not true that increased fixed-interest borrowing will always increase the risk to the investor by reducing the ratio of own to borrowed capital. There may indeed be decreasing risk over a certain range. This will be so as long as the riskiness of the venture decreases more with the total quantity of capital employed than it increases with the proportion of own to borrowed capital. It might be, for example, that the minimum practical scale of operations would leave the entrepreneur with a very small cash reserve or simply that increased scale reduced average cost. In either of these cases borrowing might well reduce the riskiness of the venture. This, however, will merely serve to postpone the operation of the so-called law, for the risk inherent in the increased ratio of borrowed to own capital must eventually, in any likely circumstances, offset the reduction in risk which the increased scale of operations, made possible by borrowing, brings with it.

of the marginal efficiency of capital in the borrower's business—for on this will depend, in the case of debentures, the likelihood of default, and in the case of equity participation, the yield.

It can be seen that many of the risk factors associated with investment affect both gaps or margins; that is, both the margin between the marginal efficiency of capital, as conceived by the entrepreneur, and the borrowing rate; and between the borrowing rate and the bill rate. Keynes referred to this when he distinguished between borrower's and lender's risk. 'The first', according to Keynes, 'is the entrepreneur's or borrower's risk and arises out of the doubts in his mind as to the probability of actually earning the prospective yield for which he hopes. If a man is venturing his own money this is the only risk which is relevant.' Lender's risk 'may be due to moral hazard . . . or to the possible insufficiency of the margin of security'. Keynes goes on to argue that 'the first type of risk is in a sense a real social cost. . . . The second however is a pure addition to the cost of investment which would not exist if the borrower and lender were the same person. Moreover it involves in part a duplication of a proportion of the entrepreneur's risk, which is added twice to the pure rate of interest to give the minimum prospective yield which will induce the investor' (*General Theory*, p. 144).

It seems to me, however, to be misleading to say that only the borrower's risk was a 'real social cost'. For this to be so the borrower's estimates would have to be in some sense objectively correct, which of course we have no right to assume. The uncertainty of a venture and the real social risk depend presumably on the probability of success as estimated by the entrepreneur and the probability that the entrepreneur's estimate is correct. The former, though no doubt very imperfectly, is reflected in the borrower's margin; the latter in the lender's margin. For if the entrepreneur is untried his estimates are prima facie less reliable than those of the successful entrepreneur, and the higher rate at which he borrows should to some extent correspond to the greater social risk of lending to him.

It is apparent, therefore, that even in this simple model, to regard the level of investment as determined by the equality of the marginal efficiency of capital and the rate of interest involves exceedingly drastic simplifications. The rate of interest, as everyone knows, is a high abstraction like the price level, for there is no single rate at which all can borrow. But even if this be recognized, it is still not true that the marginal efficiency of capital and the borrowing rate, whatever it is, will be equated. Neither can one avoid this difficulty, as is sometimes attempted, by assuming that the borrowing rate will equal the marginal efficiency of capital, discounted by a risk premium varying with the dispersion of the probability distribution of the yield; for we have seen that the borrower's margin depends on factors other than this dispersion, factors which should properly be made explicit.

Now it is clear that a capital market such as we have pictured it, comprising only owners of capital and those who ultimately employ it, would impose severe limits to the level of investment, both of each individual firm and of the economy as a whole; for the probability that an entrepreneur will be in touch with an owner of wealth who shares, or is prepared to take on trust, his estimate of the prospective yield of a venture will not be high. Many owners of wealth might indeed be unable to form an estimate of any investment project. The principal ways in which in actual markets the difficulties thus presented by the division of knowledge are substantially overcome are, of course, the growth of established business reputations and the existence of intermediaries.

Certain enterprises will be more successful than others; the fact will become known and lenders who lack more direct knowledge of ventures and men will entrust their funds to them on the strength of their reputation. The increased facility in borrowing will allow the firms to expand and secure their position, so as to further improve the terms on which they borrow. The growth of bonds of reputation and goodwill, far from being an imperfection, is an essential pre-condition of the transfer of investible funds, and I shall be concerned below with the environment favourable to it, for it is upon the ways in which reputations are gained or lost that the rationality of the allocation will depend. The function of reputation and goodwill, in common with that of conventions and customs, is to save us from the need of doing afresh all the thinking which has been done by our predecessors. They enable us to assume that there are prima facie reasons for something being the case, and thereby save us the trouble of having to investigate. This they do in a most rough and ready way; sometimes they lead us astray so that we are forced to rethink the matter for ourselves. But unless very frequently wrong, they are justified as economizing in thought, in enabling us to act in the world without having to think everything out from the beginning; and, as this would be beyond our powers, in securing thereby that society works despite the imperfections of our knowledge. Thus, for example, the fact that established firms can borrow more cheaply than those without a reputation is not necessarily a defect in the system; it may be the method in which resources are allocated in the directions in which the objective probability of their being best employed is highest.

Borrowers who have acquired a reputation need not themselves have to employ the money entrusted to them, but might lend it to others, thus interposing a class of intermediaries between the original suppliers and final users of funds. Ultimately the gaps produced by the division of our knowledge would be spanned by a complex network of intermediate borrowers and lenders each possessed of established reputation *vis-à-vis* those from whom they borrow, and of special knowledge of those to whom they lend. The conclusions reached above regarding the diversity of interest rates and the nature of borrower's and lender's margins remain essentially correct although the relationships are now more complicated. There will now be a gap between the lender's and the borrower's rate sufficient to compensate the intermediaries for their reputation and special knowledge, but the margin between the lender's rate and the bill rate will be sufficiently narrowed for the whole difference between the bill rate and the borrowing rate to be reduced. If it were not, of course, the direct channel would be used in preference.

I have been attempting to sketch, in roughest outline, the relationships which will obtain between borrowers and lenders on the assumption—the realistic assumption—that knowledge of investment opportunities was in the form of individual subjective estimates each covering only part of the field. In what way can we appraise the efficiency of these relationships as a mechanism for allocating resources between industries and firms? There exists, of course, the formal criterion that the marginal efficiency of capital should be the same in all directions. Thus, for example, Mr. R. F. Henderson proposes at the beginning of his recent empirical study of the New Issue Market that there should be 'equality of cost of finance for comparable real investment' and that 'all firms should get finance for real investment with a prospective yield above a certain level, after allowing for real risk'. Now, while this criterion is valid, it is difficult to see how it is to be applied. For we simply do not possess, *ex ante* or even *ex post*, objective estimates of the marginal efficiency of capital in every firm and industry in which it might be employed; there exist only estimates which are subjective, and may be conflicting. If we assume that the estimates of all business men, regardless of the differences between them, are the best available, we assume in fact that the capital market has already performed its primary function. The efficiency of a capital market will depend in practice on the extent to which it is likely to secure that the estimates on which investment decisions are taken will tend to correct estimates, which is mainly a question of the efficiency of the system in selecting those who are to make investment decisions; on the extent to which it provides the incentives necessary to induce these people to allocate according to their estimates; and, finally, on differences between private and social costs of the type with which we are familiar, but which are not discussed here. Seen from this point of view, many aspects of the capital market which, if we apply directly the criteria appropriate only to perfect knowledge, appear to be imperfections, or, as Mr. Henderson calls them, 'distortions', are seen to be in fact essential to the integration and improvement of the knowledge on which decisions are based.

That the market functions as a selective mechanism, and thereby improves the knowledge on which decisions are taken, is, of course, widely recognized, though I am inclined to think that in appraising its efficiency too little attention has been paid to this. Under capitalism, ideally, and to some extent in practice, the power of disposing capital will be given to those who have disposed it well in the past; successful exercises of entrepreneurial skill will produce profits which will themselves form the capital available for further investment, and will generate reputation which facilitates borrowing. Failure, on the other hand, will deprive the unsuccessful entrepreneur both of his capital and, ultimately, of his reputation. It is worth noting here that, whereas if free competition is conceived merely as an allocative mechanism only the ordinal magnitudes of profits in each line are regarded as significant, it is the cardinal magnitudes which are important in securing that those who have been successful in allocating resources in the past will obtain extended control over them in the future. Now it hardly needs saying that the selective mechanism of free competition is far from perfect; the bequeathing of private fortunes has the result that people start the race with different handicaps, and there are all the divergences between private and social cost and the dangers of speculation and oscillation which I am excluding from discussion here. But that it has worked in a rough and ready way, the existence of our highly complex industrial society seems to testify. The free economy has been lauded, sometimes rather ingenuously, for the way in which it solves millions of simultaneous equations; but in fact it does more than this: it sets up forces such as help to ensure that in the long run, and by and large, the estimates on which decisions are taken are likely to be the best available. It is important to realize that the capitalist economy does this, whether or not one believes that an alternative form of economic organization would do it better.

## IV. The conditions of efficient selection

I have argued that the efficiency of an economic system will depend, in the long run, not only on the quality of the allocation of resources achieved relative to the existing estimates, but also on the quality of the estimates themselves; that it depends therefore on the forces influencing the selection of entrepreneurs. It is to the general environmental conditions most favourable to the successful operation of this process of automatic selection that I now wish to turn.

We have already noted the absence of any general presumption that the decisions of entrepreneurs regarding the level of price and output which will effect the optimum allocation when knowledge is perfect, are the same as those most likely to do so when it is not; it can, I think, be shown that, if an environment favourable to selection is to be maintained, they will in general be different. Provided we continue to make the radical assumption that private profit and general benefit coincide, efficient selection would seem to require that an entrepreneur's control over capital should increase or decrease according to his success in the ventures in which he is engaged, for this would provide grounds for believing that he would continue to allocate capital successfully in the future. A single divergence of a realized outcome from the most probable expectation of it would, however, not provide reliable evidence of poor estimating ability; it might, for example, represent a result which the entrepreneur considered quite possible though not very likely, and even if he had forecast badly on this one occasion, only a very weak presumption exists that he will continue to do so in the future. An entrepreneur will in general be able to show himself to have or to lack foresight only if he is permitted to have several chances of exercising it, that is to say, only provided a single deviation of the realized value of any variable from its mean expected value does not remove him from business. If therefore we are relying on the process of automatic selection, there will be an optimum degree of responsiveness of the viability of the firm to errors of prediction on the part of its manager; for efficient selection will be prevented equally by an over-sensitive as by a sluggish reaction. It is important that not only should sustained miscalculation remove a firm from business, but also that a few errors should not; for even if business men were prepared to undertake any uncertain ventures on these terms, which is unlikely, few firms would survive for long: the absence of continuity and order in the ownership and control of resources would involve great social cost, and without the evidence which only long-run performance can provide, valid estimates of entrepreneurial capacity could not be formed and reputations could not grow.

The optimum degree of stability would, of course, be that which brought the realized long-run performance of the system most into conformity with the ideal allocation prescribed by static welfare economics. It would, however, be very difficult to appraise performance, and *a fortiori*, hence to estimate the appropriate degree of stability: information *ex post* about the realized values of price and marginal cost and the returns of capital in various employments would not suffice, for it would not tell us, for example, how many opportunities for investment were missed. There is certainly no presumption that, with a given degree of unavoidable uncertainty in forecasting, the optimum degree of stability will be obtained in a system of unregulated competition, in which entrepreneurs took the same price and output decisions as they would if their best estimates of economic variables could be regarded as certain. Business men do not act, however, in this way, and many of their policies, however motivated, do succeed in reducing the risk inherent in economic activity, and they may thereby derive at least partial justification, even when they are in contradiction with the formal welfare principles. A reduction in risk and a consequent gain in economic stability will be obtained by weakening the chain of connexion between the accuracy of the entrepreneur's foresight and the survival of his firm, and to do this it is necessary to damp either the effect of errors of estimation on current profits or the effect of current profits on viability. The following section presents a very summary analysis and appraisal of some of the ways in which this can be done: first, I shall deal with the holding of liquid assets in order to mitigate the effect of fluctuating profits; secondly, with price and output decisions designed to limit the effect on profits of possible shortfalls in demand; and, thirdly, with the reduction in risk secured by the grouping of several ventures.

## V. The reduction of risk

**1. Liquidity.** It is well known that a single business loss may involve the entrepreneur in further secondary losses, by obliging him to make a forced sale of his assets; if therefore a firm is to survive in the face of fluctuating receipts or costs, it is important that this multiplier effect should be minimized.

The size of this 'multiplier', that is the relation between the primary and the total loss, will depend on the liquidity of the owner's assets, which I shall define as the value in sale he expects from them divided by the valuation he himself puts upon them. By 'expected value in sale' I shall mean the price in terms of money of constant purchasing power the owner expects the assets will fetch, less an allowance representing the expected cost and delay of finding a purchaser, as measured by the quantity of money just sufficient to compensate the owner for the disadvantage entailed. By the owner's 'own valuation' of the asset I shall mean the amount of money just sufficient in normal circumstances to persuade him to part with it.

It will be observed that this definition is wholly subjective, which is as it should be; for as we are concerned with the liquidity of assets as a determinant of the owner's decisions, it is his estimate of their selling price and their value to him which are relevant. Moreover, liquidity in this sense is also relative to a particular point in time, though it might be convenient to refer to an asset as possessing a certain degree of liquidity to the extent that its owner expected it to possess this liquidity at any foreseeable date. I am aware of deficiencies in this definition; by introducing the idea of 'normal circumstances', for example, it is not quite determinate. But the whole notion of liquidity is surely one of the most imprecise and fugitive in economic theory, and the above definition seems to best represent that aspect of it which is relevant in this particular context.

Illiquidity, thus conceived as depending on the relation between the owner's valuation and that of other people, arises principally because of the imperfection, and especially the division, of our knowledge. In the case of a share or security the owner may simply take a more optimistic view of the asset's prospective yield than do others, and his view may or may not be based on particular knowledge available only to him. Or it may be that, in the case of a machine or plant, he believes the asset to be complementary with others in his possession, including his own skill and entrepreneurial capacity. It is true that in this case the entrepreneur would find it more advantageous to borrow on the security of his assets than to sell part of them, but the availability and cost of credit will also depend on how far others share his estimate of their value, that is to say, on their liquidity. In general we may say that the assets of an entrepreneur will be illiquid; that is to say, his own valuation will exceed that of the market, if only for the reason that it was precisely because he expected their yield to exceed the current normal yield that he purchased them, and, the more illiquid the asset, the higher will be the return which the entrepreneur will normally expect from it.

According to the definitions which I think are most convenient, imperfect marketability is a cause of illiquidity but not identical with it. An asset may be said to be marketable if it can be readily bought or sold, that is to say, if it is in sufficiently constant demand for buyers to be in close and continual contact. The degree of marketability will be measured by the ratio of the value in sale, as defined above, to the buying price; the degree of liquidity by the ratio of the former to the owner's own valuation. The marketability and the liquidity of an asset will therefore be equal only when its owner's valuation equals its buying price; but it is only in the exceptional case of the marginal unit of a completely divisible asset that this equality will exist. Marketability is neither a necessary nor a sufficient condition for liquidity; an asset may be marketable but illiquid when its buying price equals its selling price but is less than its owner's valuation, and may be liquid but unmarketable when its selling price approximates to its owner's valuation but falls below its buying price.

We are concerned with the liquidity of an entrepreneur's assets as a factor diminishing the multiplier effect of an initial loss, and therefore as a way of reducing risk and increasing economic stability. Most economic units will experience a continual ebb and flow in their receipts and payments, the exact magnitude of which will not be foreseeable; the direction of the net flow in the long run will determine the chances of survival and of growth, but many of the fluctuations will be self-cancelling. Were there perfect knowledge these fluctuations could be met by loans advanced by the units in temporary surplus to those in temporary deficit; but as there is not, and as the cost of bridging the gap by a network of intermediaries might sometimes be prohibitive, the need is frequently better met by the holding of liquid assets, and especially of money.

The quantity of liquid assets held will increase with the uncertainty of the yield and costs expected; and, for a given return on total capital, the return from that part of it employed directly in production will have to be the greater the smaller the proportion which it forms of the whole. Investment will therefore be pushed less far, for this reason alone, in lines in which the investor's expectation of profit is uncertain or is more optimistic than that held by others. This, however, cannot be said to be necessarily a misallocation; provided we wish to continue to rely on the forces of automatic selection, it may be the best means of securing optimum long-run performance.

**2. Price and output decisions.** The second way in which the entrepreneur can reduce the risk of his business, and thereby contribute to economic stability, is by choosing his method of production, and the price and level of his output, so as to minimize possible fluctuations in profits.

It is important always to remember that the demand and cost schedules which we employ to illustrate the price and output decisions of the individual producer should relate to subjective and uncertain estimates of hypothetical magnitudes. Elementary demonstration of the equilibrium of the firm disposes of this crucial fact by assuming complete information. It is not possible, however, to make this model serve to represent the situation with imperfect knowledge merely by replacing the uncertain estimates by certain values equal to the mathematical expectation of the uncertain estimate discounted for risk. For the business man will take a course of action in the face of uncertainty which differs in kind from that appropriate to a situation in which expectations, whatever their value, are certain.

Thus there is no presumption that the entrepreneur will adjust his output so as to equate the expected values of marginal cost and marginal revenue; indeed, there are good reasons why he should not do so, but rather seek to produce on a smaller scale. Over-estimation of demand may prove more serious than under-estimation. This is so for three reasons. In the first place actual losses will in general exceed the difference between revenue and cost whenever the firm is forced to sell illiquid assets. Secondly, it is possible that the gradient of the short-run cost curve is less for outputs which exceed that corresponding to minimum average cost than for outputs which fall below it. This would be the case where overheads were high and could not be reduced when output declined, whereas extensions could be added to the plant to enable a larger output to be produced at a cost which, though larger than that corresponding to full adaptation, was not excessively large. If demand exceeds expectations the entrepreneur will suffer an opportunity loss, through not having chosen initially a larger plant, the extent of which will depend on the difference between the levels of the short- and long-run cost curves for outputs above that corresponding to minimum average short-run cost. Similarly, if demand falls short of expectations there will be an opportunity loss depending on the difference between the short- and long-run average cost curves for outputs less than that expected. Thus if the short-run cost curve is of the shape that I have postulated, the opportunity loss which will follow from a demand which falls short of expectations will be greater than that which will be brought about by an unexpected high demand. A third and familiar final reason for inclining towards a safety-first policy is that losses are more disagreeable than gains are agreeable, provided the marginal utility of money diminishes with income.

Thus we might expect the business man to choose a scale of output less than that corresponding to the equality of the expected levels of marginal cost and marginal revenue, where expected profits, formally, would be maximized. By restricting output the difference between expected price and expected average cost could probably be increased, thereby widening the range within which demand and cost can deviate from expectations without causing a loss. Quite apart from restrictions imposed by increased risk and cost of borrowing, the output will therefore, if demand is at all elastic, be twice removed from the point where his expectations of price and marginal cost would be equal; the point which, if the expectations were regarded as correct, would be the formal optimum.

It would be proper to study under this head industrial combination, for there seems little doubt that in general it is resorted to, not in order to exact monopolistic revenue, but to reduce the hazards and uncertainties to which the participants are exposed. This they do by attempting to stabilize the receipts of the industry as a whole and, by diminishing combination within it, to stabilize the share of each producer in these receipts. But this is altogether too unwieldy a topic to incorporate here.

**3. Grouping.** The third and final method of reducing risk which I wish to consider is that of the grouping of ventures. It relies on the fact that the outcome of a group of uncertain ventures considered as a whole is more predictable than the individual component outcomes. Before discussing some of the important ways in which it differs from the forms of risk-reduction so far considered, I wish to distinguish two different ways in which it may be carried out.

In the case of risks which are objectively estimated there is no special problem. Insurance companies do, of course, consolidate risks which are estimated in this way and their business can be regarded as the pooling of a large number of ventures in each of which there is a high probability of a small gain and a small probability of a large loss. Provided a sufficiently large number of instances can be grouped, the business in the aggregate can be made substantially free from risk. In some cases, owing to the difficulty of fitting the events into a homogeneous class of similar past events, the probability estimates may be very rough and the premia demanded correspondingly great. Nevertheless all but a few of the hazards which we regard as insurable have this in common: that estimates of their probability are made by demonstrable calculation, according to acknowledged rules from known evidence about the facts. The grouping of instances therefore presents no special difficulty; the individual estimates need not all be made in one mind, for, as they are formed according to fixed rules and require no special flair, one man's estimate is directly comparable with another's. There seems therefore no limit to the number of individual instances which can be grouped without impairment to the quality of the individual estimates.

With risks which are subjectively estimated the matter is otherwise. The ordinary investor will only be able to reduce his total risk by spreading his investments, provided the estimates he forms of each individual venture do not decline in reliability. This, however, is very likely to be the case, for if investors are to enlarge the number of ventures about which they have direct knowledge, then their knowledge of each is likely to be reduced. How, then, is risk-spreading successfully undertaken?

The ordinary investor will not usually attempt to form serious estimates of the probable success of particular projects, but will invest his money in a fair number of firms of established reputation. He will thus secure a diversified and comparatively riskless portfolio at the price of accepting a lower return on each individual investment. Reputation and goodwill are here an essential part of the mechanism. But it is important to realize that investment of this kind can only be practised so long as investment decisions of quite another kind are being taken at the same time. It presumes the existence of established firms for which the chances of success may be expected to outweigh the chances of failure, and such firms would never have been established, and would not continue to be successful, unless investment decisions were being taken which relied not primarily on the law of large numbers, but on foresight, on deliberately calculated estimates of the probable outcome of particular ventures.

The problem of grouping risky ventures, without impairment to the quality of the individual estimates of their outcomes, is therefore in the main merely transferred by the ordinary investor to the units to which they lend, and there, to some extent, it is solved. It is clear that almost all estimates of the profitability of a venture are partly based on the estimating capacities of others. An investor may be able himself to form estimates of the prospects in two lines; but if he knows someone whose foresight he esteems, then he can indirectly estimate the prospects in these ventures with which the latter person is directly familiar; this person can in turn know another, and so on, with the result that the original investor can form indirect estimates of the profitability of a good many lines. It would seem, however, that the reliance which he will place in an estimate will in general be the less, the larger the number of stages between it and the basic estimate. It is true, of course, that almost all our knowledge rests upon confidence in other people's estimates or reporting, but normally the liability to error in the estimate will be slight. When the scope for error is greater a much more intimate estimate must be made of the foresight of the person on whom we are relying, so that the existence of stable relationships of mutual confidence between a number of men seems to be a necessary condition for the successful grouping of subjectively estimated risks. Such a nexus of relationships is common throughout all society; its representative form in the economic sphere is the business corporation; when it is of a much looser form, between independent units, it is referred to as goodwill.

The large multi-product firm could therefore be regarded, from one point of view, as a system of relationships devised to enable the grouping of subjectively estimated risks. Although it is the most important, it is not the only organization performing this function. An industrial bank or an investment trust can also group risks. There are, of course, important differences: an investment trust cannot hope to have as close contact with the firms to which it lends as have the managing directors of a company with their subordinate officials, and it will either have to tolerate much less reliable estimates of each individual investment or, as is more likely, to confine its lending to firms which are established, or are engaged in less risky investment, or can offer good collateral. There are, of course, yet other differences which need not concern us here.

Grouping differs from the methods of risk reduction so far considered in two fundamental and interrelated respects: it does not produce any apparent misallocation of resources, and it precludes automatic selection. We observed above that the decisions which the entrepreneur is likely to take regarding the liquidity of his assets and the level and price of his output will produce an apparent misallocation, that is to say, an allocation which is imperfect relative to the estimates on which it is based; but which, if it created an environment favourable to automatic selection, and thereby improved the quality of the estimates themselves, would be justified by the actual performance of the system in the long run. To the extent that risky ventures are grouped the need for such policies is the less, and likewise the apparent misallocation. At the same time, however, within the area of the grouping, the forces of automatic selection no longer operate; planned selection, as I have called it, intervenes. It is this latter form of selection which I now wish to discuss.

## VI. Planned *versus* automatic selection

Planned selection may exist within units subject to automatic selection, or may characterize a whole economy. In such a situation control over resources does not vary automatically with the successful allocation of them, as a result of accruing profits and increased facility in borrowing. Within the sphere in which it operates, the firm or the economy, as it may be, planned selection is incompatible with the private ownership of the resources allocated. Automatic selection, on the other hand, normally presumes it, although it may exist where there is a degree of separation between ownership and control, as in the modern joint-stock company. Ideally under automatic selection the more efficient should not only prosper, but should, by virtue of their example, educate the others; in practice, however, this does not seem to work so well, for there often remain, for a considerable period, large differences between the efficiency of the various producers of a commodity. Under a planned system the level of entrepreneurial efficiency might be raised more rapidly by deliberate education. It should, of course, be possible in principle for the planned economy to reach a level of selection at least as efficient as the free economy, simply by copying the selective as well as the allocative mechanisms of perfect competition; but although this could be done, it need not, and certainly would no longer happen automatically. The planned economy, of which I take planned selection to be the most important mark, has, of course, its own defects. If the crucial problem of selection could be by-passed and all estimates of economic variables assumed to be equally reliable, then the planned economy would appear to give the better allocation. Provided the numbers of ventures was very large, the central authority could instruct its managers to follow the Rule according to their best estimates of price and marginal cost; for in this case gains and losses might be expected to cancel out and the outcome would in the aggregate conform to the mathematical expectation. It seems, therefore, on this very formal level, that the planned economy could, by pooling all ventures, enable more risky ones to be undertaken. For a private investor will, as we have seen, discriminate against investments for which the standard deviation of the profit expectation is large, whereas the State manager need not.

But this formal analysis is far from decisive; it abstracts from any effect which the differing forms of organization might have on the psychological traits, such as adventurousness or timidity, of those who act within them. Moreover, in assuming that the estimates made by the managers of the planned economy could all be regarded as equally reliable, we assume away the crucial problem of selection. Perfect allocation on the basis of poor estimates may obviously be inferior, as judged by long-run performance, than imperfect allocation on the basis of better ones.

It would appear that the importance of automatic selection in our economy is declining. It has not, primarily, been deliberately rejected, on the grounds, right or wrong, of inefficiency, but the general climate of opinion and government policies informed by this opinion have indirectly created an environment inimical to its successful working. Taxation is perhaps the major influence at work in this direction. It acts both to inhibit entry by new enterprises and to enfeeble the selective forces at work between existing ones.

The redistribution of income has so reduced the flow of personal savings that, in the long run, the greater part of the funds available for new enterprises may have to come, directly or indirectly, from the government. That this has not already come about is perhaps due in part to transient and fortuitous factors; the conversion of the stock of the now nationalized industries into gilt-edged, and the purchase of gilt-edged by the banks, have indirectly released capital for new enterprises but cannot continue to do so indefinitely. Unless there is to be inflation, which would bias the investor in favour of shares as against fixed-interest stock, the government, if it is to prevent industrial stagnation induced by unfavourable terms of borrowing, would itself be obliged to provide funds for new enterprise. The effects on our economy of a movement towards government monopoly of new lending would, of course, be exceedingly far-reaching, and to speculate on them here would be quite outside my scope; but it seems clear enough that selection of the kind at work in the free economy would, for good or ill, almost have come to an end.

The selective forces between existing firms are at present also being sapped by inflation, and by the controls and high taxation which are its concomitant. Under inflation profits come to the efficient and the inefficient alike, and the forms of taxation by which the government recovers them often discriminate against the former class. Dividend controls, in a similar manner, will generally weaken the advantage in borrowing which the currently successful firm would otherwise enjoy.

These influences, quite apart from concentration in order to enjoy the economies of large scale or to reduce risk, may well, in the long run, render the survival of a system of automatic selection, in all but the minor sectors of our economy, very improbable. It is not impossible that economists themselves, in some slight measure, have contributed to its demise; for, neglecting the imperfection of our knowledge and the problems arising from it, they have, in their theoretical models, too often represented free competition as an allocative and not also a selective mechanism. This is understandable, for it is exceedingly difficult to lay down at all precisely the optimum conditions for selection, and it may be, as Mr. Little maintains, that 'such considerations, though in principle they ought to make the theory more realistic, would in practice only mean that we could reach no specific conclusions, because we would then be dealing formally with factors which are not in practice, nor even perhaps in principle, measurable'.

I am inclined to wonder, however, whether insistence on the need for the factors in our theory to be measurable in principle has not been overdone. It is in any case a concession to a philosophical point of view rather than to practical necessity, for what in economic theory is measurable in principle can rarely be measured in practice and has to be estimated by judgement or guess-work. Would it be too simple-minded to argue that, instead of building models which, while complying with our rigorous canons of verifiability in principle, fail lamentably to pattern the real world, it would be better, at least for some purposes, to construct theories or models which do satisfactorily explain the working of our economy, even when the relative magnitude or importance of the factors in them would have to be established by judgement rather than calculated from statistical observation?

It may be that the selective forces in the free economy were discussed much more when Darwinian theory was in the air, and probably the analogy between the working of the free economy and the operation of natural selection in the animal kingdom was pushed ludicrously far. Nowadays most people prefer mechanical to biological models, but whether they will prove the more fertile approach to the understanding of the economic system remains to be seen.

ST. JOHN'S COLLEGE,
    OXFORD

# [2]

## SCHUMPETER'S *HISTORY OF ECONOMIC ANALYSIS*

### *By* G. B. RICHARDSON

### Introduction

SCHUMPETER's long-awaited *History* will surely rank as one of the most important books on economics to be published in the last half-century.[1] It is very rare for economists so clearly in the front rank to write on the history of theory, and the present work is almost certainly the greatest yet written in that field. It is also a great deal more. Its author's encyclopaedic knowledge and wide vision, his psychological insight, personality, and style enabled him to make it not only a history of economics but also an immensely readable study of how thought develops in general, a study, as the author would say, of 'the ways of the human mind'. Schumpeter died before the book could be finished, but by far the greater part of it was written up in manuscripts which were put together by his wife. Thanks to her immense and complex labours, and to the assistance which she received from several scholars, the *History* now published is reasonably complete.

The great range of Schumpeter's learning as displayed in the *History* will inspire most readers with humility, and does so particularly in the case of the present reviewer, who has independent acquaintance with only a small part of the field surveyed. Each of the separate parts of the work merits a separate review article, and any discussion of the whole must be general and selective. I have attempted to deal first with Schumpeter's view of the nature of the subject and with the principles on which it seems to me his assessment of particular performances is based. I turn later to the way in which the subject develops and to the chequered life-history of some economic ideas.

### 2. Schumpeter on the Nature of Economics

The first part of the *History* contains a discussion of the nature of economic science which, besides being of great intrinsic interest, also serves to present the author's programme and to justify his approach. He is well aware of the futility of much methodological controversy and of the lack of correspondence frequently, and fortunately, found between our methodological professions and our actual practice. But the philosophical and methodological issues raised by the subject have a strong fascination

---

[1] *History of Economic Analysis*, by Joseph A. Schumpeter. (New York, Oxford University Press, 1954. $17.50.)

for his mind and he clearly felt that they could not be by-passed on this occasion, since 'the possibility of treating the history of economics like the history of any other science is controversial' and 'the very rules or principles that are to guide the historian's pen are open to doubt, and what is worse, misunderstanding' (p. 3).

The subject of the *History* is to be economics in its strictly analytic or scientific aspects. 'What distinguishes the scientific economist from other people who write and think about economic topics is', he maintains, 'the command of techniques which we class under three heads, history, statistics and theory' which 'together make up what we shall call Economic Analysis'. A 'science' is defined as 'tooled knowledge', being a field where special techniques of fact-finding and analysis are developed, and it is the story of economic thinking which is scientific in this sense that he proposes to tell. Schumpeter then identifies two pretenders who are allowed to figure only in so far as they influence Economic Analysis in the strict sense. The first of these is Systems of Political Economy which are 'expositions of a comprehensive set of economic policies that their authors advocated on the strength of certain unifying (normative) principles such as . . . economic liberalism, socialism and so on' (p. 38). These systems, apart from the economic analysis they incidentally embody, being, according to Schumpeter, 'mere formulations of the ideology of an epoch or country without validity for any other', are banished to the background of the *History*. The same sentence is pronounced for the same reasons on Economic Thought, by which is meant 'the sum total of all opinions and desires concerning economic subjects, especially concerning public policy bearing on these subjects, that at any time float in the public mind' (p. 38). With these out of the way the author now turns to his chosen field of Economic Analysis as he has defined it. Our knowledge is the product of Analytic Effort operating on raw material provided by our Vision. Only after Vision, which is 'a pre-analytic act', has isolated the set of phenomena which interest us does the analytic work of devising a suitable conceptual attire and of testing against reality properly begin. It appears that Schumpeter uses the term 'economic analysis' in two senses, as originally defined to cover 'history, statistics and theory', and in the narrower sense as a process subsequent to and excluding Vision.

Now this careful sifting, by Schumpeter, of economics as loosely defined is of course undertaken in order to separate scientific economics in as pure a form as possible from the mass of ideologically contaminated views with which it may be entangled and confused. Schumpeter accepts, with significant qualifications, Marx's doctrine of ideological bias, according to which mans' ideas and systems, while claiming objectivity, are in fact distorted by unconscious desires to justify, exalt, or further a particular nation, class, or interest. Such systems of thought, which help us to conceive society as we would wish it to be, and which therefore correspond to rationalizations in the sphere of personal conduct, are entitled ideologies. Now once we accept the inevitability of ideological contamination of our views on economic matters, doubt is cast on the very existence of an objective and developing body of economic knowledge comparable with the established sciences. Not even Economic Analysis is free from suspicion, for ideology enters in 'on the ground floor' via the pre-analytic cognitive act referred to as Vision, which Schumpeter holds to be 'ideological almost by definition'. Our Vision 'embodies the picture of things as we see them, and whenever there is any possible motive for wishing to see them in a given rather than in another light the way in which we see things can hardly be distinguished from the way in which we wish to see them' (p. 42). On the other hand, the rules of scientific procedure followed in our analysis are 'almost as much exempt from ideological influence as vision is subject to it' and tend in the long run to purify our vision of its ideological contamination 'automatically and irrespective of the desires of the research worker' (p. 43).

This barest of outlines does scant justice to Schumpeter's arguments; but some readers who have read the original brilliant exposition may still be inclined, while agreeing in general terms, to differ on the matter of emphasis. They may feel that Schumpeter gives rather too much ground to the view that our economic opinions are invariably subject to ideological distortion and that he is therefore driven to place excessive reliance on the purifying influence of the process of technical analysis.

Should one say that 'vision is ideological almost by definition'? It may be that Schumpeter lays insufficient stress on the distinction between two different things: the existence of the more or less involuntary self-deception which we call rationalizations, and the fact that we can never think *ab initio* or view reality quite freshly, in independence of the categories and opinions which form our intellectual inheritance. The first of these represents ideological distortion in the proper sense. The unconscious motives for it may be remote and obscure. A Marxist, let us say, may convince himself, against the evidence, about the existence of certain fatal defects in the capitalist system; he may misunderstand the present reality so that it will not conflict with the principles of his faith, the unconscious reasons for accepting which—such as the desire for the security afforded by a dogmatic and all-embracing creed—may be very difficult to discover. But such distortion is not an inevitable characteristic of our vision. The second phenomenon, the fact that no one can escape from the categories in which he is trained to think, is inevitable but is not ideological delusion. It characterizes all fields of knowledge irrespective of subject-matter and is associated with no unconscious motive except perhaps that of avoiding the unpleasantness occasioned by the disruption of established beliefs.

As our author observes, a great part of general economics is scarcely of a nature to involve us emotionally, unless we are pathologically inclined to such attachments. This applies of course particularly to work concerned with the refinement of existing conceptual schemes as opposed to the representation of reality in new ones. But even where the subject is inflammatory, can we not often hope substantially to discount our biases by consciously recognizing our fears and wishes and forbidding them to enter our scientific work ? One would think that our wishes in connexion with the working of the economic system were more readily accessible to consciousness, and therefore more easily kept in order, than those, dealt with by psychologists, which cause us to have recourse to rationalizations in the conduct of our personal lives. Where ideology can and does find an easy breach is where, in considering particular cases, we have to estimate the importance of different, and almost imponderable influences, so that our guesses naturally take colour from our prejudices. But some comfort may be derived from the fact that while our judgement of particular situations may be highly susceptible in this regard, the analytical schema, or general theory which we employ, may remain much more immune.

Schumpeter, as has been said above, places very great reliance on analysis, on applying the rules of scientific procedure, as a process which tends to 'crush out ideologically conditioned error ... automatically and irrespective of the desires of the research worker'. One might wonder whether this was not rather optimistic and underestimated the importance of the student of the subject cultivating in himself (and in his pupils) an appropriately detached attitude of mind. Intelligence is not sufficient; the detached radical intellectual who regards everyone as the victim of ideological delusion except himself is, as Schumpeter says, often 'just a bundle of prejudices which are held with all the force of sincere conviction'. Nor is the command of an apparatus of modern stainless-steel techniques a protection; it can very easily be combined with extreme susceptibility to ideological delusion. What is required is something of the self-consciousness and intellectual integrity which Schumpeter possessed in such full measure, and which was the product both of his own particular personality and of the civilization by which it was formed.

A strong conviction in the benefits to be derived from modern techniques, and in particular mathematical techniques, runs through Schumpeter's whole book. He justifies it with powerful arguments which have nothing to do with ideological contamination; but could it nevertheless be that Schumpeter welcomed these techniques also because they seemed to lift the subject on to the securer level occupied by the physical sciences? Be this as it may, it remains curious that Schumpeter should have had such faith in mathematical methods while they feature so little in his work and hardly seem characteristic of his type of mind.

The depth of Schumpeter's concern with the problem of ideological bias is of course immensely interesting for what it reveals of the style and outlook of the man. The width of his experience of persons and places, together with his quite Protean capacity for comprehending different viewpoints as it were from the inside, must have implanted in him a deeply rooted conviction as to the relativity of human beliefs. Keynes's frequently quoted dictum that 'ideas and not vested interests are in the long run dangerous for good and evil' might have seemed to him a shallow, rationalistic dichotomy, attributing as it does to ideas an autonomy and independence of our desires which they rarely acquire. Indeed the possession by most English economists of a relatively untroubled confidence in their working philosophy and moral ideas may have been felt by him to stem from provinciality and lack of depth, though he may have envied the more comfortable assurance which it was able to afford.[1]

I wish now to turn to the general principles which seem to me to inform Schumpeter's assessment of the work of various economists. We may say that economics comprises a stock of models, a stock that is of logical patterns, of functional relationships representing schematically general cause–effect regularities in the real world. These are of all shapes and sizes, the most general isolating regularities which characterize, approximately, economic activity at almost any time or place. Others claim to represent the cause–effect relationships in a particular type of economy or over a short period of time. In any case the models have to be tailored to suit particular cases. Now economists can be classed according to the particular levels of generality at which they find it congenial to work. 'Economics', says our author, 'is a big omnibus which contains many passengers of incommensurable interests and abilities', and it is part of his greatness to be able sympathetically to understand and present all the passengers' points of view. Nevertheless we can perhaps detect the type to which he is characteristically most attracted, although the many-sidedness of his nature permits only partial validity for any such generalization. The author's personal approval seems to go out most strongly to economists of a broad and deep vision who seek to bring as great a variety

---

[1] Schumpeter holds that although economics 'has frequently been vitiated by the political attitudes of economists, it has not been shaped at any time by their philosophical opinions'. One wonders whether Schumpeter would still think this true in the case of contemporary Oxford. At least philosophical preconceptions influence the terms in which we wish to state our theorems, e.g. the recent behaviourist trend in the theory of consumer demand and elsewhere.

of human activity as possible under unifying general principles, and who impress us by the grandeur of their conception rather than by its immediate practical utility. They may be contrasted with writers whose work often arises from attempts to deal with current economic problems and who concern themselves not so much with the elucidation of extensive patterns of independence but with isolating just those relationships which they believe to be important for practical purposes. Marx and Walras, in their best-known work, incline towards the first group, Ricardo, Marshall, and Keynes more to the latter.[1] Schumpeter complains of the poverty of the vision of the English classical economists, who, although they lived 'at the threshold of the most spectacular economic developments ever witnessed ... nevertheless saw nothing but cramped economies struggling with ever-decreasing success for their daily bread'. He contrasts this with the magnificence of the Marxian vision, which, 'though ideologically vitiated at the roots, hopelessly wrong in its prophecy of ever-increasing mass misery and inadequately substantiated both factually and analytically', nevertheless conceived the evolution by an inherent logic of all the interdependent activities of human society. Not everyone, however, feels the intellectual appeal of the system as strongly as does Schumpeter, for its very generality may repel as well as attract. Keynes, for example, could find nothing in it except out-of-date controversializing. Neither Adam Smith nor Marshall would probably have denied that economic change must influence some of the non-economic institutions of society,[2] but may have refrained from embodying this formally in a general theory simply because, it being extremely difficult to predict the precise form of the influence, they had no interest in formulating a relationship to which they could hope to give content. Marshall clearly states, in Appendix C to his *Principles*, that he believed a unified social science to be unattainable. What may sometimes appear as lack of imagination may, in part at least, be temperamental aversion to theorems of great generality, arising from a conviction that there is a great deal of the social process about which we have to be agnostic.

Schumpeter's predilection for theoretical generality and the glamour of great systems is suggested also by his treatment of Walras and Marshall. Walras he considered, as far as pure theory was concerned, 'the greatest of all economists', and claims that his system 'is the only work by an economist which will stand comparison with the achievements of theo-

---

[1] It may seem strange to bracket Marx and Walras. The similarity in their systems to which I refer is simply preoccupation with general interdependence. Marx's system illustrates interdependence of a 'vertical' kind, between the different layers of social activity, economic, political, and cultural: the interdependence in Walras is of a 'horizontal' kind, existing between all the units in economic activity.

[2] Cf. Smith's discussion of the different political structure of societies of shepherds and hunters, *Wealth of Nations*, Book V, ch. 1, part 1.

retical physics' (p. 827). Indeed there is a tendency, not necessarily un-justified, to regard the general equilibrium system as the divine event to which the whole creation moves, and to judge performances according to whether they hastened or retarded its arrival. Ricardo in particular is held responsible by Schumpeter for a 'great détour'. His patched-up labour theory of value stood in the way of advance, as did his theory of rent which 'carries meaning only within that [i.e. Ricardo's] theoretical set up and is nothing but an obstacle to the recognition of important symmetries within any other'. These charges, which are repeated empha-tically by Schumpeter, may seem, at least as far as value theory is con-cerned, difficult fully to justify. By being based on embodied labour, Ricardo's theory of relative prices deserves to be characterized as a detour, distracting attention from the influence of demand and the whole process of evaluation of goods and productive services. Yet it may equally well be viewed as a stepping-stone, for the heavy qualifications which Ricardo places on his theory clearly point ahead. His recognition of the time element in production points in one direction, and his theory of the return to one fixed factor, that is land, can easily be generalized to cover others such as different kinds of labour. All this is to his credit, quite apart from the fact that he brought into economics a new spirit of analy-tical sharpness and precision.

Marshall is likewise charged by Schumpeter of obscuring the pattern of mutual interdependence. This he did in the famous scissors analogy, by claiming that the demand and utility analysis of Jevons and others, and the cost analysis of Ricardo and the classics, were each only half the story. In fact, Schumpeter argues, a proper general equilibrium analysis shows that both blades of the scissors 'consist of the same material. . . . both demand and supply . . . can be explained in terms of utility'. It is difficult not to agree with Schumpeter that Marshall was generous to Ricardo at the cost of being less than just to Jevons; more important is it to notice that from the point of view of partial analysis (whether or not we believe the usefulness of this simplification to outweigh its dangers) Marshall's ap-proach is quite appropriate.

Now, the conception of general interdependence was, as Schumpeter points out, within Marshall's range and is actually set down in embryonic form in Note XXI of the Mathematical Appendix to the *Principles*. It was not lack of imagination, and certainly not lack of mathematical ability, which prevented Marshall from elaborating it; but rather, it would seem, instinctive moral scruple at formulating theories which he felt to be of aesthetic rather than utilitarian interest. He seemed to have wished to select only those parts of the whole skeleton of economic relationship which he could clothe with flesh and blood and to keep all the rest in the background. Schumpeter quotes his highly revealing remark that his 'whole life has been given and will be given to presenting in realistic form as much as I can of my note XII'. Marshall's characteristic approach derives no doubt from his particular temperament and from the nature of the motives which led him to devote his great talents to the service of the science. The driving force in Schumpeter seems to have been the spirit of pure intellectual inquiry, which in Marshall was secondary to the desire to ameliorate human life through the relief of poverty. Thus we see again that there is no simple criterion for assessing performance even in theoretical analysis; for concepts may be appraised on their purely intellectual appeal, which usually derives from the way in which they co-ordinate under a few unifying principles a wide range of ostensibly separate phenomena, or to the extent that they form 'short links' (to use Marshall's term) of great use in the study of particular economic situations.

So strong was Marshall's desire to hold his discussion down to real economic life, his 'bent', as Schumpeter calls it, 'towards misplaced realism', that the opaque façade of his work partly conceals the careful analytical scaffolding he has erected behind it. The danger in such an approach is that it may gain the very doubtful short-run advantage of applicability only at the cost of retarding the progress of the science. But the reluctance to expose theoretical schema in clear and naked outline may have arisen from Marshall's fear that they might harden in the minds of others into a more reliable representation of reality than he himself, with his sense, as Schumpeter calls it, of the 'intimate organic necessities of economic life', ever believed them to be.

Though Schumpeter appreciated Marshall's greatness as an economist and pays generous tribute to his insight into the facts of economic life— which made him speak 'as one who has power and not like the scribes'— yet one clearly notices how different the personalities and philosophies of the two men were. To Schumpeter, Marshall's manner, his tendency to patronize and his 'propensity to preach', and his lack of generosity in acknowledgement, are clearly uncongenial; his conception of the Noble Life ludicrously naïve and insular, and his utilitarian approach an obstacle, at least on occasions, to the progress of the science.

Schumpeter's appraisal of Keynes has already been recorded, before the publication of the *History*, in the magnificent memorial article[1] which recalls, in the skill with which understanding the man is related to appreciation of his work, Keynes's famous essay on Marshall. And the appraisal is particularly revealing both of our author's approach and of the nature of our subject. There were similarities between the personalities of Schumpeter and Keynes, but in approach to the subject they differed greatly.

[1] *American Economic Review*, 1946.

Keynes's kinsman in aims and method was, according to Schumpeter, David Ricardo. He says of the latter:

In all the questions he touched he was on the side that would have won out anyhow, but to the victory of which he contributed a usable argument, earning corresponding applause. Though others did the same, his advocacy was more brilliant, more arresting than was theirs; there is no superfluous sentence in his pages; no qualification *however necessary* weakens his argument; and there is just enough genuine analysis about it to convince practically and, at the same time, *to satisfy high intellectual standards* but not enough to deter. His polemical talent, which combined to an altogether unusual degree readiness, force and genuine politeness, did the rest. People took to his theory because they agreed with his recommendations . . . (p. 473). [Author's italics.]

He then adds, in a footnote, that every word of this applies to Keynes. Ricardo's method of work is also found to resemble that of Keynes, and he says of the former:

His interest was in the clear-cut result of direct practical significance. In order to get this he cut that general (economic) system to pieces, bundled up as large parts of it as possible, and put them into cold storage—so that as many things as possible should be frozen and given. He then piled one simplifying assumption upon another until, having really settled everything by these assumptions, he was left with only a few aggregate variables between which, given these assumptions, he set up simple one way relations so that, in the end, the desired results emerged almost as tautologies (p. 472).

Keynes is also found guilty of this 'Ricardian Vice' by which Schumpeter means 'the habit of piling a heavy load of practical conclusions upon a tenuous groundwork, which was unequal to it yet seemed in its simplicity not only attractive but also convincing' (p. 1171).

Keynes's work is offered by Schumpeter as a striking example of the distinction between analysis and the vision which precedes it, the vision in this case being that of England's ageing capitalism, 'the arteriosclerotic economy whose opportunities for rejuvenating venture decline while the old habits of saving formed in times of plentiful opportunity persist'. In writing the *General Theory*, he argues, Keynes 'bent to the task of framing an analytical system that would express his fundamental idea *and nothing else*' [author's italics].

These criticisms point very clearly to the different approaches to economics described above. Keynes, like Marshall, though of course susceptible to the intellectual appeal of the subject, regarded economics primarily as a useful art designed to guide policy. Given this outlook, the model he sought to construct had to be usable and had therefore to bear close reference to the particular reality with which he was concerned and had to be reasonably simple. The 'General Theory' is therefore a tailor-made model, though it is surely of much wider applicability than Schumpeter would allow it. It can, for example, as everyone knows, be used in the analysis of inflation as well as of slumps. It does not of course represent the working of any conceivable capitalist economy; a really general theory of this kind would probably be of little practical use.

Keynes's procedure of making severe assumptions so as to reach clear-cut conclusions is of course risky, and one relies partly on his judgement and intuition that the conclusions would still approximately hold even if the conditions did not quite strictly obtain. But before reaching a policy decision judgement or guess-work inevitably come in at more than one stage, both in framing the model and in the application of it. All we must demand is that the assumptions or guesses be fairly explicit and if possible capable of verification, a condition which the 'General Theory' reasonably satisfies. Finally there is the ultimate test, also met, of success, not in the sense of gaining adherents, but in having in fact actually assisted policy-makers in choosing the right means for the end they desire.

## 3. The development of the subject

We have noted that Schumpeter's conception of the *History* is based on a distinct view of the nature of economic science: further testimony to the systematic character of his mind is that the division of the book into historical periods is likewise according to a clear principle. Advance in the subject is seen as neither steady nor uniform, but as involving many detours and the loss of positions gained earlier. A certain pattern is, however, to be observed, in which long periods of confusion and controversy are followed by a time of systematic consolidation, characterized by general agreement between economists on fundamentals and self-satisfied confidence in the validity and permanence of the positions reached. Such periods of repose are referred to as Classical Situations, and Parts II, III, and IV of the book deal with the three great periods which culminate in this way. Part V presents a sketch of modern developments, which though of great interest, is not comparable with the previous parts. The first and longest part is 'from the beginning', up to the second half of the eighteenth century. It covers principally the ancient world, the medieval schoolmen, the 'more boisterous stream' of Consultant Administrators and Pamphleteers, the Physiocrats with Turgot, and finally, as the great figure of the Classical Situation with which the period closes, Adam Smith. The second period ends with the 1860's and is 'summed up in the typically classical situation . . . of John Stuart Mill, who underlined the fact by his attitude of speaking from the vantage point of established truth and by the naïve confidence which he placed in the durability of this established truth'. The third period is rounded off by the leading works of the last decade of the nineteenth century which again created 'in the superficial observer, an impression of finality'.

This development exhibits, to a much greater extent than in the sciences of matter, waste and inefficiency. First, there is no orderly inheritance of ideas; the gains of one generation are frequently jettisoned by the next according to the swing of the doctrinal pendulum. Secondly, many ideas find their way only belatedly into the corpus of knowledge, having been entirely ignored when first expounded.

The history of interest theory offers a splendid, or rather melancholy, example of how established positions can be lost. It begins effectively with the remarkable contribution[1] of the late scholastics, particularly Molina, who conceived of interest as depending on the demand and supply of money and went a long way to explaining the factors which determine its rate. The demand for money was seen to arise directly from the fact that it was the 'Merchant's Tool' and therefore indirectly from the fact of business profit. Payment for the supply of money was justified not only on account of the risk and trouble of lending but as a compensation for any losses which forgoing command over money might involve. This view of interest would appear to have persisted in the seventeenth and well into the eighteenth centuries when it was expelled by a simpler doctrine enunciated probably first by Barbon and supported by Turgot and Smith. This concentrated solely on changes in saving and productivity as affecting the demand and supply of loans. Indeed it went further; it insinuated that interest was *directly* dependent on productivity and thrift so that money could be left out of the analysis. This tended to result from the language employed. 'Interest is commonly reckoned for Money', said Barbon, '. . . but this is a mistake; for the interest is paid for Stock'. 'It is the Rent of Stock and is the same as the Rent of Land.' Thereafter the complexity of the factors affecting interest through the demand and supply of money (which had thus been effectively short-circuited) were ignored except by a few writers (one of them, Thornton, of great distinction) until relatively recent times.

Further light is thrown on the wayward nature of the development of our science by the fate of the foreign-trade theories of the mercantilists. To Smith and the economists of the classical period these theories and 'that imaginary organon, the mercantilist system', were the object of indignation and derision, as simply error, and pernicious error at that. Later on an equally excessive reaction developed, principally among German nineteenth-century economists with protectionist leanings. In attempting to strike a proper balance Schumpeter himself distinguishes between two questions: whether mercantilist policies offered adequate means towards rationally defensible ends, and whether the theoretical

---

[1] This was not the only remarkable contribution of the schoolmen, as Schumpeter, in one of the most interesting parts of the *History*, clearly shows.

arguments used to justify them were valid. On the first count the mercantilists acquit themselves quite well, given the fact that they lived in underemployed and underdeveloped economies and were deeply concerned with international power politics. But the arguments offered were mainly pre-analytic and popular 'in the most distressing sense of that word'. They did, however, have important insight and the protectionist arguments seemed to be remarkably up to date—infant and key industries, home employment, military needs, even the terms-of-trade argument all put in an appearance.

Now what we have to note here is that both the contempt and the favour with which the mercantilists were alternately viewed was in fact stimulated, not by their contributions to the science, but by their policy opinions, according to whether these appeared in harmony with the prevailing ideology. So strong were emotional attitudes towards 'monopoly' or 'free trade', that they denied to later critics the detachment required to separate the scientific contributions from the policy recommendations. Adam Smith in particular was content to ridicule a mere caricature of mercantilist doctrine and, thereby, because of his immense authority, to do disservice to the science.[1] The situation as Schumpeter puts it was 'comparable to the waste which would result if successive teams of workmen smashed the products of their predecessors whenever they disliked the latter's politics'. It certainly goes a long way to justify the stress which he places on the importance of ideological influence on economic thinking. It also suggests an important reason why, at any particular time, at least a few economists should be studying the history of the subject in an attempt to regain lost ideas.

So far we have dealt with the abandonment of economic theories because of the policy views or ideologies with which they were associated, and notwithstanding the real insights which they may have contained. Economic theory may also be retarded simply because new ideas failed to be noticed or did not catch on. The marginal utility theory of value, for example, for which credit usually goes to Jevons, Menger, and Walras, was in fact anticipated not only by Gossen and Dupuit but also by a Student of Christ Church and Drummond Professor of Political Economy, at Oxford, W. F. Lloyd, whose demonstration was, according to Schumpeter, 'quite straightforward' and had 'nothing deterrent about it'.

The causes of this phenomenon are probably several. In the first place, as Schumpeter observes, 'analytical progress—not only in economics— hinges in great part on making things explicit which have been implied

---

[1] This is not to say that Smith's condemnation did not have a beneficial influence on the policies of governments and on world affairs, and that the influence would have been less strong if the condemnation had been more qualified.

or implicitly recognised for ages'. We are capable, that is, of 'knowing' an economic fact on two levels, on an everyday, unanalytic level, or systematically, in such a way that the relations of this fact to the rest of our economic knowledge is observed. An example of this is the unwillingness and difficulty with which professional economists right into the twentieth century admitted into their general schemes of thought the fact that banks create credit. Secondly, until the nineteenth century the study of economics was comparatively unprofessional, so that it was possible for the views of individual thinkers to fail to gain a substantial audience and thereby to be accepted into the corpus of doctrine. But this is far from the whole story, as the previous example of W. F. Lloyd clearly shows. A deeper reason may be that innovation in economics consists not so much in the discovery of new facts but in conceiving a new way in which these facts can be viewed. Theories are indispensable for any understanding of economic phenomena, but once entrenched in our minds they bitterly resist any successors by which our understanding may be improved. 'New ideas', as our author observed, 'unless carefully elaborated, painstakingly defended and pushed, simply will not tell.'

The conditions for popular success are discussed by Schumpeter with reference to the most famous of all books on economics, the *Wealth of Nations*. He regards it as the conclusion of the first of the three great periods. It is seen not as the foundation of the science but as a work of consolidation, the fact being, Schumpeter claims, that 'the *Wealth of Nations* does not contain a single analytical idea, principle or method that was entirely new in 1776'. Originality is, however, surely difficult to define in this field, where ideas rarely tend to rise fully armed but tend to grow, by increasing clarification, from obscure origins; and, as Schumpeter himself observes, if eminence in an economist be judged solely in terms of entirely new results not only Smith, but Ricardo, Mill, and others might fail to justify their reputations. Schumpeter accounts for the spectacular and enduring success of the *Wealth* partly from the fact that it marshalled things the way they were going; it offered cogent and eloquent arguments in favour of policies which, as Schumpeter points out, already commanded increasing popular support. Moreover although, to quote Schumpeter, it 'entirely lacked the graces of the *Esprit des Lois*', yet it was immensely readable, free from recondite truth or difficult methods, never moving 'above the heads of even the dullest readers' but leading them on 'gently, encouraging them by trivialities and homely observations'.

Although Smith may bear a large part of the blame for the impoverishment of the theory of interest and, perhaps, of international trade, yet in other directions the *Wealth of Nations* would not seem to have too narrowly conditioned future development. For the consolidation effected by Smith was of a loose and unsystematic kind, and those who have studied the *Wealth* to discover his views of particular subjects will know how difficult it is to extract any single consistent doctrine. But this very defeat made the book a fertile source of future work, both Ricardo and Malthus, as Schumpeter says, representing different ways of recoining the *Wealth*. Smith suffers a probably justifiable reduction in status at Schumpeter's hand; his mind was not remarkably original and certainly lacked the cutting edge of, say, Turgot or Ricardo. Even his confusions, however, are, I suspect, worthy of study, for they may sometimes embody an obscure insight not given to clearer-minded economists. Schumpeter's attitude to Smith is fair if unsympathetic. He clearly finds uncongenial the personality of the painstaking, circumspect, professorial Scot, to whom 'the glamours and passions of the world were just literature', 'everywhere turning his Chair into a seat of judgement and bestowing praise and blame' on the basis of his 'dry and uninspired wisdom'.

The different rates of progress which economics has made at different times and places leads our author to some interesting reflections on the conditions most favourable to analytic advance. The pressure of great current economic problems often provides the stimulus for development, but it is far from being a sufficient condition. The great contributions arising from the controversies over the Restriction Act of 1797 and subsequent monetary crises were the work of men of affairs primarily interested in practical measures, but of men who also possessed the 'taste and ability for theoretical analysis' without which experience by itself fails to promote scientific advance. Ancient Romans had economic problems in plenty and had great ability; but what remains of the writings suggest that they lacked the necessary scientific curiosity and bent to theoretical speculation. The absence of important original work in the United States during the second of Schumpeter's great periods is attributed to similar causes. Practical problems once more were there and also the demand for economic teaching, but the tasks and opportunities presented by the business environment absorbed the energies of the best men, so that 'the brains that could have done the job were producing boots'.

Schumpeter refers more than once to the great difficulty which the human mind has in forging the most elementary conceptual schemes. One is led to reflect that in economics, as elsewhere, any original improvement in our knowledge of reality is only made possible by withdrawing from it. Under the immediate pressure of reality, in its particular or everyday aspects, we cannot hope to escape from the tyranny of the conventional categories through which we view it. To see problems in the obvious and to find the familiar strange is an indispensable, if unnatural, step to take.

## 4. Conclusion

The *History* is surely one of the most readable books ever written on economics, a quality which it owes above all to the remarkable personality of the author, which enlivens every page. One is obviously tempted to make comparisons with Keynes. Clear brilliance, authority, quickness and flexibility of mind, and a sense of fun seem common to both. Both seemed in reaction against the bourgeois virtues and had a strong personal aversion to utilitarianism as, to quote Schumpeter, 'unsurpassably shallow as a philosophy of life'. But in other ways they differed fundamentally. Schumpeter was, I should imagine, Keynes's superior as a scholar, at least within the field of economics, where the latter's knowledge of the literature, to quote our author, was 'not of the first order'. Not that Schumpeter is academic in the derogatory sense; he himself rather despises the intellectuals 'who know business only from the newspapers'. To some, Schumpeter's vision of life will seem less space- and time-bound, deeper if more pessimistic than that of Keynes, his work more systematic and thorough. Largely it is a difference in nationality; Keynes was surely exceedingly English and in direct descent from the English empirical philosophers. At least in one sense he was more successful than Schumpeter in that he probably made a greater impact on economic thought; though Schumpeter refers with scepticism and wry humour to the former's belief 'that he had led economics out of 150 years of error into the land of definite truth'.

No simple account of Schumpeter could be true. His thought displays both strongly metaphysical and strongly empirical strands, and has both Germanic and Anglo-Saxon affinities. The whole book is charged with his electric personality, yet scarcely any mention is made of his own contribution to the subject. His English style is both dignified and familiar, his vocabulary both scholarly and colloquial. He displays, in fact, all the bewildering contradictions of genius.

ST. JOHN'S COLLEGE,
    OXFORD.

# [3]

# DEMAND AND SUPPLY RECONSIDERED

## *By* G. B. RICHARDSON

## 1. Introduction

The subject of this paper is the adjustment of supply to demand in the private enterprise economy. The first part finds the usual analysis of the determination of price and output in competitive markets to be unsatisfactory, not only because it is unrealistic (which is acknowledged), but because it is logically unsound, and because, far from being a useful first approximation, it can and often does lead us to wholly false appraisals of economic systems, according to which perfect knowledge and perfect competition are seen as the requirements of ideal allocation, while anything incompatible with them is represented as an imperfection or defect. The second part of the article attempts to be constructive and sketches out very roughly what seems to me to be an appropriate theoretical framework. The arguments which I advance reflect, and seem to me to justify, a particular point of view, the view that models based on so-called perfect knowledge are fundamentally unsound and that it is only by discussing the conditions of knowledge explicitly and realistically that an understanding of economic processes can be obtained.

The traditional analysis in question proceeds in terms of the most famous of all economic's conceptual instruments, schedules of demand and supply. The demand schedule sets out the quantities which consumers are prepared to buy at different prices. The supply schedule purports to indicate, on the basis of certain assumptions, how much producers are prepared either to produce or to sell at different prices. The intersection of the two curves is said to determine the equilibrium price and output, for all other values there being a tendency to expansion or contraction. The whole analysis rests on several assumptions; the first, the existence of perfect competition, and the second, profit maximization, we shall discuss no farther now. The third assumption, the most interesting but usually the least explicit, is about expectations. What assumptions about expectations are appropriate in this case ? This is the question to which we must turn our attention.

## 2. The Supply Curve of the Perfectly Competitive Industry

Given the functions relating price to demand and supply, expectations enter very obviously into the discussion of how equilibrium is reached, but, in addition, the supply function itself involves implications regarding them, which merit our very careful scrutiny. My criticism of the ordinary analysis of the determination of price in the competitive market will in fact principally rest on the contention that the significance of the industry's supply curve as normally constructed, has been misunderstood, and that a new meaning has to be given both to this curve and to its point of intersection with the demand schedule. Let us first confine our attention to what is usually called the long-run supply curve of the perfectly competitive industry, the curve which purports to indicate how much will be produced for each level of price, assuming that there is time for new firms to enter and for the full adaptation of all the factors of production. I wish for the moment to leave aside all questions about stock changes, speculation, and short-run adjustment.

Now, strictly, according to the principle of its construction, this schedule relates not price to planned supply, but marginal cost to output, where total output is produced in the cheapest way. In building up the curve, we simply relate a given volume of output, produced in the cheapest way available, to the cost of producing an extra unit. If the supply of all factors were infinitely elastic, the curve would be a horizontal line; if it were inelastic, the curve would rise. Entrepreneurs fit somewhat uneasily into this construction, but presumably they likewise are treated as a factor of production, the remuneration of which, 'normal profits', enters in as a cost. To maintain perfect competition one must also assume that some limit is set, as for example by 'managerial diseconomies', to the scale of their individual operations. Now, although the supply of entrepreneurs to the economy as a whole might be inelastic, in the sense that less efficient ones had to be employed as total output increased, their supply to any one industry is unlikely to be significantly so. This will of course depend on whether the expansion in the demand for one industry is accompanied by contraction elsewhere, so that entrepreneurs can transfer, but these matters, so often left obscure, do not particularly concern us here. I shall assume that the level of entrepreneurial efficiency does not alter with the output of the industry. Now the question which concerns us is whether this curve, which deals essentially with costs, can in fact legitimately be interpreted as a supply function relating price to planned supply, and, if so, under what conditions. I propose to entitle the function, the construction of which I have just described, the Optimum Supply Function, and the output corresponding to any particular value of the ordinate, the Optimum Supply. I do so now simply to facilitate reference, though I hope to justify the usage later. Our question, therefore, is whether we can postulate any conditions of expectation which will permit us to represent this Optimum Supply Function as what we may call an Effective Supply Function relating price to the supply which will be planned.

Now for the optimum supply curve to be represented as an effective supply curve, it must have as ordinate not the cost of a marginal addition to the industry's output, but price. It is also clear that the price referred to must be, in effect, the price expected at some future date, for it is to this that planned supply is directly related. Any fixed relationship between actual price and planned supply is necessarily indirect and possible only if the price expected depends solely on the current price, as many writers presumably assume when they treat them as identical. We shall have to assume further that the price expectations which constitute the ordinate are universal, unanimous, and subjectively certain. These, for the sake of brevity, I shall henceforth call Perfect Expectations; they are to imply that everyone entertains an expectation of future price, that expectations are the same for all and are believed by all, rightly or wrongly, to be single-valued and certain. Anyone who wishes to represent the optimum supply function as an effective supply function must postulate expectations with all these attributes. If they were not universal, then supply would depend on the number of people who held them and not merely on costs. If they were not unanimous, then price as ordinate would have no ordinary meaning. If they were not certain, then the supply offered would no longer depend simply on prices and production functions, but would vary with the shape and dispersion of the probability expectation, the differing attitudes to risk, and so on. The replacement of the uncertain expectations by some certainty equivalent is of no use here; it merely assumes away the specific influence of uncertainty and difference of opinion.

If then we represent the ordinate of our optimum supply function as a perfect expectation of the product price, can we say that the corresponding output is the supply which will actually be planned? Clearly as yet we cannot, for planned supply will also depend on expected factor prices, about which nothing has as yet been said. Now there seems to be no doubt that one has to assume perfect expectations of factor prices if there is to be any hope of securing the equivalence in question; otherwise planned supply would depend on the difference and uncertainty of the expectations and on the number of people holding them, a situation clearly ruled out by the way in which the optimum supply function was constructed. Thus we are forced to assume perfect expectations for both factor and product prices.

We must now inquire whether, for a given expected product price, there will be certain expected factor prices which will ensure that the output planned is that given by the optimum supply function. It is in fact easy to show that there are no possible combinations of expected factor and product prices which will give any finite, non-zero planned supply. If the factor prices are such, given the expected product price, as to yield profits less than normal, planned supply will be zero; if they imply a yield equal to or greater than normal profits, planned supply is infinite. This is so provided that normal profits are being earned elsewhere, which seems the appropriate assumption for this model, but if they were generally higher the argument would need only slight modification. We must conclude therefore that there are no possible assumptions about expectations, however unrealistic, which enable us to interpret the optimum supply function as an effective supply function.

There seem to be fewer difficulties in interpreting the short-run supply curve as a function relating planned supply to price. As expansion in output can come only from existing plant, and as the marginal costs of production from each plant must clearly rise after a certain point, there is no danger of an infinite planned supply. But a further logical objection applies to both short-run and long-run functions. In order to have a planned supply equal to the optimum supply in question, the factor prices expected will have to be those employed in the construction of the optimum supply function, those, that is, which would come about if the demand were that implied by the particular optimum supply. In other words, the equivalence of planned and optimum supply requires that the factor prices expected should be those which execution of the plans would bring about, or, more simply still, factor prices would have to be correctly foreseen. But it is inconsistent with the conditions of atomistic competition to assume that entrepreneurs could obtain this particular knowledge. In order to forecast future factor prices correctly any producer must be able to forecast total planned supply and, therefore, the production plans of his competitors. Their plans, however, depend on his own and cannot be made until his own are determined. There is, moreover, no way out of this well-known circularity, except collusion, which is excluded by the assumption of perfect competition. I conclude, therefore, that producers may not be assumed to have this particular knowledge, from which it follows, that there are no possible legitimate assumptions about expectations which permit us to interpret even the short-run supply curve as a function relating price to planned supply.

The argument so far may briefly be recapitulated. I set out to consider the accepted discussion of the competitive equilibrium in terms of demand and supply schedules. In this account, these schedules are regarded as functions relating price to plans to buy and plans to produce or sell, and the equilibrium price is that for which these plans are matched, so that the market is cleared and no one has any motive for altering them. This analysis has often been criticized on the grounds that producers could not be expected to foresee the equilibrium price, or that adjustment by stages, as in the cobweb cycle, does not always ensure that it is reached. In my view, however, the objection lies deeper. The basis of the whole analysis is unsound, for what is traditionally called the industry's supply curve, constructed from costs, cannot be interpreted as a function relating price to planned supply, no matter what legitimate assumptions we care to make about expectations.

We must now ask ourselves, first, what meaning can be given to the demand and supply schedules, and, secondly, what, as an analysis of the conditions of equilibrium, is to take their place. The so-called supply curve of the perfectly competitive industry is no more than that which, by the principle of its construction, it initially purports to be—the relationship between the output of a commodity and the marginal cost of producing it in the most economical way. In itself it does not imply, and cannot be made to imply, any relationship between actual output plans and price, whether present or expected, for it has to do not with actual, but with ideal, situations—for which reason I entitled it the optimum supply function. Provided we make all the assumptions and qualifications familiar to the student of welfare economics, which I shall not enumerate here, the curve will tell us, for any particular price, what the volume of the optimum output will be. It is appropriate to centrally planned resource allocation; it tells us what output would be planned by an omniscient authority. It is wholly erroneous to imagine that, by endowing the individual entrepreneurs with similar 'perfect knowledge', we can represent the curve as an effective supply function. The intersection of this curve with the demand curve should therefore be described as representing not equilibrium price and output, but optimum price and output, in the usual qualified sense of optimum.

There are many difficulties in the interpretation of this sense of optimum which have not been much considered in formal welfare economics. If it is the long-run supply curve with which we are concerned, then the optimum defined by its intersection with the demand curve is that appropriate to the assumption that the technical conditions of production will not change, and that the level of demand will be constant, over a period no shorter than the life of any of the durable factors of production. For different assumptions a different optimum supply curve would have to be drawn.

So far we have arrogated to ourselves supernatural insight into the minds of consumers, so that the magnitude and duration of the demand was known to us with certainty. But clearly consumers are liable to change their minds; even to the supernatural observer there may be not imperfect knowledge, but absolute uncertainty. If this is so, a gradual increase in supply may be optimal, for this will both leave time for the permanence of the level of demand to show itself and for its magnitude to be sounded out empirically. For example, we may imagine that there is no way of testing the capacity of a ferry except by gradually admitting passengers until it is low in the water. The meaning which we attach to optimum adaptation will therefore depend on whether, in setting the conditions of the problem, we postulate a demand curve which is or is not certain. Moreover, in practice, successful adaptation will be a matter of degree, depending not only on how closely actual supply approached the optimum but also on the rapidity with which it does so. Further difficulties of this kind, however, must no longer detain us now.

The optimum supply function presumably came to be regarded as a function relating planned supply to expected price partly because of the insufficient attention which economists pay to their assumptions about expectations. One is reminded of the unwillingness to distinguish between savings and investment *ex ante* and *ex post*, which caused a good deal of confusion in early discussions of interest and employment theory. In the present example, however, confusion is perhaps still easier, because of the ancient difficulty in disentangling norms from facts.

Let us now turn to our second question: by what is the analysis of the determination of price in the competitive market to be replaced ? The analysis purported to show that, given perfect competition and, in some sense, perfect knowledge, price and output would tend to equilibrium values given by the intersection of the demand and supply schedules. I have maintained that the basis of the analysis was unsound, that the initial assumptions about expectations, once made explicit, were easily shown to be illegitimate. There is therefore no point in further inquiry as to how, given these assumptions, price would be determined; the question is better approached in a different way. I have argued that the point of intersection of the two curves should be regarded, not as an equilibrium, but as an optimum, position. It seems, therefore, that the question which should properly concern us is this; under what realistic assumptions about knowledge, market structure, and the like, will the optimum be reached and maintained ? This will in fact be the subject of the rest of the paper. It is important to free ourselves from the outset, from the assumptions of the rejected model of competitive price determination; they are misleading in that they suggest that perfect knowledge, whatever it means, is important for the attainment of equilibrium, so that the more widespread and certain is the knowledge of the equilibrium price, the more likely is it to be realized; and that, conversely, uncertainty and ignorance regarding it are likely to prevent its realization. This assertion regarding perfect knowledge and equilibrium is certainly very frequently made, in my view quite wrongly, and with pernicious results, for it often persuades those who make it to regard as imperfections or distortions many aspects of the economy which are in fact essential to efficient adjustment and allocation within it.

In discussing the conditions for successful adaptation, for the attainment, that is, of the optimum position, I shall assume from the beginning that expectations are not held universally and may be uncertain and differing.

The first part of the argument is to do with the conditions of knowledge and considers how producers obtain information about the future demand for their products, how different market structures affect the supply of this information, and how it has to be spread and how expectations have to form, if adaptation is to be successful. All this I have called the communication process. The second part of the explanation of the adjustment of supply to demand is to do with the determinants of the firm's response to its expectations, and the third with the interaction of the communication process and responsiveness to produce adaptation. These three subjects, the communication process, responsiveness, and adaptation, form the three main sections of the rest of this paper. They attempt to offer a very rough theoretical framework for discussing the problem before us. They do not comprise a model in the formal mathematical sense; such models have their function, but if I am right that uncertainty, difference in expectations and responsiveness, and consequently non-simultaneity of decisions are essential to the working of the adaptive process, this function may be more limited than seems the general opinion. 'Short links' to quote Marshall, rather than extended logical concatenation, may be what we want.

## 3. The Communication Process

In this section I wish to consider what conditions of knowledge or belief are most favourable to successful adaptation, and how different market structures may affect them. 'Full' or 'perfect' knowledge, I have argued, is an obscure and misleading notion, even as an ideal to be sought after if the system is to work well. We have to ask ourselves what dosage or distribution of knowledge among producers is necessary in order that the optimum adaptation is brought about, and this will depend on the responsiveness of prospective producers to it. Once more, as an example, we may take a ferry with room for, say, fifty passengers, and discuss what expectations are required about the likelihood of getting a place for just the right number of prospective travellers to turn up. One solution would be for fifty people to be sure that they would get a seat and for all the others to be sure that they would not. But once we allow them to hold uncertain estimates, and to have different degrees of willingness to go to the ferry on the chance of a seat, then there is clearly an infinite number of distributions of expectations which would produce just the right number of people to put in an appearance. The same situation holds for producers in the economic case; in order that they should plan just the right increase in supply, not perfect knowledge is required, but a distribution of knowledge which is appropriate to the conditions of responsiveness prevailing.

In order that producers should have sufficient information on which to base an output decision they need not know the whole of the demand schedule; each is concerned as to whether he can sell the output from a level of capacity which will be limited by the firm's resources, its borrowing power and so on, and at a price which is bound to lie within a limited range. Now the degree to which this information is vouchsafed to him depends to an important extent on the character of the market, of which I shall consider three principal aspects: the degree of attachment, the degree of price stability, and the number of sellers.

I use the term degree of attachment to refer to the extent to which a firm's customers tend to be the same people, who do not change their supplier except for definite reasons. Where there is attachment, producers have their own private markets and the degree of attachment refers to the frequency of frontier-crossing. In certain markets, such as those for raw materials or for securities, it will be minimal, while in others, where there is monopoly or formal market sharing, it may be complete. Attachment may result from a variety of causes, from inertia, conservatism or personal connexion; from product differentiation, or from the justifiable importance of reputation (and the inevitable risk of change) where the quality of the product cannot easily be judged; from after-sales servicing, or spares, or from tacit or formal market-sharing arrangements.

Now it is according to the degree of attachment that a general increase in demand will reliably indicate an increase in the possible sales of an individual firm. If attachment is complete the only uncertainty is about the duration of the increase; if it is zero, very little useful information is provided, for producers do not know how the demand is distributed between firms and what each others' plans are. Moreover, without attachment, price is much more likely to be flexible, which is highly significant for the efficiency of the communication process.

When there is marked attachment, existing firms will have a clear advantage over prospective entrants, whose expectations regarding the demand for their products must be more uncertain. Although this has obvious demerits from other points of view, it favours efficient communication, for it enables those in the industry to be more confident about future demand than they would otherwise be and it also prevents an excessive response to an increase in demand. In the short run, in Marshall's sense, entry is of course precluded by definition, which is one reason why short-run adaptation is likely to be successful.

The stability of price in the face of variations in demand varies, as does the degree of attachment, between different markets, there being in fact a connexion between these two factors. Where, as in manufacturing business, producers are intensely concerned with the attachment of their customers, they will be very unwilling to freeze them off by an increase in price when demand rises, but will do all they can to keep them on their order books, waiting patiently until the firm can expand its output. Very frequently, moreover, producers have formal agreements not to vary their prices. Now whatever the motives for this action, it appears to be beneficial as far as the communication process is concerned. Where, as in the raw material markets figuring in cobweb theorems, price is fully flexible, producers have very little evidence as to the extent of an increase in demand at the long-run equilibrium price: whereas if price is kept stable at this level the length of order books offers a tolerable indication. It might be objected that price stability impairs allocation in other ways; but I find it difficult to believe that at least short-run stability is of any harm, bearing in mind the inelasticity of supply in the short run and the fact that the price which consumers can pay in the short run may not be a good guide to the socially desirable allocation.

The number of firms in a particular industry has an obvious bearing on the ease with which each can estimate the likely increase in the demand for its own product. A monopolist has of course only the uncertainty of total demand to contend with, but where there are only a few sellers, there is the possibility, at any rate, that they will be acquainted with each others' investment plans. The limited empirical evidence that I could find suggests that at least some oligopolists calculate the demand for their product by assessing the total future demand and conventionally assuming that their share of it will remain roughly constant.

Now these three characteristics to which I have referred, the degree of attachment, price stability, and the number of firms in the industry can of course be considered as aspects of the restraint of trade, and one may ask why I have preferred not simply to talk about the degree of monopoly. The first reason is that attachment may not give the power to raise the price against the consumer except in the very short run and may, as we have seen, keep the price down. Secondly, it is the communication aspects of market arrangements which I wish to stress here. To these aspects economists have given astonishingly scant attention, for the very reason that the traditional theoretical framework is in terms of known demand and supply schedules and of all the other unreal constructions which derive from the pernicious assumption of perfect knowledge. When business men try to defend their restrictive practices in terms of 'orderly marketing', 'rational distribution', and the like, they may be arguing speciously, but they may sometimes be suggesting that we look at these arrangements from a special point of view, from the point of view of how, in an uncertain world, they can get tolerably reliable indications of what sales to plan for.

Of the various sources of information about future demand, binding contracts are obviously the most reliable, but in many cases, and especially where the remote future is concerned, much weaker evidence will have to suffice. Trends will be projected, and estimates will be influenced by the sense of norms, either as to the level or the growth of output, or as to a firm's proportionate share in it. Knowledge of changes in total demand, obtained for example by market research, will only be of use if some stability in the shares can be presumed or if a firm obtains it before its competitors. Some decisions will be taken on the basis of careful estimates, others as a matter of routine, or stock reaction to changes in certain indicators, such as increased orders. The commonest form of routine is simple repetition which may be rational where there is little positive knowledge, or where knowledge is costly in time and money to acquire, and where decisions are reversible and the consequences of error slight.

As a determinant of the efficiency of the communication process there lies always in the background the skill of the forecasters themselves and the efficiency of the system in selecting them; but this is a large subject in itself which I have discussed in another place.[1]

## 4. Responsiveness

Of importance for the process of adaptation is the fact that, even if two firms entertained the same expectations regarding an increase in demand, they need not respond in the same way. Most obviously, their directors may have different attitudes to risk and gain, they may be cautious or bold; but the expansion of the firm will depend on factors other than this. Of these the most important are the quantity of available reserves, borrowing power, and the rate at which the management can digest the organizational change associated with large or frequent increase in scale. Where the increase in demand is not very great, expansion may be timed to fit in with the replacement of a major unit of capital. For all these reasons, willingness to increase the size of the firm will depend on the time which has elapsed since the last major expansion and on the age of the existing equipment. Now if, as is likely, the growth of the industry was originally gradual, firms' capital equipment and organizational structure will be of different ages and, in consequence, their responsiveness will likewise differ.

Responsiveness will also depend on the importance of discontinuities in the planning of output, which will arise from the fact that units of capital are frequently of minimum size or minimum durability. If such discontinuities dictate a certain minimum economic expansion, a firm may be willing to increase its capacity only if it can count on drawing customers from its competitors, so that the greater the degree of attachment in the market the more important will be the deterrent to an indivisible capital

---

[1] 'Imperfect Knowledge and Economic Efficiency', *Oxford Economic Paper*. June 1953.

expansion. Should these indivisibilities be very important, the attached market would seem to find itself, from time to time, not only with excess capacity of the Chamberlin monopolistic competition kind, but with capacity less than or more than is appropriate to the level of output. When we regarded attachment from the point of view of communication we saw that it was clearly beneficial; but when we consider responsiveness as well, its existence, if strong, may, where there are important discontinuities, work against proper adaptation. But this is a complex matter the detailed discussion of which falls outside the scope of this paper.

## 5. Adaptation

It is now time to consider how the communication process and the conditions of responsiveness together determine the nature of the adaptation of supply to demand.

I have already said something about the nature of the optimum adjustment, which will vary according to whether we regard it as relative to an increase in demand of known size and duration or to an essentially uncertain increase. In the former case it is immediate complete adaptation which is optimal; in the latter it is gradual adaptation. The optimal technical character of the adjustment, in the sense of the optimal combination of durable and non-durable agents of production, will also depend on the likely duration of the increase in demand, in a way which is fairly easily comprehended. One point alone is perhaps worth mentioning in this very sketchy treatment; that is the fact that industry as a whole may secure full adaptation, with fixed equipment, to a temporary increase in demand, even where an individual firm could not; for it is at least possible in principle, given an appropriate age structure for the existing capital stock, for the total fixed capital to be raised to meet a temporary demand and be reduced again shortly afterwards simply by the failure of other firms to replace.

Several classifications of adaptation may be made. I shall call adaptation 'uniform' when the structure of production is altered in one move, and it may be either anticipated or belated. 'Successive adaptation' takes place when supply alters by stages, and it may be either oscillatory or not. Oscillatory adjustment, as in the cobweb theorem, is usually associated with simultaneous investment decisions based on misleading expectations. By non-oscillatory adjustment, I refer to the gradual building up of supply which is associated with successive rather than simultaneous investment decisions. Where the adjustment of supply to demand has itself no affect on the level of demand, adaptation may be called simple; where it has, adaptation is 'complex'. Complex adaptation, of which multiplier theory is an example, is not discussed in this paper, concerned as it is with particular industries rather than with the economy as a whole.

We may spend very little time on the adjustment of supply to very temporary changes in demand. In the very short run attachment is strongest and prices most stable, at least in the case of manufacturing business, so that reliable indication is provided of the change in demand, which can be met by changing stocks or by a different degree of utilization of the existing equipment. Provided the adaptation is 'simple', error is unlikely and the consequences of error are not serious.

It is the adjustment to relatively permanent changes which is interesting. Two principal types of adaptation may be compared; uniform and gradual. From the point of view of an increase in demand the duration and size of which is assumed somehow to be certain, uniform adaptation is clearly best; if the increase in demand is taken to be uncertain, the optimum adjustment, as we have said, will generally be gradual.

What are the conditions which favour uniform adjustment ? A high degree of attachment and price stability are clearly important, for without them each producer is very much in the dark about the likely demand for his own goods. Even if attachment is not very strong, producers may behave as if it was, in that they assume that their share in any total increase in demand (which they may be able to estimate) will remain constant, and should they do this, direct adaptation will be feasible, although of course the permanence of any increase in demand still remains uncertain. It is also important that the minimum economic unit of capital equipment be small, for otherwise uniform adjustment involving expansion by all firms will not be able to deal efficiently with small changes in demand. This last condition is stringent and must exclude the possibility of successful uniform adaptation in many cases. Of course the needed increase in capacity could be produced by the simultaneous expansion of some, but not all, firms, but it is difficult do see any reason, short of collusion, why just the right number should do so.

Progressive adaptation occurs when supply is built up gradually by one firm after another. It can claim four advantages. It shows the remaining excess demand as supply gradually increases, so that a very uncertain increase in demand may be determined empirically, and it leaves time for a judgement to be made as to the permanence of the change. Thirdly, if the increase in demand is temporary, there is the possibility that it can be met by the full adaptation of the fixed factors, provided one or two firms expand and others subsequently do not replace. Lastly, where the minimum economic unit of capacity is large, the appropriate increase is much easier than by direct adaptation by all firms.

What are the conditions which will favour the successful gradual adaptation of supply? The first is the existence of difference of opinion regarding the expected future demand. Given sufficient variety in the estimates, successive rather than simultaneous reaction will result, those firms which are the most sensitive to upward movements in the indicators being the most optimistic and investing first. The same effect would be achieved, all expectations being the same, if there is sufficient variation in responsiveness, and this, we have maintained, will normally be the case. Finally, it is important that the construction period be small, so that the effect of the increased supply coming on to the market be manifest before too many investment plans are under way. Of the three conditions for successful progressive adaptation this is probably the most stringent and therefore the most likely cause of trouble.

From this discussion of the conditions for successful adaptation the likely causes of failure are evident by implication. An unattached market, price flexibility, and the simultaneity of investment decisions, as may be quite unavoidable as in agriculture, are probably the most important. When 'complex' adaptation is considered, the likelihood of maladaptation would seem to be greatly increased, but this falls out with the scope of this paper.

In this discussion I have talked about the conditions for adaptation rather than the conditions for equilibrium, which, to my mind, is as it should be; for the maintenance of equilibrium is simply a particular case of the adaptation of supply to demand, either a constant demand, if we consider a stationary equilibrium, or to a regularly varying one, if we consider a moving one. The conditions for success are the same for this type of adaptation as for any other. The so-called equilibrium conditions relating present prices to marginal and average costs are merely a description of the optimum point; they do not describe a position to which output and prices must, in competition, necessarily tend. It is widely admitted that a perfectly competitive system could not cope with adjustment, but maintained, nevertheless, that there are forces at work in it which will maintain the 'equilibrium' once it has somehow been reached. But realistic conditions for equilibrium, as for any other adaptation, must be stated in terms of the state of knowledge and of responsiveness, both of existing and of potential producers. Output decisions are, in principle, dependent on expectations in every case; there is no essential difference here between replacement and net investment. We may note that it is possible to have progressive adaptation to a constant demand as well as to an increase in demand; decisions to replace capital equipment are in this case taken successively and any error by one firm may be corrected by the investment decisions of those that come after it. Normally, of course, it will be easier to adapt to a constant rather than to a variable demand, and perhaps expectations have a natural bias in favour of the *status quo*—but this is only a question of degree.

I have maintained in this paper that technical production functions, together with functions relating the demand for the product and the supply of factors to their respective prices, should be regarded as defining the optimum price and output, but that they cannot be coupled with the assumptions of a perfect market and perfect knowledge so as to form a model system with an equilibrium position corresponding to these optimum values. I then proceeded to argue that we would discover the requirements for successful adaptation, that is to say for the attainment and maintenance of the optimum price and output, only by comparing market structures from the point of view of efficient communication and by making explicit and realistic reference to the conditions of knowledge.

ST. JOHN'S COLLEGE,
     OXFORD.

# THE ECONOMIC JOURNAL

## *JUNE* 1959

---

## EQUILIBRIUM, EXPECTATIONS AND INFORMATION

THE central thesis which this paper will seek to justify can be quite briefly asserted. We shall argue that the familiar " general equilibrium of production and exchange " cannot be properly regarded as a configuration towards which a hypothetical perfectly competitive economy would gravitate or at which it would remain at rest. We attempt to support this assertion by showing that the activity required of entrepreneurs would require a certain minimum information; that the availability of such information is a function of the nature of the economic arrangements or system postulated; and that the conditions necessary for adequate information are incompatible with perfect competition.

These conclusions, even if accepted, may be regarded by many as of little importance, on the grounds that the perfect competition model is known to correspond very imperfectly to reality. Nevertheless, its use as an analytical instrument is very widespread, both in positive analysis and by virtue of its normative significance as a Pareto Optimum.[1] While the disturbing effects of indivisibilities and external economies may be freely admitted by all writers, it is commonly assumed that, in the absence of these factors, there would be a tendency to move towards, or at any rate to remain in, general equilibrium. In denying this belief, we shall concentrate on the informational aspect of economic systems, the importance of which in the analysis of group equilibrium is not confined to perfect competition.

The function of the equilibrium concept in economics is to enable us to say what particular activities will be undertaken in response to certain postulated conditions. The association between these may take a strong or a weak form; we may assert either that the activities would ultimately be undertaken or merely that, if undertaken, they would be persisted in, provided, of course, that the specified conditions do not change. Our ability to forge these connections derives from the use we make of the idea of compatibility; we argue that no activities will be undertaken or maintained unless they are compatible, first, with the particular constraints imposed

---

[1] Vide G. Stigler, " Perfect Competition, Historically Contemplated," *Journal of Political Economy*, February 1957. " Today the concept of perfect competition is being used more widely by the profession in its theoretical work than at any time in the past. The vitality of the concept is strongly spoken for by this triumph."

No. 274.—VOL. LXIX.      Q

by the assumed environment, and, secondly, with the objectives of the agents.

It is obvious that no direct connection can exist between objective conditions and purposive activity; the immediate relationship is between *beliefs* about relevant conditions and *planned* activities which it may or may not prove possible to implement.   Only those activities will be planned, we assume, which are compatible both with the agent's objectives and with the opportunities he believes to exist.   In certain situations only one projected course of action may meet these conditions.   The simplest way to proceed from here to the establishment of relationships between objective conditions (as opposed to beliefs) and actions (as opposed to plans) is by assuming that the agent has full information.   We, the model builders, postulate an agent with certain objectives and opportunities from which we can deduce the course of action which would be best for him; by then assuming that he is fully acquainted with the " determinants " of his choice, and that he will pursue his objectives, we convert our system into a model of behaviour in response to given conditions.   The ordinary account of consumers' behaviour is clearly of this kind; we can recognise that our model is no more than an incarnation of the logic of choice.   What the agent needs to know are the conditions of the allocation problem as laid down by the model builder.   What we may call the " informational requirements " of the model are simply that the agent have knowledge of the determinants of the equilibrium (*e.g.*, preferences, prices, income, etc.); if this is so the equilibrium activities will be immediately undertaken and persisted in so long as the determining conditions remain unchanged.   For all simple models constructed in this way the informational requirements are the same; they cease to hold good, however, when we pass from the equilibrium of an individual to that of an interrelated group.[1]

It seems clear that a sufficient condition for a group, or for a system as a whole, to be said to be in equilibrium, is for all the component units individually to be in equilibrium.   The condition, however, should not be regarded as necessary, for stability in the aggregates (*e.g.*, levels of output) by which we describe the system might be maintained without stability in the contributions of individual units.   Nevertheless, we shall concentrate our attention on the more obvious possibility, and assume that group

---

[1] All models of individual equilibrium are not of this simple kind.   Though full information is a sufficient condition for attaining the equilibrium, it is not necessary.   All that is required is, first, that the man should believe a particular action to be optimal and, secondly, that the process of carrying it out should provide no information which is inconsistent with, or would cause him to doubt, his belief.   By and large, however, economists have concentrated on the case where equilibrium is secured because beliefs are actually correct, though attention has also been given to hypothetical constructions in which the execution of a plan formed on the basis of inadequate information brings new evidence to light, so that full information, and therefore equilibrium also, are obtained gradually by a process of trial and error.   What concerns us is to note that in no case can we identify equilibrium activities without reference both to objective conditions and to states of belief.

equilibrium is reached when individual equilibrium is universal.  This implies, as we have seen, first, that everyone believes his projected activities to be optimal, and, secondly, that their implementation goes according to plan, so that there is no reason for changing them.  In the case of the isolated individual we could regard this latter condition as met, provided his estimates of the given external conditions were not contradicted by the evidence brought to light in the execution of his plan.  These external conditions were viewed impersonally as fixed opportunities and restrictions, and no attention was paid to the activity of others which lay behind them.  Now that the activities of related individuals are being considered explicitly, however, it is important to draw a distinction between two different kinds of conditions which any agent has to attempt to estimate.  By " primary conditions " we shall mean the technical possibilities of production and the existing state of consumer preference; " secondary conditions " will refer to the relevant projected activities of other people in the system, of customers, competitors and suppliers.  It will be convenient to refer to information, or to uncertainty, as primary or secondary according to whichever of these it is related.  This terminology is meant to convey no difference in the importance of these two kinds of conditions; a distinction is made between them because of the different ways in which information about them has to be obtained.

Now if a plan is to be carried out as intended, the estimates on which it is based must not be contradicted by events; this will be ensured in the most obvious way if the estimates are correct.  The agent must therefore have adequate primary information about his own preferences and the more or less technical relationships to which his plans cannot run counter, as well as adequate secondary information about what other people, whose actions concern him, may or may not do.  From the point of view of an observer external to the system (as opposed to an agent within it) this requirement can be put in slightly different terms by saying that the activities of all agents must be compatible both with primary conditions and with each other.

With these considerations in mind, let us now examine the celebrated attempt to identify a general equilibrium of production and exchange under perfect competition.  Perfect competition is a hypothetical system characterised, as is well known, by the existence of many buyers and sellers of homogeneous commodities and by the absence of any artificial restraints on their activities—a condition sometimes referred to as perfect mobility.  Most writers also recognise that these buyers and sellers must have certain necessary information, but this requirement is usually left obscure,[1] and its relationship with the other conditions of the model is not examined.  Given perfectly competitive conditions, an equilibrium pattern of economic activities is identified and made to depend on external conditions represented by the preferences of individuals, the endowment and original distri-

---

[1] For a notable exception, see F. A. Hayek, " Economics and Knowledge," *Economica*, 1937.

bution of resources, and the state of technique.   We shall now briefly state its properties in terms of a simple objective description of the activities pursued and their relationship to the " fundamental determinants " of the system; any reference these activities might have to the wishes or intentions of those engaged in them will be postponed.

The equilibrium configuration has two kinds of special properties, the first relating to the situation in which each individual unit finds itself, the second to relationships between the aggregate levels of the activities in which they are engaged.   Every consumer has an expenditure equal to his income and a pattern of consumption such that his marginal rate of substitution between any two goods is equal to the ratio of their prices, which are the same for all.   Each producer can be observed to be producing as efficiently as possible, given the state of technique, and the price paid to any of the factors of production is equal to the value of its marginal product in that use. These conditions suggest optimality; the others, consistency.   The aggregate current production of each commodity is neither more nor less than is used either by other firms or in final consumption.   (We avoid saying simply that supply and demand are equal, for this would involve a reference to plans and expectations which are not to be introduced at this stage.)   All scarce resources are likewise fully employed, and the expenditure of any individual is equal to the income derived from the sale of the resources at his disposal, as determined by the distribution of skill and property originally assumed.[1]

These, then, are the relationships which characterise the perfectly competitive economy in what is believed to be its equilibrium state.   But, as has been observed, equilibrium is not secured merely by the existence of a particular set of economic activities in themselves, but by their co-existence with a particular set of beliefs.   Therefore we have to discover what beliefs must be associated with the configuration we have described in order that it can be regarded as self-perpetuating.   One of its properties consisted of the correspondence of marginal rates of substitution to relative prices, so that consumers were each objectively in an optimum position, provided their incomes and the prices of commodities were regarded as fixed and given. They would themselves believe their situation to be optimal, and therefore have no wish to change it, provided we endow them with certain information and beliefs.   It would be sufficient to assume that they were fully acquainted with their own preferences and with the prices of all goods, and that they expected that neither these preferences and prices, nor their income, would change in the future.   Producers will also wish to persist in the activities the configuration allotted to them, if they know all the production possibilities, if they know all product and factor prices and expect them to remain the

---

[1] This account of the conditions of equilibrium is of course loose and inadequate; but, for our particular purposes, there is no need for a full elaboration.   We shall ignore questions as to the " existence " and " stability " of equilibria, at least in the sense which these terms are used in current theoretical discussions.

same, and finally, if there is some reason for preventing them expanding the current scale of their operations.  (The significance of this third and final condition, for which the equilibrium of the consumer had no simple counterpart, will be developed in due course.)  Similar conditions of belief will ensure that the suppliers of productive resources are also content with the rôle they have been allotted.[1]

The second set of properties of the equilibrium configuration, those concerned with the consistency of the various component activities, now ensures that the plans of consumers and producers can be successfully carried out and the beliefs or expectations which formed their basis will be proved correct.  We are now entitled to say that, in every particular market, demand equals supply, in the sense that the aggregate amount which buyers plan to buy equals the amount which sellers plan to sell.  It seems therefore that the conditions of belief required for equilibrium have been established; they consist in the possession of primary information about preferences and production functions and in the belief as to the permanence of existing prices, though it is necessary to add, somewhat untidily, that each producer must feel unwilling or unable to raise the level of his output.

Before examining the value of this conclusion, let us consider whether the conditions of belief which will ensure the maintenance of equilibrium activities will also ensure their adoption.  This question can be interpreted in either of two ways.  One may ask whether the universal expectation of equilibrium prices could produce a direct movement to equilibrium. Alternatively, one may ask whether the universal belief that current prices, whatever they are, will be permanent, could, through some process of successive adjustments, produce a gradual, if indirect, movement to the equilibrium.  Each of these possibilities must now be considered in turn.

Let us assume that the existing pattern of output, prices, etc., is not that which would exist in equilibrium but that everyone concerned happens to expect that the equilibrium prices will rule in the future.  Will the system move to equilibrium?  Here it is important to distinguish between two different assumptions which may be made about entrepreneurs.  The normal assumption, or at any rate the assumption implicit in most treatments, is that entrepreneurial skill is undifferentiated, in the sense that no entrepreneur can have a comparative advantage over other entrepreneurs in any particular line.  We shall adopt this assumption first and then take up the

---

[1] These conditions, though sufficient, are not necessary.  Producers, for example, might be content to persist in their current activities if they expected their own output and input prices to remain the same, but were unable to form any estimate of the future level of any other prices in the system.  There are in fact an indefinite number of expectational conditions which would, under reasonable assumptions as to human motivation, secure the maintenance of the general equilibrium. And though some of them no doubt appear less unrealistic than others, there seems no clear reason why any one set is most appropriate.  Our concern will be with the way in which expectational conditions are commonly introduced into equilibrium analysis, rather than with the merits of some conditions in comparison to others.

alternative one, according to which no entrepreneurs are alike, there being between any two of them differences of comparative advantage in different lines of production.

Under the first of these assumptions it is clear that, given the expectations postulated, the actions of any entrepreneur are wholly indeterminate. The product and factor prices he expects are such (*ex hypothesi*) that afford normal profits in all lines, and there is no reason why he should choose one rather than the other. There is therefore no reason why the equilibrium configuration should come to be established. The situation is altered, however, once we assume the presence of differences in comparative advantage between entrepreneurs. If this is the case the equilibrium configuration will no longer leave the allocation of output between firms undetermined; for each entrepreneur there will be one particular niche in which his income will be a maximum. Immediately equilibrium prices come to be expected, therefore, all entrepreneurs will move directly to their appointed stations, equilibrium will be established and expectations fulfilled.

We ought now to deal with the second version of our question as to the beliefs required to ensure the adoption of equilibrium activities. Will the expectation that prices will maintain their current values suffice for our purposes? Now clearly if current prices have any values apart from those appropriate to the equilibrium configuration, any universally held expectations as to their continuance will be immediately disappointed and plans based on them will prove impossible to fulfil. Equilibrium in this model could therefore be shown ultimately to come about only as a result of a process in which expectations were continually revised; the execution of plans would have to produce a set of prices which were again projected into the future and used as a basis for fresh plans and so on. In this way a model can presumably be constructed which would exhibit movement to equilibrium in a group of related markets, but an examination of the work done in this direction would lead us too far afield. There exists in any case a fundamental objection, which we must now consider, to this whole approach.[1]

In order to establish the general equilibrium it was recognised that we had to postulate certain beliefs; the universal expectation that prices would stay the same was an example of what was required. No attempt was made, however, to explain or account for these conditions, which were introduced

---

[1] There are in fact serious objections to the simple cobweb theorem, let alone a generalised version of it. These are discussed in the author's article, " Demand and Supply Reconsidered," *Oxford Economic Papers*, June 1956. Some of them may be overcome, however, if we are prepared to postulate differences in the comparative advantages of entrepreneurs. Needless to say, it is unrealistic to assume that current prices will always be projected with certainty into the future, notwithstanding persistent disappointment of this expectation; and if we suppose that each entrepreneur holds identical expectations as to all prices, we thereby renounce any claim to solve the essential problem of decentralised systems—that of how economic order is secured despite the fragmentary and diverse character of the information possessed by individual entrepreneurs.

as a *deus ex machina* in order to convert our postulated set of consistent, optimalising activities into the equilibrium position of a hypothetical system. But are we entitled thus to conjure up expectations as we please? Our interest is to establish a cause–effect relation between objective conditions and the activities of the group. Although this must come about through the mediation of states of expectation, we are surely obliged to postulate such of these as have some inherent plausibility or can somehow be accounted for within the framework of the model. Expectations are based on information, the availability of which, as we shall see, is a function of the kind of economic system or arrangement we choose to assume. They cannot be properly regarded as a wholly extraneous element for which we need have no responsibility.

It is commonly believed that expectations are satisfactorily taken care of merely by assuming their functional dependence on other elements of the system. Entrepreneurs are represented, as we have seen, as expecting future prices to maintain their current level or to be equal, let us say, to some average of the values they have attained in the past. Such " rules " for the formation of expectations may be simple or complex; although they usually in fact imply unanimity and certainty, and are rarely assumed to be modified by experience, yet these restrictions could presumably be removed. Nevertheless, the propriety of this whole method of approach seems questionable. We are rightly accustomed to assume that economic agents generally act rationally on the basis of their beliefs; we ought similarly to assume that beliefs or expectations themselves are rational, that they are based, that is to say, on adequate evidence or information.

The special significance of this requirement in the analysis of group activity has perhaps not been fully appreciated. The availability of primary information (about technical production possibilities, etc.) does not depend, in any obvious way, on the kind of system or organisation under consideration. If therefore we postulate a certain " state of the arts " or " given production functions," we are justified, for most purposes, in simply assuming that the average entrepreneur is acquainted with them. We cannot do this, however, in relation to secondary information (*i.e.*, information about what related members of the group will do), for the availability of this kind of information is quite certainly a function of the economic arrangements, or system, which we postulate. If we assume that consumers are fully informed about their own preferences and about the properties of all the goods they may buy, then the models we construct will indeed suffer in terms of realism and will offer a less than perfect account of the workings of the actual economy. Nevertheless, this simplification of actual circumstances might be appropriate in an idealised system, which, for some purposes, offered a tolerable approximation to reality. If, however, we assume that a producer has some secondary information regarding the projected activities of others with whom he is economically related, then we are committed to assume the existence of an economic system in which such information would be available. We could assume, for example, that members of the system planned their activities in concert, or that they renounced their independence to put themselves under the orders of a central planning authority, which, by itself deciding what everyone would do, could dispense with any need for secondary information. But if both these solutions are put aside as inconsistent with free competition, how, then, are we to suppose that producers become adequately informed about such activities of others as will affect the profitability of their own investments? Although this may be the most fundamental of all the problems of group organisation, it is one to which our accepted theory of the perfectly competitive economy offers no satisfactory solution.[1]

The problem arises, as we have said, from the fact that the activities of the members of the system, though inter-related, are taken independently. No individual member, it is clear, can decide what to do on the basis of primary information only, of information, that is, about such factors as production functions and consumers' preferences. He could not, for example, judge whether to invest in any particular direction without a minimum of knowledge about the supply plans of his competitors. In other words, it is of the essence of the competitive system that the profit opportunities open to one seller depend on the actions proposed by others, so that, for example, if A, B, C, . . . are all equally well placed to supply a given market, then A cannot rationally decide upon a particular level of output without some knowledge of what B, C, . . . *et al.* may do, while each of these similarly need some prior secondary knowledge of the intentions of A and others. This mutual interdependence clearly presents, for entrepreneurs, a barrier to obtaining the necessary secondary information, and, if we are to hope to show how a system can work, we cannot escape the obligation to explain how the barrier is overcome.[2]

---

[1] As is well known, both Walras and Edgeworth suggested procedures for the attainment of equilibrium. But neither the system of prices "*criés au hazard*," nor "recontracting," are convincing solutions to our problem, and in any case they involve a measure of concerted action which is inconsistent, at least with the spirit of perfect competition. The proposal that we should consider a model of perfect competition with an infinite number of markets embracing goods for sale at any future date likewise circumvents, rather than helps to solve, the real problem.

[2] An analogy may help to reinforce the point. The opportunities open to an entrepreneur in a perfectly competitive market might be compared to an unusual kind of lottery. Entry, let us suppose, is invited on the following basis. If subscriptions amount, by a certain date, to say £1 million, they will simply be returned in full; should they amount to less than this, they will be returned together with a share of a certain prize money; but should they exceed £1 million, they will be returned subject to a deduction depending on the excess. Now evidently, unless it were possible to make some assumptions about factors which independently restrict or condition how many people would enter the lottery, and what stakes they might make, it would be impossible for anyone to form a rational estimate of the chances of success. In the analogue of the competitive market there would be no basis for a rational investment decision; here also the possibility of making profits or losses depends on the total commitment of resources, while it is by no means obvious that any way of obtaining information about this is available.

The discussion in this article makes no mention of the theory of games, which is concerned with

This difficulty has frequently been noticed, but only to be pushed aside as a tiresome logical catch. Yet this reaction is curious in view of the attention which has been given to oligopoly and the so-called indeterminacy inherent in it. If there are only a few firms, then A, in formulating an output policy, must consider B's reaction to it, which may itself depend on what B thinks A might do in return; this being so, it has been recognised that without additional data we cannot hope to predict what the strategies and counter-strategies might be. The existence of many sellers, however, is supposed to eliminate this indeterminacy—but why should this be so? Where there are many producers, an individual entrepreneur planning his output still needs some knowledge of what the total supplies of competitors will be. It is true in this case that their plans will not be affected by knowledge they might have of what he in particular will do, for we can assume that his output will be small compared to the total; but this in no way makes their plans any more predictable by him. Their large number and their independence of his own particular actions do not obviously make competitive supply any easier to forecast than in the oligopolistic situation; the actions of individual entrepreneurs therefore appear equally indeterminate. Presumably the conviction that perfect competition, unlike oligopoly, has a determinate equilibrium is based on the fact the entrepreneur in perfect competition cannot affect the price at which he sells, which therefore acts as a fixed parameter in his decision-taking; but this is to ignore the fact that it is the expected future price which is relevant to him and that it is not known. One is not entitled to claim that prices, widely known and freely determined, constitute a sufficient system of communication; the current levels of prices are quite inadequate signals from an entrepreneur's point of view.

We have suggested that de-centralised systems can work only provided their constituent members can obtain the minimum necessary secondary information, and that the first objective of our analysis of them should be to explain how this is made possible. Yet although adequate knowledge is the basic prerequisite of purposive action, it cannot, of course, ensure that action will be taken or that it will be in a socially desirable direction. If therefore we are concerned to demonstrate how individual activities, though subject to no deliberate co-ordination, may yet, under certain conditions, produce a socially desirable result, our analysis must meet essentially two requirements. It must first explain how opportunities are made available and known to people in the system, and then go on to show that the opportunities will be of such a kind that action taken in response to them, and under the influence

---

what courses of action may be rationally chosen even when information is lacking as to which of several courses others may take. Our present concern, however, is not with the logic of choice under uncertainty, but with how, in a competitive economy, this uncertainty may be reduced to the extent compatible with purposive economic activity. Beyond a certain point, uncertainty would become intolerable to average entrepreneurs, and institutional change would be made in order to reduce it. Business may proceed in an informational twilight, but not in utter darkness.

of the type of motivation we assume, will further whatever is considered to be the general interest.   The former requirement is, in a sense, the most fundamental, for purposive activities could not take place without an adequate basis of information, whether or not they resulted in desirable results; nevertheless, it is this requirement that our models of the competitive economy most strikingly fail to meet.

There appears to exist in our theory of the competitive economy no adequate analysis of how the supply of secondary information is functionally related to the structure of the system assumed.   Certainly this cannot be provided here; but it is possible to set out, very briefly, some of the elements.[1] Producers could obtain information about the prospective activities of those to whom they are inter-related in three principal ways.   The first of these, explicit collusion, needs no explanation; it is clearly inconsistent with perfect competition.   The second, which we propose to describe, with some hesitation, as " implicit collusion," will be explained presently.   The third, which is of a quite different character, exists by virtue of the existence of factors which condition or limit the activities of entrepreneurs independently of their estimates of the plans of those in a competitive or complementary relationship.   These factors, which we shall simply call " restraints," will be explained more fully later.

The significance of the second way through which information may become available, implicit collusion, may be illustrated in connection with the general equilibrium " configuration " discussed above.   This represented a set of activities which would be persisted in provided everyone expected prices to remain unchanged.   We have now to ascertain the conditions under which it would be rational to entertain these expectations. An entrepreneur could rationally expect prices to remain the same if everyone else in the system continued in his present activities, but this they would do only if they could likewise expect all others (including the entrepreneur in question) to do the same.   We seem therefore to be involved in the old difficulty; no one can decide upon his optimal activity without knowledge of what others (who are in the same difficulty) will do.   Nevertheless, it seems that it may be possible, in this case, for a continuance of the *status quo* to be rationally expected.   Let us suppose that everyone in the system expects primary conditions to remain unaltered and knows that profits are everywhere normal, thus realising that he cannot improve his position so long as others maintain their current activities; and let us suppose further that everyone knows everyone else to share his beliefs.   Under these conditions, which though manifestly unrealistic, are possible in principle, everyone would be induced not to alter his activities, for they would see that each individually was powerless to improve his lot, but that if they all kept their course, at least no one would be worse off.   Such a state of affairs may

---

[1] An adequate treatment of this subject is precluded by reasons of space; the author has been engaged in writing a book which endeavours to provide it.

perhaps be usefully described as implicit collusion, on the grounds that there is a general understanding that no one will alter what they are doing. It cannot, it would seem, be regarded, in this context, as anything but a somewhat fanciful possibility, but it is difficult to see how else, in a perfectly competitive economy, entrepreneurs would be entitled to entertain rational and certain expectations that all prices would stay the same.[1]

Although equilibrium might be maintained, it clearly could not be reached by means of implicit collusion of this kind. If a number of people were asked to write down each a number, in the hope that the sum would equal 100, they would clearly have, in the absence of explicit collusion, only an infinitesimal chance of success. But if they did miraculously happen to choose an appropriate set, and knew that they had done so, it is reasonable to expect that they would then write down the same numbers if invited to play the identical game on further occasions.

We have to conclude therefore that the beliefs required to maintain the perfect competition equilibrium could be rational (*i.e.*, based on information which is available in principle), though only under very special conditions and in a very special way. If, however, any configuration other than the equilibrium is assumed to exist, we have as yet discovered no way in which entrepreneurs could obtain any information about each other's projected activities and therefore no way in which rational expectations could be formed.

We are, of course, frequently inclined not to take this sort of difficulty very seriously, for the reason that it is overcome somehow in the real world. But the real world is not perfectly competitive, and there exist in it (apart from collusive arrangements) a variety of factors, usually classed as "frictions" or "imperfections," which make possible a third, and practically important, way in which secondary information becomes available. According to the forms and strengths which such "restraints" assume in particular markets, adequate information and therefore economic adjustment may or may not be possible. Only the briefest account of this can be given here.

Let us suppose that there arises a demand for a particular commodity. This may be assumed to create a general profit opportunity, but it need not at the same time create particular profit opportunities available to individual entrepreneurs. A profit opportunity which is known by and available to everybody is available to nobody in particular. A situation of general profit potential can be tapped by one entrepreneur only if similar action is

---

[1] The notion of implicit collusion has a respectable history. Hume, for example, in discussing respect for property, refers to it in these terms: "When this common sense of interest is mutually expressed, and is known to both, it produces a suitable resolution and behaviour. And this may properly enough be called a convention or agreement betwixt us, though without the interposition of a promise; since the actions of each of us have a reference to those of the other, and are performed upon the supposition that something is to be performed on the other part. Two men who pull the oars of a boat, do it by an agreement or convention, though they have never given promises to each other." (*A Treatise on Human Nature*, Book III, Part II, Section II.)

not intended by too many others; otherwise excess supply and general losses
would result.   In other words, a general opportunity of this kind will create
a reliable profit expectation for a single entrepreneur only if there is some
limitation upon the competitive supply to be expected from other producers.
Corresponding to this negative condition appropriate to the production of
substitutes there is a positive condition appropriate to complementary production.   In general, a producer will need to know both that the production
of complements (such as raw materials) will be adequate and that the production of substitutes will not be in excess.   For the sake of brevity, however,
we shall ignore the existence of complementarity and concern ourselves only
with the necessary restrictions on competitive production.   We have seen
that we cannot in general assume that producers could have knowledge of
their competitors' plans.   But there is no logical objection to them having
information about the *maximum possible* competitive supply in some relevant
future period, if supply is bound by restraints.   They may also be able to
estimate likely minimum supply (either competitive or complementary) if
this is determined by the momentum of previous commitments.

Let us glance briefly at the nature and effects of these restraints.   They
will impose themselves, at any particular time, with different force on different firms so as to limit their ability to increase either production or sales.
An entrepreneur need fear no threat of increased competitive supply if others
are unaware of the unsatisfied demand; he enjoys a form of monopoly, until
of course the knowledge which he alone possesses becomes diffused.   In
this way, paradoxically, the imperfect distribution of information may
sometimes facilitate economic adjustment.   But even those firms who are
aware of the increased demand will have a limited capacity to meet it,
depending on the reserves and the limited external finance which is currently
available.[1]

Firms which were able to mount the required increase in production
might still experience difficulty in penetrating the market in which demand
has increased.   Not only do the firms already in the industry have " economies of experience," they also, as Marshall indicated, have " particular
markets," in which, by virtue of goodwill or other ties, they have a significant advantage.   These restrictions or " imperfections " could reasonably
be regarded as natural, but they shade into others which are artificial, in the
sense that they were devised for the purpose.   A tacit agreement to live and
let live may become formal market sharing, and entry may be impeded by
deliberately erected barriers.   Firms may agree to bind their hands and seek

[1] Here we may recall the celebrated criticism of perfect competition made by Sraffa, when he
pointed out that the conditions of the model left the size of the individual firm indeterminate.
Sraffa was concerned to point that, as the supply response of the individual firm in perfect competition was indeterminate, the continued survival of many firms in the industry could not be relied
upon.   We require limits to the supply potential of each firm and to the number of firms which can
respond, but for a different reason.   Unless a firm can set some upper bounds to the possible
volume, in the near future, of competitive supply, it will not be prepared to invest.

to bind those of others.  All this helps to make the world a safer place for entrepreneurs; by narrowing the possibilities of competitive supply it makes the market of each more secure.

Almost all the protective or restrictive influences to which we have alluded are inconsistent with the letter or the spirit of perfect competition; moreover, they are commonly the objects of criticism; if natural, they are regretted; if artificial, they are often condemned outright.  And of course this long-standing attitude has its good reasons.  It is certainly necessary, in a decentralised economy, that the activities of different firms be kept in step, and these so-called imperfections are part of the machinery which ensures this.  But there are other objectives which may sometimes be in conflict with this one.  Entrenched monopoly positions may bring about the misallocation of resources and may weaken the process of competitive selection by which the efficiency of the private enterprise economy is furthered.  Many would therefore be tempted to regard the restrictive influences which we have described as " necessary evils," comparable, let us say, to the position of the laws in civilised society—but it is well to remember the highly paradoxical nature of such a classification.  In addition, one cannot assume that *any* degree of restrictive influence will be injurious; factors which give only short-run stability to a firm's market will rarely tempt it to exploitation and to neglect of efficiency.  It would be helpful in practice if we could assume that natural imperfections were tolerable, whereas artificial man-made ones were not.  But whether or not such a division might be a useful policy guide, there seems no theoretical justification for it; there seems no reason to believe that the optimum degree of " imperfection " is reached exactly at the point where ordinary market restrictions begin to be supplemented with protected measures designed specifically for the purpose.

If, then, we are right, and our model of the purely competitive economy s seriously deficient in the way we suggest, it is interesting to speculate on the reasons for its adoption and for the strong grip which it continues to hold on our minds.  The comparative neglect, in accepted economic doctrine, of the informational aspects of hypothetical systems may, perhaps, be the result of a variety of causes.  The broad rationale of the private enterprise system was, of course, appreciated long before the development of modern equilibrium analysis.  It was realised that, if the demand for an article increased, the profit opportunities created would permit private self-interest unwittingly to further the public good—subject, of course, to qualifications which were paid a varying degree of attention.  It was realised also that if the total supply of the article were in single hands, then the terms of sale could be influenced to the benefit of the seller, but at the general disadvantage; and it could also be shown that both ignorance, and the artificial restriction of enterprise, could hamper the invisible hand.  These ideas, in the latter half of the nineteenth century, were expounded with a new degree of logical rigour and precision and fitted together so as to form a hypothetical system purporting to represent the workings of the economic system reduced to essentials.   There were to be no artificial restrictions and no impediments due to ignorance; by assuming atomistic units and the absence of collusion between them, the terms of any exchange were safely withdrawn from individual control.   Such a system of " perfect competition " was not represented, at least by reputable economists, as accurately describing the actual state of free-enterprise economies, from which all elements of restriction, ignorance and monopoly had not been purged.   But it stood as an ideal or model form of organisation—strictly speaking only a logical as opposed to an ethical ideal, although the distinction was not always sharply made. Those who objected to the model in terms of realism could easily be reminded of the abstraction inherent in all scientific thinking and of the need to concentrate on essential elements.   On account both of its pedagogic convenience and its suitability as a basis for extensive formal and mathematical elaboration, perfect competition obtained a central place in theoretical discussion, and the many qualifications with which, let us say, Marshall would have hedged the concept, fell into the background.   There was little realisation that the elements which had been banished as " imperfections " were necessary, in some measure, for the provision of adequate information, that an unequal distribution of knowledge and the existence of " frictional " restraints were required in order to make the system work.[1]

One suspects that our discussion of the competitive model may also have suffered, on occasion, from a confusion of perspective, from confounding the view-point of the model builder himself and that of his creatures within the model.   For the creator there is no problem of knowledge, for the objective facts about the system appear as postulated data from which could be deduced (or so it was believed) the equilibrium configuration.   Was it always appreciated that information about these " determinants," that " perfect knowledge " in this sense, would have been of no use to the members of the system even if they could ever be assumed to possess it?   To put the matter somewhat differently, was it realised that the problem of knowledge for a member of a group was not the same as that of an isolated agent working in a passive medium—that the availability of secondary information, as we have called it, is a function of the nature of the economic system postulated, so that " adequate knowledge," far less " perfect knowledge," may in fact be incompatible with certain kinds of economic arrangements?   The question is not so much whether these contentions would have

---

[1] The usefulness of the perfect competition model has been compared to that of mechanical statics.   The latter, though it assumes no friction, nevertheless enables us to determine the equilibrium position of a system of forces.   An economic model which abstracts from all friction can, it is argued, perform a similar function.   But the analogy is treacherous.   It ignores the fact that, in economics, both the maintenance and the attainment of equilibrium require the existence of certain beliefs or expectations, which have no strict counterpart in mechanics; and by doing so it may conceal the need to show how such expectations could be rationally formed in the type of system we assume.

been explicitly denied, but whether anything approaching full weight was given to them in the construction of theoretical foundations.

The argument of this article may be briefly summarised, in conclusion, as follows. Our accepted analysis recognises that equilibrium requires the existence of certain expectations, but does not recognise that expectations, if they are to be rational, must be based on available information. Nor does it take account of the fact that the availability of certain essential information depends on the economic arrangements or system which we postulate. These contentions were maintained in connection with the so-called general equilibrium of perfect competition. This was found to represent a set of optimalising activities consistent with given constraints and with each other, but we denied that it was a position towards which a hypothetical perfectly competitive system would gravitate. Our denial was based on the fact that perfect competition, strictly interpreted, would fail to afford adequate secondary information for purposive entrepreneurial activity. If concerted action were ruled out, only the existence of certain restraints (or "imperfections") in appropriate form and strength would make available the information required for economic adjustment.

G. B. RICHARDSON

*St. John's College,*
*Oxford.*

# [5]

# THE LIMITS TO A FIRM'S RATE OF GROWTH

## By G. B. RICHARDSON

## I. The evidence of the inquiry

GIVEN the will to expand, a firm's actual rate of expansion could be limited, it would seem, by one or more of four circumstances—shortage of labour or of physical inputs, shortage of finance, the lack of suitable investment opportunities, and the lack of sufficient managerial capacity.

None of our guests said that the growth of their firms had been held up, to any significant extent, by the difficulty of recruiting labour, skilled or unskilled, or by a shortage of materials or equipment. Whether they were more fortunate, in this respect, than the majority of companies, I do not know. One had to bear in mind, however, that even although labour supplies are scarce for the economy as a whole, and ultimately limit its expansion, no individual firm need in consequence feel a shortage. To the extent that there is active competition in the hiring of labour, so that wages rise under the pressure of demand, a firm will always be able to find additional workers, even if it has to pay them highly.

Some firms said that they were never held back in any way by lack of finance. Others gave more qualified replies. Thus one firm had not in fact been short of money, but it would have gone short had it not been a subsidiary of a larger concern. Yet another did not itself lack finance for expansion, but the demand for its services—building—had been reduced in Ireland and in the United States, but not in the United Kingdom, by credit restriction. One of our guests said that his firm was not now held back by lack of funds, but that it had been in the past. One very large firm was evidently never short of finance and remained unaffected by short-term credit restriction; but were the long-term rate of interest to rise, its management would require eligible projects to show a higher rate of return. One small firm had once been marginally affected by a credit squeeze.

Shortage of capital was an effective brake on the expansion of four companies. Two of these had recently been sold to larger businesses in order to break the financial bottle-neck. The third was in a special position, in being a subsidiary of an American concern which did not wish to float an issue in this country for fear of losing control. The fourth was a family business of which the rate of growth was deliberately kept within the limits imposed by self-financing.

There is, therefore, no uniformity of experience; but it is safe to say that, for most of the firms in our sample, growth had been checked by other factors before the financial limit was felt. Only two firms were held back by shortage of money, pure and simple: they were both small and have now been taken over by larger concerns.

With one exception, our visitors did not claim that the growth of their firms had been limited by the lack of suitable investment opportunities. (The industrialist who did refer to this circumstance, moreover, did so in rather special terms; he talked of the rate at which the firm's personnel could devise new projects rather than the absolute scarcity of these projects in an objective sense.) On the face of it, this finding may appear rather surprising, all the more so as we were given the impression that the firms demanded that any project, put forward for consideration, should show a rather high rate of return.

A very striking number of our guests expressed the view without hesitation that the availability of suitable management had been, and was, the operative check on their expansion. The minority which did not represent this fact as the principal check, nevertheless gave it some weight. There could be no doubt that, for most of the firms dealt with, managerial capacity, in some sense yet to be defined, was the strongest restraint on their rate of growth.

## II. Interpretation

The notion of a managerial limit to expansion is by no means straightforward. Some of our visitors talked in terms of a 'shortage of good people', implying, on the face of it, that there were just not enough able men, in the economy as a whole, to go round. But, whatever the aggregate supply of good managers, one may still wonder why individual firms should feel a shortage. By referring to the shortage of a factor, we would seem to imply that the price of the factor is set at a level below that which would equate demand with supply. But why should the salaries of good managers not be bid up competitively, so that firms would come to refer to their cost rather than to their scarcity?

It may be that salaries are to some extent conventionally determined with the result that, at least for the senior grades, they are less than firms would really be prepared to pay. It is also possible that movement from one firm to another is inhibited, to some extent, by the existence of non-transferable pension rights and kindred factors. Such imperfections may be part of the explanation of the felt 'shortage' of good people, but it can scarcely be the whole of it.

Rather more weight can perhaps be given to a second consideration. The men in charge of a company are presumably able to size up those already working for them much more easily than they can judge the talents of those in employment elsewhere or seeking employment for the first time. 'Insiders', other things being equal, will be preferred to 'outsiders' if only for the reason that their performance will be more predictable. To hire outsiders is to invest in assets of uncertain yield; the rate of new recruitment, at least to the higher levels, may therefore be limited by considerations of risk.

There is a further set of circumstances nearer the heart of the matter. New-comers are at an inevitable disadvantage to established personnel in terms of experience of the firm's products, markets, and internal organization. No doubt there is such a thing as general managerial skill capable of being applied in a great variety of fields. Nevertheless, men differ from inanimate factors of production in that their services can be developed fully only after experience of the particular circumstances of their job. Moreover, as Mrs. Penrose has effectively brought to our attention, management functions as a team, with links of familiarity and confidence between its members. This being the case, organizations cannot simply be constructed as can the material apparatus of production; they have to grow. The pace can be forced, but only, after a point, at the sacrifice of efficiency. The point was made by one of our guests when he said that 'the real curb is the lack of managerial ability in the sense that it takes a long time to train people into the ways of the firm and its wide range of activities'. We therefore seem justified in assuming that there is a functional relationship between the 'organizational efficiency' of a firm and its rate of growth, and that the former will decline, after a point, as the latter rises.

Let us now consider why the managers we interviewed did not regard their firms as held back by the absence of additional investment opportunities. The lack of suitable opportunities, and the lack of managerial capacity, are not, it must be observed, wholly distinct circumstances. Irrespective of the general state of trade, there will usually be some sectors of industry offering good returns to investment. The exploitation of these opportunities will fall normally to those firms with the most appropriate commercial contacts, production experience, and marketing skills. But this appropriateness is a matter of degree, and versatile, diversified firms—such as those forming the majority of our sample—are able to cross many industrial and market frontiers. It can safely be assumed, however, that the degree of organizational strain resulting from expansion will depend, not only on the magnitude of the expansion, but also on the directions in which it takes place. A firm's management will be more heavily taxed by expansion into new areas than by expansion along those existing lines for which the firm's organization and experience is most appropriate. The lack of managerial capacity is therefore a more fundamental limit on growth than the fact that investment in a firm's existing lines may show diminishing returns. The managers whom we interviewed, moreover, were perhaps unusually energetic and resourceful; those less fertile in ideas, regarding new markets and products, might be more inclined to regard the growth of their firms as inhibited by lack of openings. Paradoxically, it may be the most creative and enterprising boards of directors that are most likely to stress the managerial or organizational restraint on expansion.

I have already mentioned that investment projects, in order to qualify for adoption by our firms, had usually to offer, prospectively, a rather high return. This finding is consistent with the existence of a managerial restraint and with the high level of efficiency characteristic of our sample. Boards of directors, it is true, may set high qualifying yields in order to allow for risks and in order to discount any excessive optimism on the part of those who conceive the new ventures. But I doubt if this can account for the total gap between the figure demanded (say, 20 per cent on capital) and the cost of the additional finance that would be required. If an efficient firm is already earning 20 per cent on its capital employed, then there are good reasons why it may require new projects to show a comparable return. This policy might, on the face of it, seem illogical, in that a marginal venture will add to profits provided it gives a yield greater than the cost of the funds necessary to undertake it. But this reasoning would neglect the fact that the firm's managerial resources are not, within the investment period, capable of indefinite expansion. If there is a limit to the amount of business that a firm can safely take on, without prejudicing its organizational efficiency, then the directors may be justified in requiring new ventures to show a return comparable with that the firm is already showing itself able to obtain. In somewhat different terms, one can say that management has in effect to consider the effect of an additional investment on the firm's total profitability and that this will depend both on the return from the investment, taken in isolation, and on the effect of the extra work on the organizational efficiency of the firm as a whole.

The proved success and reputation of the firms interviewed may well also explain why most of them did not suffer from lack of funds. The supply of finance to any particular firm is likely to become inelastic beyond a certain point either because those acquainted with it are few in number or because the market believes that the firm is already expanding as rapidly as its organization and prospects permit. The firms in our sample were, for the most part, well known, and they had chosen to expand at a rate that did not threaten their efficiency and their profits.

## III. Theoretical formulation

For the remainder of this paper I shall be concerned with devising a suitable theoretical formulation of the considerations we have been discussing. Ideally, for reasons of economy, one would prefer to employ the familiar categories of the orthodox theory of the firm, but I doubt if these are appropriate.

Our inquiry merely confirms, it might at first be argued, that 'managerial diseconomies of scale' do in fact exist, so that long-run cost curves are, after all, U-shaped. A little reflection, however, obliges us to reject this conclusion. The long-run cost curve is designed to relate the unit cost of producing a particular commodity to the scale of its output, it being assumed that the processes of production employed are fully appropriate to the scale of output. In constructing such a curve, assumptions have to be made, not only about factor prices and manufacturing technology, but also about organizational or managerial efficiency. Marshall's own assumption, regarding the long period, was that production was carried out with the degree of efficiency that could be attained given time for a firm's managerial organization to be built up to the necessary scale.[1]

Thus conceived, the long-run cost curve is a useful idea, but one must not try to make it perform out of context. In particular, one cannot always use it, in conjunction with a demand curve, to illustrate how an entrepreneur takes investment decisions. The long-run cost curve does not indicate the possibilities open to a firm within the investment planning period, for it takes no account of the relationship, stressed by the witnesses in our inquiry, between organizational efficiency and rate of growth. The levels of unit cost to which it refers are those attainable by a firm already endowed with an organizational structure appropriate to the corresponding scales of output, however large. These levels of unit cost are therefore irrelevant to investment decisions where the firm lacks the appropriate organization and cannot hope to build it up during the planning period. The ordinary long-run cost curve, one must therefore conclude, does not help us to determine the volume of net investment that a firm ought to undertake.

It might at first appear that the long-run cost curve could be made to serve this purpose if only we revise the assumptions on which it is based. Could one not employ a curve which took account of the relationship between organizational efficiency and rate of growth? Such a curve

---

[1] In the long period, according to Marshall, 'all investments of capital and effort in providing the material plant and the organisation of a business, and in acquiring trade knowledge and specialised ability, have time to be adjusted . . .' (*Principles of Economics*, p. 377).

would assume that fixed equipment, but not necessarily managerial organization, was appropriate to output. It would have to be associated with a particular firm as well as with a particular product, and its position and shape would depend on the size and the elasticity of the managerial resources at the firm's disposal. Would this curve, when associated with the demand curve for the firm's output, help us to determine the volume of investment that should be undertaken?

It seems to me that it will not, in fact, do so. There is first the obvious objection that the apparatus of demand and cost curves is appropriate to deciding upon the output of a single commodity rather than upon the optimum expansion by a diversified firm. But, in addition, we cannot sum up the effect of the managerial limit to growth simply by saying that costs, after a point, will increase with the size of the contemplated expansion. Such a formulation would unduly circumscribe the managerial function. Managers are not merely concerned with keeping down the costs of a given product; part of their job is to decide upon the precise character of the product, or products, to be made, and to find, or create, a market for them. Managerial difficulties, associated with an unduly high rate of growth, will show up, not just in costs, but in all of the determinants of profitability.

We are, in fact, unlikely to be able to handle with perfect success, in any simple framework of analysis, the entrepreneur's decision about the optimum rate of expansion for his firm. The framework which I shall now suggest is certainly inadequate, but seems to me to do less violence to the facts than those constructed from demand and cost curves.

If an increasing rate of growth causes, after a point, decreasing organizational efficiency, then this should be shown up in profits. Let us therefore take some planning period—say, five years—and relate the amount of gross investment planned for this period to the rate of profit expected on the firm's total capital. By the 'expected profit rate' I shall mean the best estimate of profit that management can make irrespective of uncertainty. It is meant to be calculated on the replacement cost of the *total* capital employed in the firm, and not merely on that part of it devoted to the projected expansion; and it is to be taken gross of the cost of the finance employed by the firm. Investment is to be taken as gross of replacement. Needless to say, we can envisage a relationship between investment and profit on total capital employed only by taking many things as given—such, for example, as views about external profit opportunities.

It seems to be reasonable to assume that the firm's profit rate per unit of capital employed (let us call it $p$) will generally be higher if the firm undertakes some gross investment than if it undertakes none at all. The

### G. B. RICHARDSON

capital assets in the possession of a firm are usually complementary, and if some are not replaced, others may cease to be useful. Thus $p$ will first rise with gross investment ($I$). Organizational considerations will at first reinforce this tendency; people within the firm will be more contented if it grows—and they will certainly be discontented if it contracts. Beyond a certain point, however, $p$ will fall as $I$ rises. The firm will find it costly to expand further in its existing lines, and, although it can move into additional lines, this is likely to increase the strain on management. The

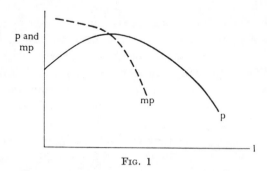

Fig. 1

shape of the curve, therefore, will be drawn as in Fig. 1, organizational efficiency being presumed to fall rather sharply after a point, with higher rates of investment. The dotted line represents the *marginal profitability* of investment ($mp$), this being defined as the change in expected *total* company profits resulting from a unit increase in the investment contemplated. Marginal profitability is distinct from the profit rate on marginal investment, in that expansion, through its influence on organizational efficiency, affects the profitability of all the firm's operations.[1]

Let us now turn from the returns expected from the employment of capital to the cost of employing it. The notion of cost is required, for our purposes, to enable us to judge the success with which the firm is employing its existing capital and to decide upon the extent to which it should add to it. Thus the 'cost' of capital is the minimum return which capital must earn in order to justify its actual or projected use.

---

[1] The curve $mp$ will always intersect the curve $p$ at its highest point, in the way shown. If $P$ represents the firm's total profits, and $I$ the gross investment contemplated, then, by definition,

$$mp = \frac{dP}{dI}.$$

If $K_0$ is the value of the firm's capital if no investment is undertaken, and $p$, as before, the profit per unit of capital employed, then we may write this equality as

$$mp = \frac{d}{dI} p(K_0 + I) = K_0 \cdot \frac{dp}{dI} + I \cdot \frac{dp}{dI} + p.$$

If $p$ is to be a maximum, then $\frac{dp}{dI} = 0$, so that $mp = p$.

How is this minimum return to be assessed? Relevant standards are provided both by the sums that have to be paid to the owners of capital for its use and by the return that the capital could provide in alternative employments. By comparing actual returns with the first of these standards we determine whether net profits are positive; by comparing them with the second, we determine whether net profits are as high as they might be. We shall assume that the entrepreneur has already selected the most fruitful lines of expansion and is concerned merely with how much, in total, to invest in them.

Let us now consider first the notional cost attributable to the capital already employed by the firm. Adopting the first of the standards referred to, this is represented by the charges that are incurred in ensuring that this capital continues to be available. Were funds always borrowed from others on uniform, fixed-interest terms, then their unit cost would be simply the going rate. In fact, however, a firm raises money from a variety of sources on a variety of terms. The amount obtained from each source, and therefore the firm's preferred financial structure or 'financial ratios', will depend partly on cost, partly on availability, and partly on considerations of risk. Thus a bank overdraft will represent a source of funds that is cheap but limited and liable to be withdrawn; short-term loans may cost less than long-term loans, but they will have to be re-negotiated on unpredictable terms; and any form of fixed-interest borrowing will involve the risks associated with constant commitments and variable receipts. Money raised from the sale of ordinary shares differs from fixed interest borrowing in respect of the risks incurred and by virtue of the fact that it has no price, in the strict sense. But one may, nevertheless, attribute to it a particular cost, equal to the minimum return that share capital will have to yield in order to maintain the firm's ability to raise fresh funds. The size of this return will depend partly on the general level of returns available elsewhere and partly on the riskiness of the business in question. The notional cost of share capital is a concept, no doubt, rather lacking in precision, but managements—for good reason—do think in terms of it.

Given the variety of ways in which a firm will raise money, the cost of capital has to be conceived in terms of a weighted average of the costs attributable to each source, the weights corresponding, of course, to the amounts obtained from each source. I wish now to consider how the cost of a firm's capital, thus conceived, will be affected by the amount of additional finance the firm seeks to raise. In appropriate circumstances one would expect a business to be able to obtain some additional funds on the same terms as can be attributed to the capital it is already employing. But the supply thus available will be limited. Some sources of funds, such as bank credit, will become exhausted and others more expensive. If the market takes the view that the expansion being planned by the firm is immoderate, then funds will be forthcoming, if at all, only on terms high enough to compensate leaders or subscribers for the greater risks they believe they are running. Thus the larger the expansion projected, beyond a certain point, the greater will be the unit cost of finance. Not only may additional finance become more expensive; the 'replacement cost' of finance already acquired may rise also in response to the market's changed assessment of risks. If there is a critical point beyond which the unit cost of finance rises very sharply indeed, then an entrepreneur may be justified in thinking in terms, not of increasing cost, but of unavailability.

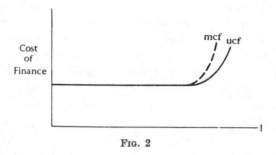

FIG. 2

It is therefore possible to represent the unit cost of the total capital to be employed by a company as a function of the magnitude of the expansion it proposes to undertake. This is done in Fig. 2 by a curve relating the unit cost of the total finance employed by the company ($ucf$) to the monetary value of the gross investment contemplated within the planning period. I have assumed that the firm can raise further money, up to a point, on unchanged terms, but that, beyond this point, further fundraising at first drives up unit costs and then (where the curve is vertical) becomes impossible. The curve $mcf$ indicates the variation, with the magnitude of the investment contemplated, of the marginal cost of finance, this being defined as the increase in the total cost of the company's capital attributable to a unit increase in the amount of the additional funds raised. I am assuming that the unit cost of funds ($ucf$) and the unit return expected ($p$) are being calculated with reference to the same base—this being the replacement value of the total capital that the firm proposed to employ. The marginal concepts, $mcf$ and $mp$, refer respectively to the changes in the total cost of the firm's capital and the expected total return from it.

Let us now examine whether it is possible, with the help of these ideas, to formalize the choice of an optimum expansion. This choice will depend,

18      THE LIMITS TO A FIRM'S RATE OF GROWTH

it is apparent, upon the objectives which the entrepreneur sets himself. If his aim is simply to maximize total expected profit, with no regard to risk, then he would choose the level of $I$ which equated $mp$ with $mcf$. If, on the other hand, he wished to play safe, he might choose the expansion which maximized the difference between $p$ and $ucf$. This would be the policy most suited to guard against the possibility that $p$, in the event, would fall so far short of expectations as to result in an actual loss. Were the entrepreneur to wish to grow quickly, even at some sacrifice of profits, and some risk of loss, he might plan an expansion nearer the size that would bring $p$ and $ucf$ into equality. These are three extreme policies; in practice a firm would be likely to follow some intermediate course.

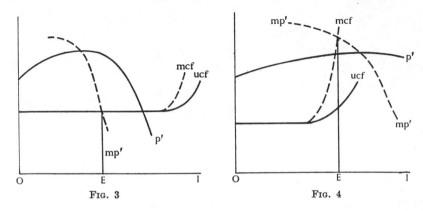

Fig. 3                                    Fig. 4

Choice in this matter can be made more determinate (but only in appearance) by associating the different values of $I$, not with $p$, but with its 'certainty equivalent' $p'$, this being defined as that rate of profit, the certain expectation of which would be as equally attractive as the uncertain expectation of profit actually envisaged. Clearly $p'$ would be less than $p$, the divergence between the two increasing with the level of investment with which they are associated. If this procedure is followed —and there are some good objections to it—one can then perhaps represent the entrepreneur as always choosing the level of $I$ which will equate $mp'$ (defined analogously to $p'$) to $mcf$.

Adopting this approach, one can distinguish between firms according to the nature of the check to their expansion. In Fig. 3 I have assumed that $mp'$ comes to equal $mcf$ at a level of investment $E$ where $mcf$ is still equal to $ucf$. This will be the position of firms, like those forming the majority of our sample, that do not regard finance as setting the limit to their growth. The operative check in this case is managerial resources, the burden upon which may be made specially heavy through the need to expand in new directions. In Fig. 4 the curves are drawn so that *mp'* intersects *mcf* while *p'* is still rising. In this situation, one can say that finance, rather than management, is the operative check on growth. If the curves had been drawn so that *mp'* cut *mcf* at a level of investment at which *p'* was falling and *mcf* rising, then both checks could be said to be effective.

If the curves of *p'* and *mp'* were as I have drawn them in Figs. 3 and 4, then the entrepreneur expects to receive a rate of profit on capital which could be called abnormal in that it exceeds the cost of finance by more than the risk premium demanded by management. (The imputed cost of finance includes the risk premiums which shareholders and others have

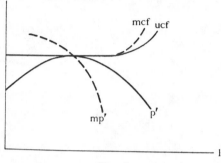

Fɪɢ. 5

to be given to persuade them to subscribe capital.) The curves are re-drawn, in Fig. 5, on the assumption that the firm, if it chooses the optimum expansion, will expect to make only normal profits; were it to expand by more or less than this, it would expect to earn less than normal profits. This might be presumed to represent some sort of equilibrium position for a firm of average efficiency and luck; it would not be safe to conclude, however, that competition would ensure that the average rate of profit in industry would approximate to the normal in this sense. We have been dealing throughout with expectations, rather than with fulfilments, and we have to allow for the possibility of some systematic divergence between these two.

The framework of analysis which I have now presented is an attempted formalization of decisions regarding the optimum expansion of a firm. I do not wish to suggest that entrepreneurs need think in terms of it. There may be no possibility of precise estimation of the extent to which expansion, beyond a certain point, may impair the organizational efficiency, and therefore reduce the profits, of the company as a whole; if this is so, then the directors may well content themselves with rejecting any proposed venture which offers less than some specified qualifying yield. The formal analysis may, however, serve to rationalize this

20        THE LIMITS TO A FIRM'S RATE OF GROWTH

particular procedure, especially where the qualifying yield is much higher than the cost of additional finance.

## IV. The level of aggregate investment

Although the availability of management and money may set limits to the investment undertaken by firms, it does not follow that we must explain changes in the level of investment in these terms. Investment is manifestly affected by the state of business confidence, by technical change, by tax policy, and the like. If these circumstances alter, so, in general, will the rate of firms' expansion, even although management

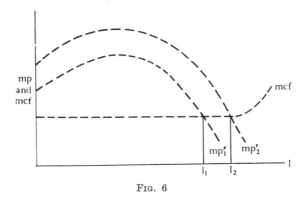

FIG. 6

(and, to a lesser extent, finance) can still properly be regarded as the ultimate limiting factor.

The joint operation of these general and particular determinants of a firm's investment plans can readily be viewed in terms of our diagrams. Changes in profit expectations will affect the position and shape of the curves of $p'$ and $mp'$; changes in credit conditions will affect the position and shape of the curves of $ucf$ and $mcf$. Let us now consider each of these changes in turn.

Most obviously, perhaps, a general change in profit expectations will affect the height of the $p$ and $mp$ curves. But if $mp$ intersects $mcf$ where either of these curves is highly elastic with respect to the volume of investment planned, then it is clear that the response of investment, to a change in the height of the curves, may be slight. Thus, if in Fig. 6, the $mp'$ curve is shifted upwards from $mp'_1$ to $mp'_2$, investment rises only from $I_1$ to $I_2$. If, in other words, a firm has exhausted the demand in its familiar markets, and is prevented, by managerial considerations, from rapid expansion into new ones, then a small change in the profit rate expected will not much affect investment plans. The same situation would obtain, more obviously, if the firm was faced with a sharply rising cost of finance.

Much more important will be the effect of a revision of expectations on the *shape* of the $p'$ and $mp'$ curves. If, for example, demand rises generally throughout the economy, firms will expect to be able to increase their sales of their established products, in their established markets. Response to opportunities of this kind will place much less strain on the firms' managerial organization than will expansion in new directions, so that

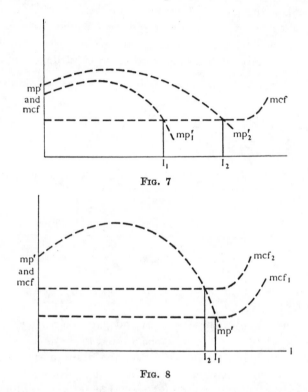

Fig. 7

Fig. 8

we may associate the revision of expectations with an elongation of the curves of $p'$ and $mp'$. A much larger expansion will be possible, in other words, before organizational strain causes $mp'$ to decline. Thus in Fig. 7 a change in the curve of $mp'$ from $mp'_1$ to $mp'_2$ will cause investment to rise from $I_1$ to $I_2$. Bearing in mind, therefore, that a general revision of expectations may be thus associated with a change in the shape of the $mp'$ curve, its possible effect on investment can be seen to be substantial.

Let us now consider changes in the cost and availability of credit. If the unit cost of finance increases for a firm (say, because of a general rise in interest rates), without any change in the supply elasticity of this finance, then the effect on investment may be slight. Thus, in Fig. 8 if $mcf$ rises from $mcf_1$ to $mcf_2$, investment will fall only from $I_1$ to $I_2$. If firms are already straining against the limits imposed by their established markets and their managerial organization, a change in *mcf* will not substantially affect investment plans. But if credit conditions change so as to alter the supply elasticity of finance, and thus the shape of the *mcf* curve, then the effect on investment plans may be more marked (see Fig. 9). The incidence of the effect, however, will be uneven. Those companies—the majority of our sample—which do not normally experience rising *mcf* may not experience it even after a credit squeeze, and their investment plans will be little changed. Other companies, working near the rising part of the *mcf* curve, will be obliged to cut their investment plans. This seems to accord with what we know from other findings.

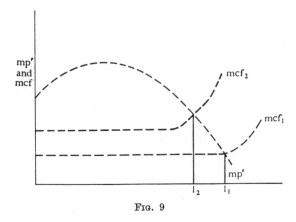

FIG. 9

These considerations lead one to conclude that the level of investment in manufacturing may be relatively insensitive to changes either in expected profit rates or in interest rates, if these are not associated with changes—using our terminology—in the shapes of the *mp* and *mcf* functions. What is needed for a substantial change in investment is a change either in the *volume* of sales that firms hope to make or in the *volume* of credit that they can raise. And, in that only some firms appear to be normally subject to a financial restraint, the latter circumstance is less influential than the former.

The relative powerlessness of interest rates to affect investment in manufacturing has been most commonly attributed to the importance of risk. Thus, Professor Meade, in looking back on a former Oxford Inquiry, comments as follows: 'What seems to have been overlooked is the extent to which our interviews were confined to risky manufacturing or commercial business, where one would expect the rate of interest to have the least affect because the "risk premium" is everything.'[1] I am myself

---

[1] Quoted in *Oxford Studies in the Price Mechanism* (ed. Wilson and Andrews), p. 4.

inclined to be somewhat sceptical of this explanation. The fact that firms contemplating investment may wish expected profit rates to exceed interest rates by a substantial risk premium does not itself imply that changes in interest rates will have a negligible affect on investment. If, in the extreme case, the expected profit rate on all projected invest-ments exceeded the interest rate by just the risk premium, however great, then presumably any rise in the interest rates would deter all investment. Nothing can be said about the elasticity of investment with respect to interest rate changes unless we know something about the elasticity of profit expectations with respect to the level of investment. This latter elasticity has usually been represented as dependent on the diminishing marginal productivity of capital and on the extent to which the cost of producing capital assets will rise, with the volume of their output, in the short run. The above analysis suggests that it will depend also on the firmness with which companies' expansion is being checked by the limits of demand in their familiar markets and by the organiza-tional restraints upon rapid expansion into new ones. If entrepreneurs feel that the marginal profitability of their total company capital would fall sharply with further expansion, then a reduction in interest rates may scarcely influence their investment decisions. It is to this circum-stance, rather than to the magnitude of risk 'premiums', that the weakness of interest rate policy ought probably to be attributed.

*St. John's College, Oxford*

# [6]

# THE THEORY OF RESTRICTIVE TRADE PRACTICES

## By G. B. RICHARDSON

WE are here concerned with that branch of economic theory which seeks to establish connexions between market structure and economic performance. This theory begins by postulating hypothetical forms, or models, of market organization and then examines the nature of the opportunities available to entrepreneurs within them; it then proceeds to predict the kinds of behaviour that entrepreneurs will adopt and the properties of the patterns of resource allocation that will thereby come to be established. Formal welfare theory provides us with the criteria of optimum allocation to serve as a standard of comparison and thus it becomes possible to judge whether particular restrictions on competition, as an element of market structure, either promote or impede economic efficiency.[1]

Private property will be the common feature of all the models of economic structure with which we are concerned, so that resources will come to be allocated as a result of decisions taken by individual businesses seeking profit. In these conditions one can distinguish at least four distinct ways in which the organization of a market can influence economic efficiency.

First, to the extent that a market provides producers with monopoly power, it will give them an incentive to fix the volumes of their outputs below the socially ideal levels; prices, that is to say, will diverge from marginal costs in varying degrees, thus indicating a departure from optimum allocation either in the proportions in which products feature in final output or in the proportions in which factors are combined in production. This is the influence of market structure that has been given most attention by economic theorists and least attention by the man in the street.

Misallocation of the kind caused by monopolistic restriction can equally well result simply from the fact that entrepreneurs, if they are inadequately informed of the circumstances relevant to their decisions, make mistakes. I shall argue that market structure affects the information

---

[1] There is also a macro-economic aspect to our subject. We may wish to know how restraints on competition might effect the distribution of income or an economy's liability to suffer unemployment or inflation. I propose to exclude these matters from consideration in order to have space to concentrate upon what seems to me the most important issue—the effect of restrictive practices on economic efficiency. I have also decided, in order to reduce the subject to manageable proportions, to confine myself to the relationship between manufacturing firms and to ignore the relationships between manufacturers and distributors or between distributors themselves.

available to them and therefore influences, in this second way also, the pattern of resource allocation that will emerge.

The efficiency with which resources are made use of will also depend on the quality of entrepreneurship. This in turn will vary with market structure in its roles as a provider of incentives, positive and negative, and as a mechanism of selection causing the control over resources to pass to those who can employ them profitably from those who fail to do so. Here then we have a third and fourth way in which structure can influence performance.

Our formal theory of markets tends to concentrate our attention on the first of these four influences—on the distortions, that is to say, caused by monopolistic exactions—although I much doubt if it is the most important. In strong contrast to this, little heed has been paid to the way in which market organization, by influencing the predictability of the business environment, determines the availability of information to entrepreneurs. I shall therefore feel justified in giving prominence to this aspect in the discussion that is to follow. The effect of economic organization on the quality of entrepreneurship is of the highest importance but difficult to handle in theoretical terms.

Before turning to a systematic consideration of the analysis of market forms, and of restrictive agreements in particular, I wish to make mention, in passing, of one general limitation to which this analysis is subject. By and large, our standard theory is founded on the assumption of profit maximization, an assumption that is, for two reasons, exceedingly *simpliste*. In the first place, the alternative opportunities before entrepreneurs cannot be ranked unequivocally in order of profitability, as they are normally associated with a range of possible outcomes. Secondly, money-making is not the only motive; business men may also value, for example, independence or a quiet life.

The relevance of these considerations to any analysis of the effects of restrictive agreements can be seen from two examples. Let us suppose that the operation of a restriction reduces the uncertainty attaching to the yield from an investment, but at the same time provides greater scope for monopolistic exaction. Will the net effect of the restriction be to increase or to diminish the volume of output planned? The reduction of uncertainty should strengthen the willingness to invest, whereas the protection from competition should provide an incentive deliberately to restrict supply. Clearly, the net result cannot be predicted without some knowledge of the magnitude of the factors at work; we require some quantitive assessment of the degree to which the restriction will reduce uncertainty and of the significance that the entrepreneur in question will attach to this. As these magnitudes will vary according to circumstances,

we will be able to assess them as best we can only in the context of particular cases or groups of similar cases.

Consider, as a second example, an industry in which the firms are too
small to exploit all the available economies of scale; and suppose, further,
that the firms agree prices. Now it is evident that the existence of the
agreement does not eliminate the gains to be had, in the form of cost
reductions, from amalgamation between two or more firms. It may be,
however, that so long as the common price level is high enough to provide
reasonable profits, the firms will not consider the gain from amalgamation
sufficient to compensate for the associated loss of independence. The proscription of the agreement, were this to cause prices to fall to unremunerative levels, might provide the jolt required to induce managements to
sacrifice their independence and overcome that inertia which takes the
form of a settled preference for the *status quo*. Nevertheless, it is possible,
at the same time, that the price agreement does fulfil useful functions;
about this I shall have more to say at a later stage. Once again therefore
we are forced back to an exercise of judgement to be made only with a full
knowledge of the circumstances of the case; and judgement is made the
more difficult by the fact that the quality of business enterprise is itself a
function of market organization. Entrepreneurs' desire for independence
has been represented as a barrier to realizing economies of scale. Independence, however, may provide positive benefits; a manager may show more
enterprise as his own master than when obliged to account for all his
decisions to higher authority. Concentration in an industry, or even the
subjection of the firms within it to restrictive regulations, may be bought
at the price of some loss in freshness and variety of decision.

In mentioning, at the outset, these several limitations, my aim is to
stress the need for a proper modesty, on behalf of economists, when they
endeavour to apply their theoretical constructions to the questions that
here concern us. Our formal models of market organization do not readily
accommodate many factors that practical judgement must take into
account; nor can we often assess the relative magnitude—which may be
crucial—of the elements that these models help us to identify. These
reservations made, we must proceed; although an appraisal of restrictive
practices may be difficult even with the help of economic theory, it is
certainly not possible without it.

Let us adopt the traditional procedure and begin our analysis of the
effects of restraints on competition by considering the model in which such
restraints are wholly absent. Perfect competition has been regarded, for
about a century, as of key importance by virtue of the fact that it is
supposed to result in a determinate pattern of resource allocation the
relevant properties of which are those of a Pareto optimum. From this

### G. B. RICHARDSON

many economists have deemed it an easy leap to conclude that the market structure defined by the model is an ideal, deviations from which produce misallocation. Thus a market structure is made to appear defective if the number of firms is small, if there exist understandings between them and if output is not homogeneous. Each of these circumstances is seen as capable as affording a firm some control over price and thereby an incentive to restrict output below the optimum level. I believe this analysis —set out here, albeit, in crudely simplified form—to be radically defective.[1]

We may begin by observing that no one has ever been able to explain satisfactorily how the equilibrium configuration associated with perfect competition might in practice be attained. The earlier writers on the subject did at least realize the existence of a problem; thus Edgeworth had recourse to the process of 'recontracting' and Walras to his prices *criés au hazard*. But these are not genuine solutions, if only for the reason that they require the mediation of very special arrangements to be found neither in the real world nor in the conditions of the model.

In order to explain how equilibrium is reached we need to provide an account of how entrepreneurs are able to identify investment opportunities the exploitation of which will cause resources to be distributed in the required way. The crucial difficulty is to show how, in perfectly competitive conditions, investment opportunities could ever be identified. I have endeavoured to set out elsewhere[2] reasons for believing that it is impossible, within the context of the model, for entrepreneurs to acquire the information on which to base investment and current output decisions. At the same time, I sought to show that investment decisions not based on the relevant information, but simply on projections of current prices, would not lead to equilibrium. This is not the place to recapitulate all the argument; suffice it to say that the profitability of investment by an entrepreneur in the production of a particular good will depend upon the relationship between the demand for that good and the total supply planned by competitors. The model we are dealing with, by postulating an indefinite number of firms ready and willing to set up in the production of any good, leaves this total volume of competitive supply quite unrestricted and therefore unpredictable.

Progress beyond this point can only be made, it seems to me, by giving explicit recognition to this most important principle; *the availability to entrepreneurs of the information on which to base investment decisions is a function of the structure of the model in which they are presumed to operate.*

---

[1] There seems no need to discuss the ways in which the analysis has to be qualified to take into account indivisibilities or divergences between private and social cost; that such qualifications are required is agreed by everyone.

[2] *Information and Investment*, Oxford University Press, 1960.

Alternative market forms may be compared, in other words, according to the predictability of the environment that they afford entrepreneurs. Perfect competition represents an environment in which predictability (of the appropriate kind) is zero;[1] only by postulating some restriction on the freedom of individual entrepreneurs can this predictability be increased. Once this is admitted, practices in restraint of competition no longer appear as so much sand in the works.[2]

It is possible for firms to undertake informed production planning, and thus promote the adjustment of supply to demand, only when competition is less than perfect—a condition which the real world, fortunately, normally grants us. But this is not to say that the restrictions on trade, such as would concern the Registrar, are always, or indeed normally, required. Sufficient stability in the business environment may be provided by natural imperfections in competition or by the adoption by entrepreneurs of codes of behaviour that regulate the relationship between rivals without the need for agreements or understandings in the ordinary sense.

The natural imperfections take the form of geographical barriers, of product differentiation in the widest sense, and of economies of scale such as leave room, in any one market, for only a few competing firms. It is not difficult to see how each of these facilitate foresight of the kind required by entrepreneurs. Geography and product differentiation reduce the dependence of the profitability of investment by one firm on the investments being planned by others; they give natural advantages to particular producers that may suffice to permit them, so long as they remain efficient, to presume that the whole of a limited market is their own to develop. The existence of only a few firms in an industry, if these are in possession of some advantage over outsiders, likewise works towards more predictable markets. The restriction in numbers makes it much easier for each entrepreneur to know what his rivals plan to do.

Although natural imperfections of the kind described will usually increase the predictability of business environment, it is clear that they need not do so, at all times and in all markets, to the extent required to permit informed investment and production planning. Their strength will vary from market to market; and according to the scale and irreversibility of investment decisions, so will the need for them. Circumstances will therefore arise in which entrepreneurs, in the absence of deliberately

---

[1] It is for this reason absurd to postulate the existence of both perfect competition and perfect knowledge. Yet this is often done.

[2] I am inclined to think that many economists, rather than give full recognition to the relationship between information and market structure, will prefer to endeavour to salvage perfect competition through the introduction of additional special assumptions. Not only industrialists may be reluctant to scrap obsolete equipment. That the model may be patched up to some extent I do not deny, although the changes that have to be imposed upon it will probably be equivalent to some kind of restriction on competition.

contrived restrictions on competition, are unable to make any capable estimates of the likely volume of supply being planned by their rivals.

The most objectionable feature of this situation, from the firms' point of view, is the risk of excess supply and negative returns on investment. They will therefore be led to modify their relationships in such a way as reduces the risk of excess supply or mitigates the effects of excess supply on profits.

The forms of behaviour adopted, though various, have for the most part this in common; each firm does something (or refrains from doing something) on the expectation that its rivals will do likewise. In this limited sense, at any rate, the behaviour in question is co-operative; the reciprocal expectations or understandings that form its content may be set out in express agreement or may be merely the silent premiss of actual conduct. The motive at work is self-interest, but self-interest enlightened by the sense that the interests of each member of the group coincide, at least partially, with the interests of the group as a whole. (Thus, for example, a firm may refrain from an apparently advantageous price reduction in the realization that if all competitors were to reduce prices, all of them would lose.) The sanctions available are of three kinds. The first is the threat of retaliation; each entrepreneur may appreciate that if he breaks the code others will do so also, with the result that any gains will be illusory or short-lived. But transgression may not always be easily detected and retaliation may take place, if at all, only after some delay. Further sanctions may therefore be provided by means of an express agreement; if it is legally enforceable, the sanction in force is the law of the country, if not, it is the fact that promises have been exchanged. The parties to these undertakings may regard their promises as binding, either from a sense of moral obligation or in the realization that others will not enter into future undertakings with those who have acquired a bad reputation. The forms of behaviour in question may perform the same function irrespective of whether the sanction is provided by the fear of retaliation or by the existence of an agreement, although it is only in the latter case that legal control or prohibition can easily be applied.

I have maintained that firms may act so as to restrict competition in the hope of thereby reducing the risk of excess supply. Were this the only aim and effect of their co-operation, then, provided excess supply were defined appropriately, the co-operation would always be in the general interest. Not only would wasteful gluts be rendered less likely; to the extent that fear of gluts inhibit investment, the incidence of scarcity would also, paradoxically, be diminished. That there is a problem of policy arises from the fact that the power to prevent excess supply may be used to limit supply unduly, just as the power to reduce uncertainty may be used to provide an easy life.

In considering in more detail the various forms of restrictive behaviour adopted by entrepreneurs, it will be convenient to distinguish investment decisions, relating to the installation of fixed plant, and output decisions, relating to the amount to be produced from fixed plant already in existence. Let us first consider investment decisions.

In the endeavour to prevent a wasteful duplication of capacity, firms might decide, with or without express agreement, to maintain constant shares of their common market. But the practical difficulties in working such an arrangment are formidable. In surprisingly many markets firms lack accurate information as to the shares they currently enjoy and are therefore unable to know whether or not they are maintaining them. And even if actual shares are known, firms may entertain different ideas about how total demand for the product will change. This being so, it would be difficult to judge from the observed investment policies of firms whether they were observing the code, in the sense that they were just maintaining their share of the increment of demand they expected, or whether they were seeking to encroach on the markets of rivals. If a firm lacked assurance that others were observing the code, however, it would not feel bound to do so itself. It is evident therefore that strict market sharing would require formal agreement, quotas being negotiated and some common forecast made of demand. Given inevitable differences of interest between the parties, these arrangements are not easy to make—quite apart from the attention they are likely to receive from the appropriate governmental authorities. And it can scarcely be denied that formal market sharing can be operated in such a way as to exploit the purchaser or retard the differential growth of the more efficient firms.

Theory cannot of course determine, in any general way, whether it is better to prohibit firms from co-ordinating their investment plans, and thus run the risk of some maladjustment of capacity to demand, or to permit such co-ordination subject, perhaps, to some form of control. Much will depend on the circumstances of the market. Maladjustment may develop more easily, and involve more waste, when much fixed and durable capital is employed in production and when this capital is installed in large and indivisible units. Where investment decisions are on a small scale and easily reversible, and when demand is on a strong upward trend, maladjustment may be less severe and less persistent.[1]

---

[1] It is worth noting that industrial organization can often be improved, in the relevant respects, without recourse to systematic co-ordination of investment plans. Arrangements can be made, for example, to ensure that firms are informed of the total sales in their market and therefore of their share of them. Decisions to install additional capacity, once taken, can be made known to competitors. A system of accounting may also be introduced

Where the losses from the maladjustment of capacity to demand are likely to be serious, then it may be desirable to permit firms (or oblige them) to co-ordinate their investment plans, subject to some control designed to ensure both that aggregate capacity is planned in accordance with the best estimate of future demand and that the more efficient firms have an opportunity to expand their share of the total market. If prices are fixed so as to yield only normal profits to a firm of normal efficiency, the less efficient firms may in any case be willing to give ground to their lower cost rivals. The danger, of course, is that too great respect will be given to vested interests, small firms or potential entrants having little or no influence on the arrangements made. State supervision may prevent some abuses but there is no guarantee that it will do so; even governments have been known to favour the industrial establishment.

It is perhaps curious that indicative planning, of the kind now in vogue in France and in England, stresses the need for the inter-industry co-ordination of investment plans while apparently accepting the absence of co-ordination between the investment plans of firms in the same industry. The co-ordination of plans within an industry seems the logical extension of co-ordination between industries; indeed if the former is not realized the latter is unlikely to be realized. Presumably the doctrine must be that the co-ordination of investments within an industry can usually come about spontaneously, by virtue of the existence of the natural restrictions on competition referred to earlier and without measures designed to this end. Theory, however, lends no support to the view that such spontaneous adjustment can always be relied upon.

Let us now turn to the way in which market structure may affect economic efficiency through its influence on entrepreneurs' decisions about

sufficiently sophisticated for firms to know the true costs of what they are producing. Surprisingly, this quite often does not exist. (There have been firms that first estimated the return from capital on particular products when required to do so by the Restrictive Practices Court.) An efficient allocation of resources, in the full sense, requires that the manufacture of particular products is undertaken by those firms best suited to that manufacture; but unless management knows the costs attributable to each of the firm's products, this specialization according to comparative advantage will not come about. Firms may fail to relinquish the production of articles which they are ill suited to manufacture simply because it is not apparent to them that these lines are unprofitable. Ideally, it is desirable for management to know (at least approximately) both its own costs of manufacture, for each of its products, and the corresponding costs of competitors either individually or, in the form of a weighted average, as a body. In the long run, no doubt, a firm that continues in too many unprofitable lines will lose ground. In this way competition works automatically so as to withdraw control of resources over those unable to make efficient use of them; but if it is to provide all its benefits it should also act as a signalling mechanism able to tell managements, in time to take remedial action, where their weaknesses lie. I make these points, in this theoretical article, to show that the efficiency of a market structure depends on factors other than those commonly taken into account. The information made available to entrepreneurs, by a particular market organization, will influence not only the process of adjustment of supply to demand, but also the effectiveness of competition in stimulating firms to reduce costs and specialize according to their comparative advantages.

how much to produce from given equipment. We know from welfare theory that, for the prices of products and factors to be consistent with optimum allocation, the output that ought to be produced from given equipment is that just saleable at a price equal to the short-run marginal costs of its production, these being the same for all firms if production is distributed efficiently among them. Many writers appear to believe that, if perfect competition were to exist, this is precisely what would happen, profits being maximized—the demand for the firms' output being perfectly elastic—where price equals marginal costs. But this would be true only if entrepreneurs were able to obtain the information with which to predict future prices, this being something, I have argued, the conditions of the model will not permit them to do. We must therefore banish from our minds the widespread but erroneous belief that allocation will be efficient if competition is perfect and inefficient if it is not.

Let us begin by noting that, in the real world, manufacturing businesses are not characteristically concerned in their short-run output decisions with the prediction of future prices. Prices do not generally move so as to equate demand and supply at every point of time. In practice, therefore, firms are normally engaged in predicting the volume of demand on the assumption that prices are steady in the short run. These predictions, which will be based on trends in sales, on stock movements and the state of orders, will not be perfectly accurate, but they are feasible and permit tolerably informed output decisions to be taken. The feasibility of the prediction, moreover, depends upon the short-run stability of prices. If the price level of an article moves continuously to equate demand to current supply, then it will no longer be possible to use changes in stocks and order books as indicators of the trend in demand. In addition, and equally important, if the relative prices quoted by different manufacturers of an article vary in the short run, then no seller will be able to assume that his share of the total demand will remain roughly constant, with the result that even if he can predict the total future demand for the article he will nevertheless be unable to decide how much to produce.

Short-run price stability, we must now recognize, is maintained by a certain code of behaviour among entrepreneurs.[1] Let us suppose that there are several producers of a particular commodity the demand for which begins to fall relative to the available capacity with the result that the price previously charged now exceeds marginal costs. In these circumstances each entrepreneur is under temptation to adopt a policy which, if he alone were to adopt it, would greatly increase his profits, but which, if all were to adopt it, would bring losses to all sellers and a net loss to society

[1] The remainder of this paper draws on my article 'Les Relations entre Firmes' in *Economie Appliquée*, 1965.

as a whole. This policy would consist in lowering price so as to divert trade from rivals and thereby ensure that the firm was working at full capacity. If the cross elasticity of demand for the firms' outputs were very high, only a very small price cut would be required; a great increase in profits would then be obtained, the actual magnitude of which would depend on the proportion that fixed costs bore to the total costs of production.

Competition in this form, if practised by all concerned, could lead to heavy excess supply. If all firms acted in this way then none of them would succeed in increasing its share of total sales. Each would find that the increased output it had produced and hoped to sell at a price only slightly below its previous level could not in fact be sold at that price. It would then have either to reconcile itself to holding an undesirably large volume of stocks or to endeavour to sell the goods it had available by a further price cut. Each producer might in fact be able to sell all his increased volume of output provided price fell to a sufficiently low level, but this level might be well below the marginal costs at which the output was manufactured. The losses sustained by the producers, as a result of the the competitive policies they pursued, might be very great, their actual magnitude depending on elasticity of demand for the product and upon how great an increase in market share each of them had hoped to achieve. The consumers of the product would gain, by virtue of the fall in price, but it is important to note that there may be a net loss to society as a whole. Economists are prone to assume that competitive price-cutting in a situation of the kind we are considering will cause prices to fall only to the level of marginal costs; this then entitles them to conclude that competitive price-cutting secures the optimum supply. But we have no right to make this assumption; that economists so often do so derives from their belief (or need to believe) that the equilibrium solutions of competitive theory are somehow always realized. There is no reason to believe that, as a result of competitive striving by which each firm endeavours to increase its share of the total market, the aggregate supply produced will clear the market at a price just equal to the marginal costs of each producer. In fact, if each producer expected a small price-cut to produce a substantial increase in market share, the total supply forthcoming would be in excess of the amount that could be sold at a price sufficient to cover marginal costs and constitute, for that reason, a misallocation of resources.

Competitive activity of this particular kind (which we may term short-run price competition) is so obviously destructive that entrepreneurs have a very strong incentive to develop codes of behaviour capable of preventing it. The simplest of such codes would consist in each firm maintaining the price of its product when capacity exceeds demand, in the expectation that its rivals would act likewise. Firms would refrain, as Marshall pointed out some time ago, from 'spoiling the market'. This restraint would have as its motive the fear of retaliation, a sense of common interest with rival sellers or even a vague feeling, almost of a moral kind, that this was 'the right thing to do'.

Very often, however, this simple form of co-operative action would give way to the pressure of individual interests. An individual seller may be tempted to reduce his price in the hope that he will enjoy a large increase in sales before his rivals discover what he has done. He may be able, for example, to offer rebates to large customers which he hopes will be kept secret, at least for some time, from competitors. If the size of an individual order is large compared to total annual turnover, the incentive to acquire it, by slightly reducing price, will be strong. If the seller also carries large surplus stocks, and is in great need of cash, the incentive will be even stronger. Once prices begin to be cut it will only be a matter of time before this becomes known to all concerned; the code of behaviour will soon be undermined and the market, in business men's terms, be 'de-moralised'. Even if there is a strong fear of price-cutting, as distinct from its actual practice, the situation will be highly precarious.

In many markets therefore one will expect more formal co-operation to develop. The next step in this direction is an agreement to exchange information about the prices actually being charged or the price changes that firms plan to make in the future. In this way firms voluntarily give up the advantages of surprise attack in return for similar assurances from their rivals. In these circumstances, when retaliation can be immediate, a firm will only cut price when it believes that it is in its long-run interest to do so; when it believes, that is to say, either that other firms will not act likewise or that it will benefit even if they do. Information agreements of this kind are very common, especially in countries where agreements on price itself are illegal, and they undoubtedly help to check short-run price competition of the kind we have been discussing. They are subject, nevertheless, to important limitations.

Complete price stability would be as undesirable as it would be impracticable. Prices ought to change when costs change and it may be desirable to change them also, to some extent, in response to changes in demand. There is then a problem of how these changes are to be brought about without at the same time causing the prices charged by different manufacturers to alter, in relation to each other, in unpredictable ways. One seller may wish to raise price but be afraid to do so in case others do not raise their prices also. Alternatively, a seller may think that conditions justify a lower level of price but may not wish to initiate a process of continuous and irregular price reductions. A solution to this problem, providing for uniform price changes, is given by the system of price leadership in which one firm announces in advance that it proposes to alter its price list and other firms then make similar announcements. Once again, however, there are limitations. The interests of all the firms in the industry will not be identical and it may therefore happen that the price chosen by the leader is unsuitable for some of them. In this case either the system may break down or it may be replaced by an agreement on prices themselves.

Of all the methods arranged to prevent short-run price competition an agreement of prices is probably the most effective. So long as it operates, firms' market shares will be relatively constant in the short run, being determined essentially by traditional connexions with buyers, reputation, quality differences, and the like. Each firm will have given up its freedom to endeavour to gain a temporary increase in market share by secret or unexpected price changes and will have obtained, in exchange, a more predictable demand than it would have had otherwise. From the point of view of the short-run planning of output—i.e. decisions about how much to produce from given plant—this is a substantial gain; the costs of the arrangement, from the community's point of view, will concern us shortly. Although less fragile than collusion based merely on the exchange of information, associated with price leadership, agreements on prices are nevertheless, as is well known, liable to break down. Being voluntary, they cannot survive without each of the parties believing that they are in their own long-run interest; given the likely disparity of firms in terms of costs, size, and ambition, this is a condition that may often fail to be met.

Let us now endeavour to draw up a balance of the gains and losses associated with the business behaviour we have been examining. On the credit side we have the fact that this behaviour may prevent such forms of competition as may result in excessive supply or may deter investment through fear of the losses that such excess supply may bring. This end is achieved by making the environment of entrepreneurs more stable and thus permitting more informed planning of output. On the debit side, there may be losses of three kinds. First, co-operation of the kinds we have described may give the firms concerned the power to restrict output unduly; secondly, it may retard the differential growth of the more efficient firm, and, thirdly, it may make profits too easy to obtain so that entrepreneurs lack the stimulus to develop their energies and inventiveness to the full.

It will be convenient to consider the effects of a price agreement—or those related forms of behaviour that perform roughly the same function—in two stages. I shall examine first the welfare implications of the fact that the volume of output from given equipment will be different when a price agreement is operated than when it is not. The long-run consequences of such an agreement—on investment, efficiency, and incentives—will be discussed later.

Ideally, we noted, existing equipment should be used to produce just that volume of output that will sell at a price equal to marginal cost. We have seen that where there is short-run price competition this is unlikely to come about, for the reason that entrepreneurs will be unable to predict the demand for their own output. If, however, price is kept wholly unresponsive to short-run demand changes, then, in these circumstances also, even if there is perfect predictability, a divergence between price and marginal cost is to be expected. This follows obviously from the fact that marginal cost is likely to be different for different volumes of output whereas price remains the same. The resultant social loss will depend on the shapes of the demand schedule and of the curve relating marginal cost to output. It will be greatest when the elasticity of demand is great and when marginal costs fall sharply when output is reduced. The extent to which these two circumstances obtain will depend on the market in question and there is therefore little that can usefully be said in general terms about the magnitude of the social loss to be expected. It would seem, however, that the range of possible divergence between price and marginal cost is greater when the divergence is the result of uninformed output decisions than when it is merely the consequence of an inflexible price. If the fluctuations in the total demand for the product, moreover, are modest, then the misallocation resulting from an inflexible price will itself be slight. (We leave until later the question of whether the level of price is too high.) Even modest demand fluctuations, however, if they lead producers to seek a larger market share by short-run price cutting, can lead to large variations in supply and therefore to more substantial waste.

If then a choice has to be made, in any particular market, between price stability resulting from price agreements and price flexibility resulting from the promotion of short-run price competition, the factors that ought to govern the choice are clear; price agreements, or some equivalent code of behaviour, are the more likely to be necessary the lower the elasticity of demand for the product, the higher the proportion of fixed to variable costs, and the larger the fluctuations in demand to be expected.

Our argument has tacitly assumed, until now, that the only alternatives were complete price stability, on the one hand, and short-run price competition on the other. But there is of course no reason why firms should not co-operate in quoting a common price which was varied uniformly according to demand conditions. This would be achieved most readily where all firms were committed to formal discussion and agreement in prices, less readily by a system of price leadership, and very doubtfully where firms felt obliged only not to spoil the market. In principle it would even be possible for a cartel to adjust supply so as to maintain equality continuously between expected price and marginal cost although, as this would not maximize profits, it is not the policy one would expect it to adopt.

A little reflection, moreover, leads one to doubt whether this policy would be practicable even if cartels had the public interest rather than profits as their objective. There is a good deal of evidence, that cannot be reviewed here, to the effect that most firms operate for most of the time under conditions of excess capacity—in the sense that marginal costs are less than average costs of production. If this is indeed the case, then it follows that under marginal cost pricing, firms would normally be making a loss, so that, for production to be profitable over the long period, they would have to make, occasionally, a level of profits that was very abnormally high. This could be done if the volume of manufacturing capacity were kept small enough to cause acute scarcities in times of peak demand and if prices were raised so as to clear the market at these times. Whether such an arrangement would be superior, on welfare grounds, to the usual practice of maintaining a steady level of price high enough to yield normal profits over the long period is, at least, open to doubt. It consists, in fact, of creating occasional bottlenecks and exploiting them, by raising price, to an extent sufficient to make profits high enough to offset the losses that firms would make normally. Would purchasers welcome such a policy? Would not the social loss produced by the bottlenecks, which might spread to other industries using the product in question, normally outweigh the social loss occasioned by a normal divergence between price and marginal costs? These are questions that can be answered with confidence only in relation to a particular, specified industry, but one might be prepared to guess that the answer would usually be in the negative.

Let us now turn again to the long-run effects of restrictions of the kind we have been examining. We may begin by inquiring whether these restrictions will result in the level of an industry's investment being less than optimal. It may be that the behaviour adopted merely serves to maintain prices in response to a temporary fall of demand below capacity, while leaving each entrepreneur prepared—and expecting others to be prepared—to endeavour to increase his share of the market by means of price reductions that his unit costs enable him to make permanent. If this is so there is no reason to expect a sub-optimal level of investment; on the contrary, the greater security offered by the absence of short-run prices competition, may make investment in the industry more attractive. Inter-firm co-operation, however, may have less modest aims. Prices may be not only stabilized, but maintained at a level that yields abnormal profits and implies a sub-optimal supply. A tightly organized cartel is clearly well placed to aim at this objective, which may be also pursued, without formal arrangements, by a group of firms small enough for each to appreciate that high prices are in its long-run interest. The obstacles in the way of this restrictive policy are, as is well known, dissension between the parties and the threat of outside competition.

If the entry into the industry is somehow blocked, then it is clear that those already in it, taken as a whole, can be made better off by the restriction of supply. It does not follow, however, that the restriction will operate so as to benefit each firm individually. The gain from it will accrue to firms according to their size and the smaller among them may not wish to perpetuate their disadvantage. Some firms, moreover, having the capital and the managerial resources that permit both expansion and the reduction of costs, will be eager to extend the market; others, with high costs and little growth potential, will oppose any reduction in price. Restriction may not therefore make every firm better off than it would be in the absence of restriction; generally, however, it would be possible in principle to arrange this, in that there will be some redistribution of the gains from restriction that would make every firm benefit from its operation. Whether firms succeed in acquiring monopoly profits will often depend, therefore, on whether they can agree on how these should be shared. In order to reach agreement and to put the terms into effect, fairly formal arrangements for consultation and for compensation may be required. Loose, informal co-operation, such as might escape legal prohibition, may be unable to resolve substantial differences of interest between the parties concerned.

No system of compensation is likely to be able to bribe the potential entrants into an industry to stay out; it is for this reason that the threat of entry is likely to be a more powerful check on monopolistic restriction than is internal dissension. What we require is that conditions of entry be such that existing firms need not fear invasion by newcomers only so long as they maintain normal efficiency and cater for all demands at prices offering only normal profits. It might at first seem that these conditions are met provided only that newcomers are at some very slight disadvantage in terms of experience, market contacts, &c. Unfortunately, however, matters are not quite so simple. Let us suppose that the firms already in the industry pursue the policy, discussed above, of maintaining prices stable in response to short-run demand fluctuations. In these circumstances it will be profitable for an outsider to enter the market even though firms already in it earn no more than normal profits in the long term. All the entrant need do is charge rather less than the established firms when capacity exceeds demand and as much as or more than they do when demand exceeds capacity.  By acting in this way it will be able to operate at full capacity and therefore to flourish at the expense of the firms that continue to maintain stable prices.

The entry of new firms into the industry, in response to these opportunities, would lead to the installation of excessive capacity and, in most cases, to the breakdown of the codes of behaviour by which price stability was maintained.  The chief deterrent to entry under the circumstances we are postulating is, of course, the fact that the firms already established may abandon their policy of price stability in order to match the prices of the intruder.  It is this same threat that may dissuade firms tempted to leave the association from doing so.  It may prove effective or it may not. If the potential entrant, or potential defector is small, then it may be prepared to take the risk that the rest of the firms in the industry may tolerate some incursion into their markets rather than give up the advantages of a stable and agreed price.  If the new firm is located abroad, and protected in its home market, then it will be strongly inclined to quote lower prices for its exports.  For these reasons, as is well known, inter-firm co-operation in price setting may frequently break down.

To what extent does the restrictive behaviour we have been examining make it more difficult for the more efficient firms to grow at the expense of their less efficient rivals ?  If a low-cost firm believes that it would gain from larger sales at a lower price, then it is difficult to believe that the restrictive arrangements that we have been considering are likely to prove a strong barrier to the firm acting accordingly.  In order to obtain the agreement of other firms to a price reduction, it can threaten to act independently ; high-cost firms will have good reasons to accept a uniformly lower price, while maintaining whatever form of co-operation is practised, rather than face an irregular fall in prices brought about through competitive warfare.  The situation is otherwise when the low-cost firm already possesses a large share of the market and considers that its interests are best served by keeping its present volume of sales at a high margin of profit rather than to increase them at the cost of a cut in this margin.  In these circumstances, price competition, by means of secret rebates and the like, may bring prices down and the restrictive forms of behaviour that inhibit it—whatever their benefits in other ways—can act so as to shelter the inefficient.

There remains the question of whether restrictive arrangements, despite their useful functions, make life too easy for all the firms concerned, with the result that the general level of efficiency in the industry suffers.  I can see no reason why short-run price stability need make producers lazy ; it would do so only if prices were set so as to give profits higher than normal to firms of no more than normal efficiency.  Provided price is low enough, the high-cost producers will be under pressure to improve their performance. If short-run price competition were practised, then no doubt entrepreneurs would have an incentive to exert themselves in a particular way—in concealing their own price reductions, in predicting competitors' moves, and in endeavouring to deduce from price changes the likely shift in consumers' demand. But there is little reason to believe that skill in this particular game deserves to be rewarded and encouraged; it is not at all evident that it is in the public interest for each entrepreneur to devote much of his time and energies to guessing what the others are going to do. It would seem in general preferable for entrepreneurs to eliminate or reduce the uncertainties that are generated by certain forms of competitive behaviour and thereby release more of their attention for directly useful activities such as improving products and processes of production.

The abuses to which the restraint of competition may lead are very well known. Both popular and academic opinion on this matter (which is subject to a good deal of fluctuation) is reluctant to accept that restrictions of certain kinds and in certain circumstances, can be to the general advantage. In considering the best forms of economic organization we are faced with a genuine dilemma and nothing is to be gained from pretending that it does not exist. If firms have the power to make their environment more favourable to informed planning they may also have the power to act against the public interest, either by the restriction of supply or by the protection of high-cost production. In the final choice, therefore, we may have to seek a compromise the terms of which will vary according to the circumstances of each particular market. Any maladjustment of supply to demand will be the more serious the lower the elasticity of demand for the product and the higher the proportion of fixed costs employed in its manufacture. The likelihood that unrestrained competition will produce misallocation depends on a variety of factors. It will be greater the higher the elasticity of substitution between the outputs of rival manufacturers, for this will determine the gains to be had from short-run price competition. It will be greater the longer the period of production in that this will make overproduction take longer to become recognized. The more frequent the periods of deficiency of demand relative to capacity, and the higher the ratio of fixed to variable costs, the stronger will be the incentive for each firm to endeavour to enlarge its share of the market by a price reduction. The codes of behaviour necessary to check short-run price competition will need to be less formal the smaller the number of firms, the longer the tradition of co-operation between them, and the easier it is to find out the prices that competitors are actually charging. At one extreme, prices may be maintained without any arrangements between the firms concerned simply by virtue of the fact that each recognizes that price reductions would be immediately noted and matched.

At the other a complex agreement may be necessary. In the former situation, there will be little or nothing that legislation can do to make firms behave differently; in the latter, co-operation on prices can be prevented, or made very difficult, by a prohibition of agreements in restraint of trade. Thus anti-trust policy is likely to have much more impact in some industries than in others even though the economic effects of interfirm co-operation, as distinct from the forms in which it is practised, are much the same.

These considerations lead us, however, to questions of public policy with which this article does not directly deal. I have been concerned with the general theoretical ideas that ought to guide us in reaching a decision for or against the restraint of competition in any particular case.

*St. John's College, Oxford*

# [7]

# THE PRICING OF HEAVY ELECTRICAL EQUIPMENT: COMPETITION OR AGREEMENT?

*By* G. B. RICHARDSON

1. *Introduction.*

This paper deals with three types of heavy electrical equipment, the markets for which have important features in common. The questions I try to answer are these. Should the prices at which the equipment is sold be determined by competitive tendering or by agreements? And, if agreements are judged appropriate, what form should they take, who should be party to them and to what controls, if any, should they be subject?[1]

Although our concern is with the way in which prices ought to be set, it is instructive to consider how they have in fact been set in the past. In the United Kingdom, the prices of the equipment that concerns us have been regulated, for the greater part of this century, by agreements between the manufacturers; although these agreements broke down from time to time, we can regard their operation as the normal state of affairs. In recent years, however, this tradition has been broken. After an adverse decision, in 1961, by the Restrictive Practices Court, the agreements relating to one type of equipment —transformers—were abandoned. The others have been referred to the Court by the Registrar of Restrictive Trading Agreements but the hearings have been held up pending discussions between the manufacturers and their chief customer—the nationalised electricity authorities.

It is difficult to determine, with confidence, the extent to which the tradition of agreed prices has held sway in countries other than the United Kingdom. Restrictive agreements have for long been illegal in the United States, but the Philadelphia Anti-Trust Cases of 1960 produced evidence of elaborate arrangements to fix prices and share markets that were in effect, covertly, for at least one period in the recent history of the electrical machinery industry. Accounts of this famous 'conspiracy', and of other anti-trust cases involving the industry,[2] leave one with the impression that violations, despite the shocked indignation which they provoke, have been by no means infrequent since the turn of the century. This is not to deny that price competition has been severe at some times, as during the so-called 'white sales' of 1955;[3] collusion, always illegal appears to have been intermittent and often ineffective. Whether the situation is better described as price competition tempered by collusion, or as collusion undermined by rivalries and the enforcement of the laws, I cannot judge. In Continental

---

[1] This article is an expanded version of a paper which I submitted to the Economic Development Committee for the Electrical Engineering Industry. I am a member of this committee and have benefitted from its discussions. My education has also been advanced through talks with representatives of the industry, but neither the EDC nor the industry bears any responsibility for the views I express.

[2] For an account of these see Corwin D. Edwards, *Big Business and the Policy of Competition*, 1956, pp. 137–41 and 163–64.

[3] When price cutting is believed to have got out of hand it is termed 'white sale'. In 1955 orders for equipment were being accepted at prices up to 50 per cent below normal levels.

Europe price agreements were generally legal, and often officially approved, until after the Second World War, but there, as in Britain, public opinion and the statute books have recently undergone much change. Whether this has brought to an end the practice of agreeing prices, however, is another matter and one on which an outsider cannot easily form an opinion.

It is safe to conclude, even on this most cursory review of past experience, that the circumstances of the heavy electrical industry must be such as put firms under pressures towards price agreements, pressures strong enough to overcome the reluctance of managers both to accept restrictions on their commercial freedom and (in the United States) to run the risk of criminal prosecution. One of our tasks must be to enquire how these pressures are generated. We should also note, at this point, the great difficulty in arguing either for or against price competition merely by reference to the way in which it has in fact worked. Such an appraisal of price competition would need to examine its effects when sustained over a long period without the degree of mitigation that agreements, of varying legality and effectiveness, have always exercised in the past. In this respect the protagonists as well as the opponents of competitive pricing are in the same boat: they must endeavour to predict, with the help of theory and limited experience, what would happen in a hypothetical situation.

The pricing of heavy electrical equipment, in this country, has already received the attention of the Monopolies Commission, the Restrictive Practices Court and the Select Committee on Nationalised Industries.

The Monopolies Commission took the view that prices, in the markets we shall be considering, ought to be determined by competitive tendering.[1] It saw no merit whatever in agreements or arrangements between the manufacturers, who were urged 'to refrain from any kind of collaboration in matters of price and tendering'. Nor were they prepared to give any support to the manufacturers' suggestion that agreements might be operated with safeguards designed to ensure that prices and profits were reasonable; free competition, they insisted, was the proper regulator for these markets. Price notification agreements, in so far as they would apply to the home market, were also condemned, on the ground that understandings on prices might follow them.

The Restrictive Practices Court was called upon to declare whether a particular price agreement, operated by the transformer manufacturers at the time of the hearing, was contrary to the public interest; it did not have to give an opinion on the wider issue of the appropriateness of competitive tendering for all three types of equipment. Nevertheless, the judgment of the Court may be regarded as in line with the views of the Commission.[2]

The Select Committee, reporting six years later than the Commission, does not show the same enthusiasm for competitive tendering.[3]

While maintaining that 'competition is still realistic between firms making smaller equipment', it clearly has doubts as to its appropriateness for markets in which 'both the Board and the manufacturers of larger equipment at higher

---

[1] *Report on the Supply and Exports of Electrical and Allied Machinery and Plant*, 1957.
[2] *In re* Associated Transformer Manufacturers' Agreement, LR, 2 RP, 295.
[3] Report from the Select Committee on Nationalised Industries; the Electricity Supply Industry, Vol. 1 Report and Proceedings.  Chapter 16.

voltages are becoming more and more prisoners to size'. It recommended that an independent arbitrator, acceptable to both the manufacturers and the Central Electricity Generating Board, be asked to inquire into the arrangements for placing contracts and fixing prices.

It is not my purpose to review the arguments and the conclusions of the Commission, the Court and the Select Committee, but the reader will find in their reports a wealth of useful background material for which space could not be found in this article. My excuse for setting out, by myself, on this well-trodden ground is twofold. First, I wish to focus more narrowly on the relevant economic analysis than did these reports. Secondly, I find myself in disagreement with the conclusions of the Monopolies Commission and with part of the Judgement of the Court. One hesitates to question the findings of these bodies, which, quite rightly, have great authority, but some comfort may perhaps be found in the fact that these are matters on which informed opinion has, in the past, suffered a good deal of fluctuation.

I shall be dealing with three quite specific types of electrical equipment, these being turbo-alternators with ratings of 30 megawatts or above, Grid switchgear and Transmission and Generator transformers all for 132 kilovolts or above.[1] I shall refer to these, for brevity, simply as 'turbines', 'switchgear' and 'transformers', or, collectively as 'heavy electrical equipment', but the readers will have to bear in mind that we are dealing with restricted types of equipment under these heads. (Roughly speaking, we are concerned only with the largest or 'heaviest' categories of each of the three kinds of equipment). The justification for grouping them for discussion is the fact that they are sold under similar conditions.

## 2.  *The Structure of the Markets.*

Let us begin by listing the common features of the three markets that are relevant to pricing policy.

(i) The first of these is the predominance, in the home trade, of the nationalised Electricity Supply Authorities. Turbines, switchgear and the larger transformers are bought, in England, only by the Central Electricity Board, and, in Scotland and Northern Ireland, by corresponding bodies. On the manufacturing side, we find three firms in turbines, four in switchgear, and about a dozen in transformers.[2]

---

[1] Electricity is generated by boiling water to produce steam, which, when applied to a turbine, strikes metal blades fixed to wheels, thus causing the wheels and connecting shaft to move at a high speed. This mechanical energy is then converted into electricity by a generator. The various bits of equipment other than the boiler necessary to do these things are referred to as a 'turbo-alternator set' and are usually ordered together. It is efficient to distribute electricity at a voltage higher than that at which it is generated and much higher than that at which it is ultimately used by consumers. The equipment which steps up the voltage when electrical energy leaves a generating station, or lowers it as the current passes to the consumer, is a transformer. Switchgear is used at the points where electricity is stepped up to voltages suitable for the main transmission lines and where it is stepped down. Its functions are to connect or disconnect a line as required or to act as a safety device cutting off a current when there has been a fault. Thus it acts like domestic switches or fuses, though the high voltages with which it deals require it to be much more complicated.

[2] The turbine makers are Associated Electrical Industries, the English Electric Company, and C. A. Parsons. Switchgear is made by the first two of these companies, by the General Electric Company and by Reyrolle. Of the dozen or so firms making larger transformers none has a share of the total markets as large as twenty per cent.

(ii) Of key significance for our analysis is the fact that the total home demand for each category of equipment is in effect totally inelastic with respect to price. This is certainly the case in the short run, as it is unlikely that the electricity authorities would alter their construction programmes in response to fluctuations in the price of this equipment. In the longer run, the price of the equipment, by influencing the cost of these programmes, might affect their scale, but the circumstance will have no bearing on the price that a manufacturer quotes for a particular order at a particular time. Although the total demand for each type of equipment is inelastic, however, the demand for that offered by any single seller will be highly sensitive to the level of his price compared to those of rivals. This very high cross-elasticity is the result of the fact that each item of equipment is produced by the different manufacturers to the same specifications, as laid down by the buyer.

(iii) Of related significance is the size of individual orders. Either because of the scale of particular items of equipment (as with turbines) or because of the inclusion of several items in one order (as with transformers), success or failure in obtaining a particular contract may have a very large effect on the total business obtained by a firm within a year. In the case of turbines, there are only about two orders, on average, per year, worth (in 1965) some £20 million each. A single order for transformers may represent a quarter of a firm's annual turnover in this equipment. The business in switchgear is in effect allocated in bulk by the Generating Board, rather than split up and put out to tender; but it is safe to say that were competitive tendering to be introduced, the size of an individual order could be very large.

(iv) Excess capacity, from time to time, is inevitable in this industry. There are several reasons for this. It is obvious, first, that if productive capacity is to be sufficient to meet the electricity authorities' demands when these are at their peak, then it will necessarily exceed them at other times. The demand for each type of equipment is on a steadily rising trend, but subject to fluctuation. The 'stop-go' policies, so much discussed in recent years, have a clear enough impact on this industry, in that they give rise to sudden modifications in the electricity investment programme. A greater stabilisation of public investment would permit a better adjustment of capacity to demand, though imbalances would never be wholly prevented. Export orders may help to fill the gap left by the falling off of home demand for a particular category of equipment, but they cannot be depended upon to become available in sufficient quantity at remunerative prices.

Excess capacity may also arise through technical advance. In the case of turbines, which form the heart of a generating plant, recent improvements have been very striking. Increases in the size of the turbine and devices that enable it to deal with higher steam temperatures and pressures have markedly reduced cost per kilowatt. The first 30 megawatts set was installed in 1930; by 1956 a 100-MW set had been commissioned and orders for 120-MW, 200-MW and 275-MW sets had been placed. The first 500-MW set was ordered in 1960. The cost per megawatt of turbine plant over these thirty years fell by more than half. (The rate of progress has been so rapid, in fact, that firms find themselves designing plant with higher ratings before they have had operational experience of plant with lower ratings.) The fall in turbine cost per megawatt is associated with a reduction in the real resources required; excess capacity, in terms of skilled men as well as equipment, can be prevented only by a sufficiently great increase in the volume of orders.

The fact that the investment plans of the independent manufacturers are not co-ordinated can also result in excess capacity. This has happened, notably, in transformer production, where the number of firms concerned is relatively large. Given fairly large numbers, there is nothing to ensure that each firm, in the hope of realising scale economies, does not count on enlarging its share of the market, with the inevitable result that total capacity becomes excessive. This tendency, I have argued elsewhere[1] is endemic in precisely those markets with large numbers of producers acting independently that often feature as the textbook ideal.

(v) We have already noted, in the case of turbines, that the industry's product is subject to continuous change. The same may be said of switchgear and transformers, which have to be adapted to deal with higher voltages. As a result, the firms concerned deploy large resources in research, development and design. There is some inter-firm co-operation in this field, particularly in the development of certain kinds of switchgear, but the Generating Board took the view that there ought to be more of it.[2] This is an important matter lying, for the most part, outside the scope of this article; its relevance to pricing will be discussed later.

(vi) Finally, we must bear in mind the export trade, which represents a significant, but diminishing, proportion of the total sales of the equipment with which we are concerned. In 1965 exports of heavy electrical equipment represented about 16.5 per cent of the value of home deliveries, which were some £100 million in value. In 1961, the value of exports was almost one-third of home deliveries. I am concerned in this paper with the pricing of equipment sold at home to the electricity authorities, but it will be necessary to consider whether this has any bearing on the exports that firms are able to make.

3. *The Criteria of an Efficient System of Pricing.*

How are we to assess the relative merits of the alternative ways in which the prices of heavy electrical equipment may be determined? Let me now endeavour to set out, very briefly, the criteria that I shall apply.

First, and most obviously, the procedure adopted should be such as sets prices at levels that are appropriate relative to demand and cost conditions. Appropriateness, in this sense, has two aspects. It would be generally agreed the rate of profit in this line of production, taking one year with another, should neither exceed nor fall short of the rate in other industries subject to an equivalent degree of risk. Considerations of equity might be regarded as sufficient justification of this equality, but the economist sees it as a condition for the proper allocation of resources in different employments. We have to consider, that is to say, whether the prices set are likely to cause the right amount of productive capacity to be installed and to ensure that the right amount of output is being produced from this capacity.

---

[1] *Information and Investment*, Oxford University Press, 1960.
[2] Report from the Select Committee, pp. 167–8.

The indirect effects of alternative pricing systems must also be taken into account. Would they permit the more efficient firms to grow at the expense of their higher cost rivals? Would they put such pressure on producers as would induce them to exploit all available economies of scale? Would they be consistent with whatever forms of co-operation between firms in matters other than price, are held to be desirable? Would they be likely to facilitate, or to hamper, the forward planning of production? How, if at all, would they affect the ability and willingness of firms to export? These are some of the ways in which alternative methods of pricing might influence the efficiency and structure of the industries that adopted them.

The simplest solution to the problem of determing prices is that recommended by the Monopolies Commission and, by implication, in the Judgment of the Restrictive Practices Court. It consists in proscribing any inter-firm agreement or arrangement and leaving prices to be determined by free competition, each producer setting his own price in independence of his rivals. The genuine merits of this solution are readily apparent. The operation of price agreements, and their public control, requires an administrative machinery which, in terms of the services of lawyers, accountants, economists and the like, represents a genuine social cost. Price agreements, if not subject to public control, may be used to further the interests of those who make them, to the disadvantage of the community as a whole; but public control may itself be abused, either to protect vested interests or to court political popularity. By relying on free price competition, we can avoid these costs and difficulties. This is a substantial advantage to which I give full weight. I shall argue, nevertheless, that price competition is not appropriate to the special conditions of the markets with which we are concerned.

4.  *Transformers.*

(i) *Alternative Effects of Abrograting Agreements.*

Let us first consider transformers. First, we have to decide whether the proscription of agreements would be likely to lead firms to compete actively in terms of price. It will be recalled that the agreement between the manufacturers of transformers was held by the Restrictive Practices Court, in 1961, to be contrary to the public interest. The Report from the Select Committee, however, quotes the Generating Board to the effect that 'while the manufacturers have observed the letter of this decision, they have flouted its spirit by adopting a system of price leadership'. Acting under this conviction the Board ordered two large transformers from Canada at prices appreciably below these ruling in this country. The manufacturers objected strongly to this decision; they maintained that the transformer market in Canada was very depressed and saw the Boards' action as an attempt to bring British prices down to similar levels. At the same time, they claimed that the system of price notification that firms had adopted was not equivalent to price agreement, in that it permitted firms to quote low prices if they believed themselves to be competitive.

No fully adequate information is available to me about the present level of prices and profits in transformer production or about the extent of the changes that have taken place since abrogation of the agreement. It is possible, nevertheless, to sketch out the general picture. The prices of the smaller transformers have fallen markedly and continue to fall; all or almost all the manufacturers appear to sell these transformers at a loss.[1] The prices of the large transformers—those which directly concern us—held up better, at least in the years immediately following abrogation.

These developments are very much what one would expect. In the first place, there is excess capacity in transformer production. A reliable measure of a firm's capacity is difficult to make, chiefly because the maximum volume of output that can be put through the works depends on the 'product-mix', this being the proportions of the total output formed by different sizes of transformers. Not all firms, moreover, make estimates of the capacity they have available. (All the members of the 'Power Transformer Conference' make returns on capacity but not all transformer manufacturers are members). Despite these difficulties it seems safe to say that the demands of the electricity authorities, together with any likely export demand, will leave a substantial margin of capacity unemployed.

In these circumstances, firms are continuously subject to the risk of getting little or no work. The magnitude of this risk varies with the number of firms making each type of transformer, being great for those making the smallest types and less for those making the larger types with which we are primarily concerned. An excess of capacity over demand of even one per cent would make it possible, in principle, for some of the smallest firms making the smaller transformers to be left without work. A 10 per cent excess would make it possible for even large firms to have no orders. Given the electricity supply authorities' system of tendering—which is such that a single order can make a great difference to a firm's annual turnover—it is clear that each manufacturer is under strong pressure to quote a price low enough to obtain some business. It is also clear that firms have an incentive to resist this pressure, because they realise that the total business available to the industry as a whole will not be increased by price reductions.

What we have, therefore, is a familiar oligopoly situation where the outcome depends on the relative strength of two opposing considerations. The larger the number of firms, the greater is the chance that one of them may be left without work; the more likely therefore is that prices will be driven down by the competitive struggle, a limit being set, in the last resort, about the level of variable costs. In the case of the smaller transformers, this is what has happened. With the larger transformers, which are made by fewer firms, prices are more likely to be sustained, if only precariously. Although the business available is insufficient to fill all the works, each producer may expect to get some of it. A sense of common interest may be sufficient to prevent price-cutting, especially if firms keep one another informed as to the terms on which contracts with them are actually placed.

In appraising the effects of proscribing agreements, therefore, it is important to distinguish between two situations, the first in which excess capacity will

[1] These smaller or 'distribution' transformers are made by about fifty firms and sold to Area Electricity Boards. The characteristics of their market create special problems distinct from those associated with the pricing of large transformers and it seemed appropriate to exclude them from discussion here.

result in competitive price-cutting, the second in which it may not. Very broadly, these alternative outcomes can be associated in this case with the markets for the smaller and for the larger transformers respectively, though it would be misleading to draw a sharp line. In the case of the so-called distribution transformers, which are sold by some fifty firms to a dozen Area Electricity Boards, conditions bear some resemblance to the text-book model of perfect competition, and prices have clearly fallen in response to the excess of capacity over demand. In the case of the larger transformers, sold to the Generating Board by a smaller number of firms, there has been a more obvious reluctance to 'spoil the market', but, given excess capacity and the practice of tendering for very large orders, more active price competition can readily develop.

### (ii) *Prices Responsive to Excess Capacity.*

Let us take first the situation in which the abrogation of a price agreement does produce active competition in tendering. On the face of it, this may seem precisely what is required; the more efficient firms will be able to undercut their high cost rivals and the general level of profits will be kept low. Given excess capacity, it will be conceded, prices will fall to uneconomic levels, but, in doing so, they will help to bring about the contraction required and thus restore profits to a normal level. This, at any rate, is what the more elementary text book models would lead us to expect; a more careful examination of the situation points to conclusions less simple and less satisfactory.

In the first place, excess capacity is likely to be chronic. Each firm may see its salvation in expansion, which will enable it to reap more of the economies of scale. The fact that the demand for transformers is on a rising trend may give further countenance to this policy, with the result that the industry's total capacity may become even more excessive. Lest the reader consider this situation too perverse, let him bear in mind that the excess capacity with which the industry is at present afflicted, and which so far has shown no tendency to disappear, did in fact develop over a period of steadily rising demand. Nevertheless, it is reasonable to suppose that firms will not for ever persist in such unprofitable courses, that some will leave the industry and others cease to expand with the consequence that capacity will come to equal, or even fall short of demand. What chance is there that these developments would lead, in the long run, to a steady growth of capacity in balance with demand?

To my mind, very little. Losses are indeed likely to check investment and thus bring capacity, for a time, into rough equality with demand; but, given the continuing presence of a large number of competing firms, there would seem to be every reason to expect further bouts of excessive investment. Economists with faith in some kind of tendency to equilibrium may envisage a fluctuating balance between demand and capacity, firms gaining on the swings of excess demand what they lost on the roundabouts of excess capacity. But, in the special circumstances of this market, these conditions need not result in normal profits. Firms would certainly lose, through price competition, in times of slack, but it seems to me unlikely that they would be able to gain very high profits at other times. In the first place, supply conditions are likely to be fairly elastic, firms being able to take on extra work without much rise in marginal costs. But even although there were bottlenecks, it is difficult to envisage the Generating Board or even the Area Boards deliberately bidding up prices against themselves. No one has yet seen a one-man auction. Normal profits would be compatible with the conditions we are postulating only if excess capacity could be avoided at all times. This is unlikely to be assured and it is undesirable that it should be; the public interest requires that the investment programmes of the electricity authorities are not held up through bottlenecks in the capacity to supply equipment. If peak requirements are to be met, excess capacity must develop at normal times and must be tolerable to the industry.

There is a further circumstance that would make active price competition often incompatible with normal profits even in the absence of unused capacity. Part of the output of the larger transformers is exported and at prices below those ruling at home. It seems to be very generally the case that heavy electrical equipment is sold abroad by all the main manufacturing countries, at prices that approximate more to marginal than to full unit costs of production. The gap between home and export prices is of course evidence that price competition within the home markets of the manufacturing counties is somewhat attenuated. If producers were to fight for domestic contracts in the same way as they fight for foreign contracts, home prices would move down towards the export levels and the profitability of the total output would fall. Many see the differential between home and export prices as proof of our fallen state and would welcome its erosion under the stress of more active competition. But, as far as British manufacturers are concerned, the low level of the export prices of these capital goods is simply a fact of life which neither our industry nor our government has by itself the power to alter. Were our export quotations to move up to the level of home prices, we should fail to export; if our home prices were to move down to the level of export prices, the total business would not be remunerative. This is a conclusion that those most eager to promote price competition in the home market are rarely seen to draw.

Let us now return to the main course of our argument. Given fairly numerous independent manufacturers, faced with a totally inelastic home demand and in active price competition for orders, there will be chronic tendency to excess capacity and low returns. This tendency is unlikely, in the nature of things, to continue indefinitely, but an end to it could be brought, it seems to me, only as a result of change in the structure of the market. The logic of the situation is likely, sooner or later, to lead producers to concentrate production, in the hope that this will both limit the extent of excess capacity and reduce the likelihood that excess capacity will induce firms to cut prices. There is no telling how long this change would take to come about and no assurance that, once it had come about, it would not subsequently be reversed.[1]

[1] Of key importance in this connection is the magnitude of scale economies in the production of transformers. If these economies are insignificant then concentration within the industry might prove short lived; small firms would be attracted by the prospects of entering the business in the hope of prospering under the umbrella of the larger producers. Given, that is to say, the maintainence of relatively stable prices by the established firms, even in the face of some excess capacity, there would be a living to be made by the outsider willing to charge a slightly lower price in order to get a full load on this works. Assuming free entry therefore, the viability of a regime of concentrated production and stable prices would depend on the existence of significant scale economies.

(iii) *Prices Unresponsive to Excess Capacity.*

We have now, in effect, moved on to the second of the alternative situations that we proposed to analyse. We have been assuming that, in the absence of a price agreement, active competition would cause prices to be flexible and to fall in response to excess capacity. Now we assume that the producers, chiefly because they are less numerous, succeed in maintaining stable prices in the face of a changing balance between demand and capacity. This of course is the situation in the generality of manufacturing industry. When the demand for cars suffers temporary decline, their prices do not fall to the level of variable costs; the total burden of adjustment is usually met by a fall in output. For adjustment to take this form, there is no need for manufacturers to make an agreement; each of them takes it for granted that price reductions would without delay be noted and matched by competitors with the result (given the prevailing elasticity of demand for cars) that all would stand to lose. The circumstances of the markets for heavy electrical equipment, however, are vastly different. The size of individual orders relative to a firm's turnover puts management under very strong pressure to cut prices in order to be sure of getting work. Where the largest and most advanced types of equipment are concerned, to miss an order does not only produce unemployment of men and machines; it may also cause firms to fall out of the race in technical development. In order to be able to tender for the most advanced type of equipment, firms require experience to draw upon and this experience cannot be acquired if they fail to get orders. The willingness of firms to cut prices at the risk of 'spoiling the market' would also be influenced by the fact that competitive prices, instead of being 'posted' as with cars, would be quoted in closed bids. Firms would not normally know what prices their rivals were quoting and might be tempted to reduce their quotations substantially in order to make sure that they were not undercut. It is of course open to firms to exchange information about prices at which contracts have actually been placed, so that it would be possible for them to know, after the event, whether rivals were in fact reducing their bids below some normal level. This arrangement might go some way in inhibiting firms, eager to increase their share of a fixed market, from starting a price war.

These considerations suggest that price stability, based on the wish not to spoil the market, is possible but by no means assured in the circumstances we are considering. Let us now ask whether it would be in the public interest.

If prices can be maintained, in the face of temporary falls in demand, then producers certainly enjoy a more stable prospect than they would have otherwise and will be more willing to create facilities large enough to meet their customer's peak requirements in the knowledge that the associated excess capacity, in normal times, will not bring them heavy losses. Only very grudging recognition, if any, is usually given, in this context, to the benefits that society as a whole can derive from a more predictable business environment. If the context is economic planning, and the need for a more stable rate of investment, then most people are prepared to see virtue in arrangements that enable firms better to insulate their expansion plans from short-run fluctuations in the balance between demand and capacity. But there is a strange reluctance to perceive that arrangements or conventions leading to short-run price stability fulfil just this shock-absorbing function.

But there is another side to this matter. Can one reasonably assume that price competition between firms, in these circumstances, will be suspended only in conditions of excess capacity? Is it not possible for mutual tolerance to be so developed that firms will refrain from use of the price weapon to compete for larger market shares even when demand rises above capacity? The force of rivalry might or might not be strong enough to ensure that abnormally high profits were rapidly removed by competition. In the case of large transformers, where there are a dozen producers, it may seem unlikely that a struggle for market shares could for long be in abeyance; but where there are only three or four companies—as with turbines and switchgear—mutual accommodation is less unlikely. Abnormally high profits might, in the long run, induce entry by new suppliers, but entry in these fields is not sufficiently easy for this to be an adequate discipline. My own view is that neither theory nor experience enables us to say, with certainty, whether the producers of heavy electrical equipment would or would not, in the absence of agreements between them, have the power consistently to maintain prices such as yielded abnormally high profits. What one can say is that the proscription of agreements cannot be relied upon always to give either the electricity authorities or the public at large the *assurance* of reasonable prices.

Here then we have a dilemma that those who advocate merely the abolition of agreements have to face. Either the abandonment of the agreements results in active price competition and flexibility of prices in response to the changing balance of demand and capacity, or it does not do so. In the former eventuality, prices are likely to be chronically depressed, thus leading to an undesirable shrinkage of capacity or to a movement towards further concentration. In the latter case, the purchasers and the public lack sufficient assurance that profits will not be unduly high. These are the considerations that lead me to conclude that the mere abolition of inter-firm agreements, whether or not it results in prices flexible in response to supply and demand, does not ensure suitable regulation of the markets for transformers. But before examining the available alternatives, let us turn to consider the working, in the absence of price agreements, of the markets for turbines and switchgear.

5. *Turbines.*

(i) *Special features of the market.*

Those features of the transformer market that made price competition unsuitable are to be found also in the market for turbines and in a much more marked degree.[1]

The manufacture of turbines has of necessity to be on a very large scale. Very large investments are required in terms of research, design and training as well as

---

[1] At the time of writing, there were three producers of turbines, each with its own design. But there has been talk of a desire, on behalf of the Generating Board, to have only two designs. This desire could achieve fulfilment only through structural change in the industry, but I lack the information required to discuss this matter. Whatever changes might be promoted seem likely to weaken the case for price competition yet further.

fixed equipment. The rate of technical advance in the industry has, as remarked earlier, been particularly rapid and the firms operate continuously at the frontiers of new development. Overheads (taken to include the teams of designers and other skilled staff) are high relative to turnover, and are, in effect, completely specific to manufacture of turbines. The firms concerned do all the research and development relating to the equipment they produce and bear the costs of rectifying it when it fails to work.

Of central significance, for our purposes, is the magnitude of individual contracts in this industry, the value of which, at £20 mill. or more, exceeds the average annual turnover in turbo-alternators of any one of the firms.[1] The size of order is to be explained, in this case, not in terms of the buyer's preference for inviting firms to tender for a bunch of different items, but by the remarkably rapid increase in the scale on which it proves possible and economical to build single turbo-alternator sets. This development, moreover, is not yet complete and we may envisage even larger sets, and therefore larger, and to that extent fewer, orders in the future.

A nice balance between demand and capacity is no more possible to maintain in this market than in the market for transformers. The electricity authorities cannot avoid some fluctuation in their requirements, nor can the producers hope to expand their total capacity at a continuously appropriate rate. In addition, excess capacity is likely to develop, in the absence of a strong upward movement in demand, simply because rapid technical advance has made it possible to generate the same amount of electricity, from larger sets, with reduced inputs of capital and labour in turbine construction.

These special circumstances, taken in combination, are very unfavourable to effective regulation by price competition. Failure to obtain a contract will certainly burden a firm with heavy financial losses and may indeed threaten its survival as a producer of turbines. Given that an interval of four years may elapse between the ordering and final commissioning of a turbo-alternator set, it is apparent that management will be obliged to attend, not to the current load on the works, but to the chances of getting work in the future. Each firm will be well aware of the disastrous effect on profits of competition, in terms of price, for a share in the total business; at the same time, it cannot fail to realise that failure to obtain an order may put it out of the race.

The buyer also will be faced with its own dilemma. Presumably, according to the advocates of regulation by price competition, the Central Electricity Generating Board will award a contract to the firm that makes the lowest bid, allowing for differences in performance between rival equipments. But is it really conceivable that it could thus ignore the effects of its actions on the structure of the industry? It is perfectly possible for the distribution of its orders to cause a firm to be starved of technical experience or to be obliged to give up production for good. To place contracts blindly, in these exceptional circumstances, merely according to the lowest bid, would be to credit market forces with quite magical authority.

---

[1] Twelve years ago, orders rarely exceeded £2 millions in value. It is worth observing that circumstances have therefore changed in this respect since the Monopolies Commission studied the industry—changed moreover in a way less favourable to the suitability of price competition.

I find it very difficult to predict what the effects of abrogating the price agreement between the turbine makers might be. It is worth while, as with transformers, to distinguish between two possible outcomes, the one in which prices fall in response to excess capacity and the other in which they do not.

### (ii) *Alternative effects of ending an agreement*

Prices could fall sharply, given the threat of some excess capacity, if the firms strove, by endeavouring to under-cut their rivals, to get work. The export trade, it should be noticed, could not be called upon to redress the balance caused by a falling off of demand at home, for the prices at which it is conducted are below full cost. Inevitably, if this were to happen, firms would suffer losses; investment would be checked and, if the situation were sufficiently grave, the currently available productive facilities might be contracted with an associated dispersal of design teams and other specially trained staff. Expenditure on research and development seems to me one of the forms of investment that would suffer a check or an absolute reduction, although the Restrictive Practices Court denied, in their judgment on the transformer case, that this kind of result would be likely to happen. The Court apparently took the view that, if conditions were to become more competitive, firms would be obliged to spend more rather than less on research. The superficial plausibility of this argument rests on an ambiguity in the term 'competitive'. The market for turbines, even with agreed prices, is already highly competitive, in that firms have to strive hard, with the help of sustained investment in research and development, to stay in the technological race. Were the price agreement to be given up, the market would not become more competitive in this sense; the chief effect would be for receipts to fluctuate more widely (given periods of excess capacity) at a lower level. The decision as to how much to invest in research and development (never easy) will rationally depend upon the magnitude of the expected yield. If the general profitability of turbine business is to fall, then the yield from investment in research, aimed at securing for the firm a larger share of this business, will fall likewise. The Restrictive Trade Practices Court, in arguing as they did, would seem to believe that a man could be induced to increase his stake in a lottery provided only the value of the prizes were lowered.

It is theoretically conceivable that the check to investment, occasioned by poor returns, could ultimately so reduce the volume of capacity relative to demand as to restore profitability. But, for reasons given in the discussion of transformers, this result, even if it could be assured, would not be in the public interest.

Let us now assume, alternatively, that the producers would not make competitive price reductions when capacity came to exceed demand. Their resistance to the temptation to use the price weapon might find strength merely in a keen sense of common interest, but might be further re-inforced by the belief that the buyer would in any case choose to allocate business in such a way as ensured the survival of all three firms. In this case the disturbances set up by price instability would be avoided, but it is still necessary to ask, as with transformers, whether the public interest would be sufficiently safe-guarded. The fact that we have here only three producers, rather than the dozen found in transformer production, strengthens the chances that mutual accommodation might serve not merely to stop prices falling to an unduly low level but to keep them permanently higher than they should be. We need not take a view as to whether firms would in fact choose to exercise any joint monopoly power; the point to be noted is that there would be no automatic competitive force sufficiently strong to *ensure* that they did not.

These considerations seem to me to suggest that competition would fail to be an efficient regulator of prices in this market irrespective of the alternative assumptions one may prefer to make as to the outcome of abandoning the practice of agreement.

### 6.   *Switchgear.*

The market for switchgear differs little, in basic structure, from that for turbines, but it is marked by a more developed system of co-operation between the four producers and between them and the Central Electricity Generating Board.

Let us begin by noting that the cost of supplying electricity must depend upon the rapidity with which potential gains from improved technology can be realised through their embodiment in equipment actually in use. There are in fact substantial gains to be had in particular from increasing the power load with which a transmission system can deal, and the rate at which this can take place depends on the time taken to get the more advanced types of switchgear into service. This circumstance creates in itself the need for close co-ordination between the investment plans of the Generating Board and its suppliers.[1]

Under the current arrangements, the plans of the two sides are co-ordinated at several stages. A forecast of the Board's switchgear requirements is made known about a decade in advance, thus enabling the manufacturers to take certain steps—such as acquiring factory space—that are an essential preliminary to future production plans. The second and most important stage is reached when the Board makes a bulk allocation of work between the manufacturers and thereby enables them to make their own production plans as well as to inform their own suppliers (the makers of porcelain and bushing) of their projected needs. The point to note here is that the arrangement permits firms to go ahead with their programmes without having to wait for the Board's requirements to be articulated in detail. Binding contracts are entered into only later and on the basis of prices listed on a schedule agreed between the manufacturers.

I find it hard to conceive that this procedure, or any other procedure equally able to save time, would be fully compatible with competitive price tendering. If the allocation of work were to be determined by competing bids, then the Board would have to be in a position to specify its needs in appropriate detail. The producers would then take longer to learn of the amount of work for which they had to prepare, with a resultant delay in dates of commissioning. It may be

---

[1] The reader will recall that Scotland and Northern Ireland have their own separate electricity generating authorities. What is said, for brevity, about the Central Electricity Generating Board should be taken as applying to these bodies also.

asked why the same degree of expedition could not be achieved by the Board's making its plans earlier, but, were this to be done, these plans would be based on less information about future demand and on a less advanced technology. Also relevant is the fact that detailed specifications are at present decided upon, not by the Board alone, but by the Board and the appropriate manufacturer after the bulk allocation of work.

It is worth noting that the system of bulk allocation enables the Board, if it chooses, to distribute work among the firms in accordance with their relative advantages in capacity, skills, experience and the like. Competitive bidding, of course, is itself a system of allocation which, ideally, ensures that orders go to the firms able to execute them most cheaply. It seems doubtful to me, however, that it could in practice promote as efficient a distribution of work as it is possible to achieve directly, with only one buyer and four sellers. Different firms have different methods of costing and may have different ideas about the bids that others will submit, so that the prices quoted for particular jobs need not closely reflect the relative ability of firms to undertake them.

Work has, in the past, been distributed between the firms in such a way that intertrading has had to take place on a fairly considerable scale. Up to 40 per cent of the value of a particular contract obtained by one of the firms may be represented by components bought from the others, the prices paid being those listed in the agreed schedules subject to a handling discount. Where there are significant economies of scale in the production of particular components, this arrangement has much to commend it, but I cannot believe that it would for long endure under a regime of competitive pricing. In the absence of the agreement, firms would be free to vary both the prices they quote to the Board, for main contracts, and the prices they quote to each other for the supply of components. Thus a firm competing for a main contract could demand prohibitive prices for the supply of essential components required by its rivals. If all four firms had given hostages to each other in this way, then one might hope that they would refrain from any attempt thus to hold each other up to ransom. But at present there is one firm nearly self-sufficient and therefore in a stronger position for this type of warfare than the others. It seems to me, therefore, that the present measure of rationalisation, let alone further extension of it, would clearly be prejudiced by the introduction of price competition. Each firm would be likely to strive for self-sufficiency, as far as its rivals are concerned, or run the risk of being put out of business. This consequence of price competition, as most of the others, cannot be predicted with certainty; it would be foolish to imagine that we are able to identify simple and dependable links between cause and effect in affairs of this kind; new or unperceived circumstances can easily upset one's speculations. The point I make is that, on the face of it, price competition is incompatible with rationalisation of the kind described; it is up to the protagonists of such competition to show either that this incompatibility is illusory or that the rationalisation achieved, or capable of achievement, is not worth preserving.

Further co-operation takes place, between the buyer and the producers, and between the producers themselves, in the development of standardised equipment. The aim is to provide components that are interchangeable, thereby reducing the average quantities that have to be held in stock, and at the same time incorporate the best ideas of the four design teams. I am unable to estimate the gains from collaboration of this kind, but there seems little reason to doubt that the Generating Board, which took the chief initiative in this matter, regards them as valuable. What concerns us here is the compatibility between this exchange of ideas and the practice of price competition. Although it would be perfectly possible for firms to compete in terms of price while co-operating in development, I cannot believe that they would be likely to do so for long. There are bound to be times at which some firm is convinced that it has less to get from an exchange of ideas than it has to give and succumbs to the temptation to make use of this advantage in the competitive struggle. The temptation exists, of course, even under the price agreement, but abrogation, by obliging the companies to struggle for their share of the market, would greatly strengthen it. It is likely, moreover, that firms would seek some shelter from the full vigour of price competition by developing non-standard products which, by the very fact of being incapable of substitution, have a low cross-elasticity of demand.

### 7.   *The Summary case against Price Competition.*

The unsuitability of price competition, for the three markets under discussion, seems to me the consequence of several quite particular circumstances taken in conjunction. It is certainly not my intention in this paper to offer a general apology for restrictive agreements; circumstances alter cases and, in this field, can do so decisively.

To sum up, the policy of promoting price competition, in the sale of heavy electrical equipment, is inappropriate for two main reasons.

In the first place, it will fail to attain its own objective. The size of single orders, the inelasticity of demand, the gap between marginal and average costs and the predominance of one buyer, all taken together, make it impossible to combine normal profitability with price flexibility and periodic excess of capacity over demand. Something has to give. Normal profitability must be assured, if the firms concerned are to stay in the business. Excess capacity could be completely avoided, if indeed at all, only at great social cost. Price flexibility is avoidable only if firms make an agreement or are able to refrain from active price competition even without one; in this latter eventuality, however, there will no longer be any guarantee that prices are not kept unduly high.

Secondly, price competition would prejudice the attainment of other objectives important in this context. It requires only a very limited faith in the principle of planning as such to recognise that the particular character of the markets which concern us offers a special opportunity for the deliberate co-ordination of plans. Such co-ordination is made difficult, in the generality of industry, by the number of firms on both sides of the market; but the domestic requirements for turbines, transformers and switchgear depend on programmes made by a single nationalised electricity authority and framed several years in advance. Co-operation between the suppliers and the Generating Board has developed furthest, I believe, in switchgear, where, as we have seen, there is a system of bulk allocation. The utility of such co-operation, in matters of design and development as well as the planning of investment, seems to me something no reasonable man could deny; in the nature of things, it would seem appropriate for the manufacturers and the Generating Board to work together as a team. I am indeed inclined to think, as an outsider, that co-operation might be closer, but even its maintenance would be threatened by the practice of price competition. Thus the real problem before us is to devise arrangements that permit the manufacturers and their customer to work together as a team without sacrificing the objectives for the attainment of which price competition, in other circumstances, is a useful device.

8.  *The Alternative to Price Competition.*
   The alternative to price competition is agreement, but I do not wish to suggest that we should be satisfied with agreements such as have been in force during the last few decades. The electricity supply authorities have surely a right—indeed, a duty—to insist that the price they pay for equipment is not such as provide the manufacturers either with abnormally high profits or with a shelter for inefficiency. The agreements in operation hitherto have not given this guarantee; quite apart from whether they did promote high prices and costs—and on this we need not express an opinion—they offered the buyer no assurance that they did not do so. Neither, I have argued, would price competition provide this guarantee; some other way has to be found of providing the purchaser and the public with the assurances to which they are entitled.
   It might at first be supposed that the pricing policy of the firms operating an agreement would be subject to two forms of check or sanction, the first provided by the threat of new producers entering the market, the second by foreign competition. In fact, however, it is very difficult for new firms to enter the heavy end of the industry, in which much capital and experience is required. Nor would it be expedient for the Generating Board to purchase equipment from abroad. Obviously the balance of payments would suffer, and, in any case, the prices quoted by foreign suppliers would not provide a standard for home producers, as export prices seem generally to be below the level of full costs. We have to conclude, therefore, that there are no natural checks such as would prevent a price ring from abusing its power.
   The need is clearly to devise an agreement to which both the Generating Board and the manufacturers are party and into which appropriate safeguards have been built. This could be done in a variety of ways, the details of which ought to be the subject of another paper. Clearly the level of price must be related to production costs, these being calculated as a weighted average for the firms concerned and set so as to provide a rate of return on capital comparable to that obtained in industry generally and not less than is required to finance expansion and provide a normal yield to shareholders. A fairly loose form of control would seem preferable, prices being set for a period of—say—three years and revised subsequently if they did not provide the agreed rate of return on capital. The firms would be obliged to employ the same accounting techniques and their calculations would have to be submitted to some independent body, neither the producers nor the purchaser being left as judge in their own cause.

Negotiations along these lines have in fact, I believe, been under way between the parties concerned, but I am not informed as to their progress. Needless to say, there are important issues of principle and of practical administration that require to be resolved. One of these is the appropriate allocation of costs between home and export sales.

First, in the production of heavy electrical equipment there are important overhead costs the allocation of which, between home and export sales, is essentially arbitrary. Capacity installed to make switchgear for the CEGB for example may be used at a later state of its life to produce for export. The development work done to produce ever larger turbo-generators will likewise serve both the home and export markets. In so far as these costs are concerned, any net contribution to them that the manufacturers can obtain from exports will reduce the level of home prices necessary to secure a reasonable return overall. Even if almost the whole of these overheads were attributed to the cost of producing equipment for the home market, it could not be said that the home customer was subsidising exports; without the exports he would have to pay more.

Secondly, it appears to be the case, throughout the world generally, that the domestic price of heavy electrical equipment exceeds the export price. Foreign manufacturers, that is to say, rely on their home markets for recouping the greater part of their overheads. Whether or not we approve of these arrangements, they are a fact of life and the British industry cannot hope to compete overseas unless it operates similarly.

Thirdly, there are no statistics known to me that can provide us with the return earned on capital, in industry generally, on home sales alone. The available figures relate to the return on capital on total business. This is important in that the permitted rate of return on the production of heavy electrical equipment —assuming that this were to be employed in fixing prices—would have to be related to the returns in other industries. If like were to be compared with like, then it is the manufacturers' return on their total sales of the electrical equipment in question that must be considered.

For these three reasons, it seems to me that the prices fixed in any agreement between the industry and the supply authorities ought to be such as afford a normal rate of return to a firm of normal efficiency on its total business, home and export, subject to the condition that export prices are not actually below marginal costs.

A further problem concerns the computation of the capital employed by the firms concerned and, more generally, the structure of production in the industry. The prices set ought to be such as to compensate producers for having installed an amount of capacity sufficient to meet the buyer's needs when at their peak even although that capacity is not currently in full use. But it is possible for excess capacity to exist to an extent greater than that required to meet peak requirements, through lack of co-ordination between the firms' investment plans, technological change, a falling off in export orders or for some other reason. The Generating Board has no obvious obligation to take this particular burden off the firms' shoulders, and yet it may in practice be difficult to measure the quantity of excess capacity attributable to one circumstance rather than another. I can see no hope of precise solutions to this problem, but it should not be so difficult for reasonable men to reach a compromise appropriate to the particular circumstances of each case.

These considerations lead us to the question of the structural efficiency of an industry as a whole. Let us assume for example that it could be established, beyond reasonable doubt, that the number of, say, transformer makers was too great to permit full exploitation of all the available economies of scale. Were this the case, the firms would have an incentive to form larger units in order to reduce costs, but it could be that this incentive was not strong enough to counter the effect of inertia and the desire to maintain independence. In these circumstances price competition does offer some remedy. Firms that did merge would strive, by price reductions, to enlarge their share of the market and would thereby force rivals to follow their example; even the threat that this might happen might encourage firms to exploit such scale economies as became available. A general fall in prices, produced by competition in conditions of excess capacity, would at least help to concentrate the minds of manufacturers on the need to improve their position.

Under these conditions, it would be hard to justify any agreement that left firms, on average, with a normal return on capital employed and thereby prevented an unsatisfactory structure from registering itself in the way most likely to lead to its improvement. It ought to be understood that an industry is not entitled to enjoy the legal right to operate a restrictive agreement that serves to perpetuate inefficiency. But it would be wrong to turn to price competition as the sure way of bringing about desired rationalisation. No doubt poor returns, in the long run, will reduce an excessive number of producers, but they may also weaken the incentive and the ability, even for the most efficient firms, to invest in the development and installation of up-to-date productive equipment. It is conceivable that general impoverishment might prove the only way, in practice, of forcing the required changes, but I should hope that a less costly and more rapid method might be found in cooperative action in which both the manufacturers and the electricity supply authorities would take part.

A policy of agreed prices, based on a weighted average of the firms' costs, is open to the further objection that it ensures only that a company's profits are commensurate with its efficiency relative to rival producers as contrasted with its efficiency relative to industry as a whole. And the point could be made, in this connection, that three or four producers, as in both turbines and switchgear, represented a very small sample. The most obvious reply to an argument along these lines is that, given the difficulty of entering these markets and the objections to buying from abroad, competition would do no better; each firm would fare according to its efficiency relative to its two rivals irrespective of the level of efficiency of three firms as a whole. It is conceivable that, in fixing agreed prices, one might even do better, in that the buyer might be able to produce evidence of costs in other countries or to make his own estimates of what costs, employing the latest equipment and techniques, ought to be.[1]

---

[1] Sir Robert Shone, in a comment on an earlier version of this article, pointed to the steel industry's experience of price control based on calculations of this kind.

Whether such developments would eventually be feasible, I cannot readily judge, but it would be wrong to rule them out of consideration. In a similar way, the buyer could claim that any very marked spread between the costs of the firms concerned was *prima facie* evidence of structural inefficiency or of the use of different accounting techniques.

Some readers, dismayed by the number and difficulty of the problems bound up with the choice of an agreed level of prices, may feel that their sympathy for the policy of price competition is now being re-kindled. But reliance on such a policy, although it might encourage us to forget about these problems, would not ensure their solution. It would not, I have argued, guarantee that profits were neither persistently above nor persistently below those earned generally; it would not automatically correct any structural inefficiency, and it would not ensure that firms were in a position to compete, by differential pricing at home and abroad, in the international market as it currently exists.

Other readers may blame me for not following, to their proper conclusion, the logic of my own arguments. They may see the plurality of producers as a permanent obstacle to the co-ordination of investment plans, the importance of which I conceded, and recommend that not only the generation and distribution of electricity, but also the manufacture of the equipment used in these processes, should be put under the control of a state monopoly. Such a proposal can appear reasonable, however, only if we focus on some of the requirements of economic efficiency to the exclusion of others no less important. Given that we cannot hope to know, in advance, the forms of research and development that will prove the most fruitful, the designs that will be most effective, the techniques of organisation and management that will show themselves superior, the decentralisation of decision-making provided by a plurality of firms is a sound strategy. Nor must we imagine that, price competition being appropriate, all forms of inter-firm rivalry serve no useful social purpose. We should see ourselves not as obliged to choose between competition and monopoly but as confronted with the problem (an economic problem quite strictly) of devising arrangements that provide, even approximately, an optimum balance between competition and planning, freedom and order. We should aim at getting (as far as is possible) the best of both worlds.

*St. John's College,*
*Oxford.*

# Price notification schemes

## The legal position

Ought firms to be allowed to make arrangements to exchange information about the prices they are charging? 'Price notification schemes' or 'open price agreements', as they have been called in the United States, have attracted attention since the passing, in 1956, of the Restrictive Trade Practices Act. The Registrar, in his Report published in January of this year [1967], expresses the opinion that these arrangements are 'spread rather widely over industry in substitution of price agreements that have been condemned or abandoned'. He remarks, moreover, that it is 'unnecessary further to argue the proposition that registration and examination by the Restrictive Practices Court of information agreements are desirable, since I think that it has been accepted by all parties in Parliament'.[1] My purpose in this article is to examine the circumstances and the ways in which these particular agreements can influence competition and to inquire whether this influence is economically desirable.

Let us begin, however, by taking note of the legal position. Some notification schemes, even under the present state of the law, are considered restrictive and are therefore registrable; this much was made clear by a Judgement of the Restrictive Practices Court given in June 1966. The matter before the Court was an agreement between tyre manufacturers regarding the supply of tyres for buses. The practice had been for manufacturers to contract with a transport operator to provide, maintain, and renew tyres for his fleet of buses. In 1961, the manufacturers entered into an agreement called the 'Rate Notification Scheme'. It had two parts, the one binding upon the parties, the other optional or permissive. The compulsory part obliged members to inform each other of the rates they had quoted to operators; the permissive part left them free to inform the others, if they so chose, as to the rates they provisionally intended to quote. The understanding was, under this second scheme, that members were free to change their intended quotations after learning of the rates others had in mind; they could then inform others of these changes with the result that a fresh set of revisions might be set in train.

The Registrar of Restrictive Trading Agreements did not contend that the first or compulsory part of this scheme, referring to rates actually quoted, was restrictive and the Court did not pronounce on the matter. [359] He maintained, however, that the permissive part of the scheme was a restrictive arrangement and that, being to the like effect as the previous agreement that the firms had undertaken to abandon, there had been contempt of court. In the Judgement, delivered by Mr. Justice Megaw, this point of view was sustained. The Court was not moved by the argument that the manufacturers had not *agreed* to operate the permissive part of the scheme; the fact that they did operate it, over a period of some $3\frac{1}{2}$ years, was evidence that an arrangement was in fact in existence. A quotation from the Judgement puts the point forcibly:

The law is not so subtle or unrealistic as to involve the conclusion that, while an arrangement can come into being as a result of information as to one another's intentions supplied in word or writing or by a nod or a wink, it cannot come into being as a result of information as to one another's intentions derived from their actual and continuing conduct towards one another.

There would appear to be two general principles, of considerable scope and importance, established in this case. First, the mere practice of exchanging information about prices, even though there is no agreement to do so, would seem to constitute an arrangement in the meaning of the Act. And, secondly, such an arrangement is restrictive – and therefore registrable – where the prices in question are those that the parties provisionally intend to quote.

### Short-run price competition

So much for the present legal status of information agreements; what must now concern us is their economic effects. What is their influence on the pricing policies of firms and, indirectly, on the public interest? We may begin with the distinction between agreements according to whether they provide for the notification of prices before or after contracts have been placed. First, let us assume that firms inform each other, as in the optional part of the tyre scheme, of the prices they intend to quote. On the face of it, it might seem that this would promote competition, in that each firm would supply to the others the information they need to make an effective rejoinder. But no one now needs to be told, in this world of deterrents and a balance of terror, that improved opportunities for retaliation may reduce rather than augment the chances of conflict. It has been suggested that if the Russians were given an early-warning radar station on the Rhine, and the Western Powers a similar establishment on the Oder, the likelihood of war would be diminished. In similar fashion, in cowboy films, two potential contestants used to put their guns on the table in order that neither of them might have so great an advantage from being quick on the draw. Schemes for prior notification of prices seem to me to [360] fulfil the same kind of function; each of the parties gives up the opportunity to make a surprise attack on the understanding that the others do so likewise.

Post-notification schemes (as contrasted with prior notification schemes) provide for the exchange of information about bids after the contracts have been allotted or at any rate after the closing date for tenders. They do not oblige firms in effect to invite competitors to match the prices they are quoting on outstanding tenders and, for this reason, will be less effective in preventing them from trying to steal a march on their rivals. Nevertheless, evidence that one seller has been quoting low prices on past deals is likely to persuade his competitors that he will do so again and induce them to retaliate at the next round; and the threat of such retaliation may sometimes be sufficient to cause those considering price reductions to hold their hand. The restraint exercised will be weaker than under systems of prior notification, but not altogether without force.

We can describe this effect of information agreements, rather conveniently, in terms of a distinction between different forms of price competition. In some circumstances, a seller may be induced to cut his price by the prospect of the gains to be made before his rivals become aware of his move and seek to match it, or he may cut his price in order to forestall others from securing such gains. If sellers act in either of these ways, I shall say that we have *short-run price competition*. A firm may, however, reduce its price even though its rivals are free to retaliate instantaneously; in this case it seeks the more durable gains which it believes its efficiency and productive capacity can enable it to obtain. When firms make price reductions for this reason, or in order to match such reductions made by others, I shall say we have *long-run price competition*. I do not claim that, in practice, every example of price competition will fit neatly into either of these two categories; the distinction is crude but important and I hope serviceable. Its relation to price notification arrangements is obvious; such agreements inhibit short-run price competition but leave the parties to them free to engage in long-run price competition if they are in fact minded so to do. Let us now consider these effects more closely.

The opportunities that a market will provide for short-run price competition will depend on two principal circumstances, the first being the duration of the interval that elapses before a price reduction becomes known and is matched by other firms, the second being the volume of business that can be transacted during this interval. In these two respects, markets differ widely. No time need elapse before the manufacturer of the typical consumer good finds out what his rivals are charging, as prices – for good reason – are made public knowledge. (Even here, however, there [361] may be some scope for clandestine discounts to large retailers that take time to be detected.) In the case of contract work, on the other hand, rivals may remain ignorant of the bids being submitted by others unless they have made an arrangement designed to keep themselves informed. There are likewise differences between markets in the value of the sales that can be made during the interval before retaliation takes place. A single order for large turbo-alternators may be worth some £20m and represent more than the average annual output in that product of a large firm; the incentive to steal a march on a rival is therefore, in these circumstances, very strong, as it can make a substantial difference to the load on a firm's workers. In few industries can the natural unit of sales be so large – although one can think of others – but even in the absence of such large natural indivisibilities, there may be the possibility of obtaining, through an unmatched price cut, the disposal of a large volume of stocks or large orders for delivery over a substantial future period.

It is worth noting, in this context, that the distinction between prior and post notification, now apparently crucial in law, may be of very variable significance in terms of economic effect. Where a firm's sales are made up of sufficiently small individual transactions to amount to a continuous flow, as for example with most consumer goods, convenience usually dictates that prices are changed at relatively infrequent intervals; in this case knowledge of a firm's present or immediately past prices usually gives a good indication of the price it will charge in the immediate future. It is generally where sales take the form of large and relatively infrequent transactions that past prices are no reliable guide to current or future ones. Prior notification schemes are often adopted in precisely these circumstances because of the likelihood that short-run price competition would take place without them.

For manufacturing business as a whole, short-run price competition, at least in the home market, is probably the exception rather than the rule. Most national markets are dominated by a few firms which are aware of each others' prices without the need for special arrangements designed for the purpose. In these circumstances, a firm will normally reduce its home price level, not in the hope of taking its rivals by surprise, but because it believes that it stands to gain even after they have reduced their prices in retaliation. Notification schemes, by converting otherwise 'closed price' markets into 'open price' markets, cause the pricing policies that they influence to conform to the general pattern. As the successful operation of these schemes usually demands that competitors are reasonably few and reasonably trusting, their effective scope rarely extends beyond home markets into the wider and less restrained field of international trade. [362]

The natural differences between industries are therefore such that short-run price competition can be promoted in some of them merely by prohibiting notification arrangements, whereas, in others, it could be made to prevail, if at all, only through radical changes in structure such as might be brought about by the measures of dissolution, divestiture, and divorcement recommended by the more enthusiastic American supporters of anti-trust. But in these matters, it may be pointed out, consistency is not everything. We might decide to seize the opportunity to encourage short-run price competition when this could be done simply through the prohibition of agreements, but prefer to tolerate its abeyance rather than incur the risks and costs of a policy of enforced deconcentration. In this case, short-run price competition would take place in some industries and not in others, its incidence being in no way associated with its appropriateness.

These matters of policy, however, are not my immediate concern and they cannot in any case be resolved until the underlying economic issues are settled. Is short-run competition essential to the fully efficient working of the private enterprise system? What are its likely effects on the incentive to invest and upon the adaption of supply to demand in particular markets? How does it compare, in terms of social utility, with long-run price competition? These are the questions that we shall now have to consider.

## Stable v. fluctuating prices

Let us begin by observing that short-run price competition will make prices responsive to the balance between demand and productive capacity in the industry affected. When firms are working at less than normal capacity output, so that their physical equipment and skilled labour force are underemployed, the additional or 'marginal' cost of executing a further order is no more than the so-called variable expenditure on materials, labour, etc. necessary for the work. Considered in isolation, therefore, a further order will appear remunerative provided the price obtained for it exceeds marginal cost. Nevertheless, where only long-run price competition is practised, firms will usually be unwilling to quote prices below the level sufficient to make a full contribution to fixed overheads. They will appreciate that a general reduction in the industry's prices will normally fail to produce an increase in the volume of sales sufficient to compensate for the fall in their average value. It is where conditions favour short-run price competition, that successive reductions are likely to drive prices down towards the level of marginal costs. The firms concerned, needless to say, will not want this to happen and would generally be prepared to maintain their prices provided that they knew that others [363] would do likewise. In fact, however, they will have to quote in ignorance of rival bids; by making even a small price cut, they may gain a large increase in their share of the business, by failing to do so they may be left without work.

Excess capacity is not the only condition to cause prices, under the influence of short-run price competition, to be driven down to the level of marginal costs. The extra business that a firm hopes to gain by means of a price reduction may serve, not to fill unused capacity, but to replace some other less profitable work to which capacity is, in part, currently devoted. Many, if not most, British industries appear to be selling more cheaply abroad than at home and in some cases export prices are well below full normal average costs. The fact that this gap exists indicates that short-run price competition is not practised, for, if it were, each firm would seek, by means of a slight reduction in the prices it quotes on the home market, to replace export business by home business so long as the latter remained the more remunerative. And the ultimate result of these endeavours, in the great majority of industries, would be to bring home prices down towards the level of export prices on the international market.

Short-run price competition, I have argued, will give us fluctuating prices, which may fall to the level of marginal costs when capacity exceeds demand. If only long-run price competition is practised, on the other hand, prices will remain relatively stable in response to temporary changes in demand. Let us now consider which of these alternative forms of price behaviour is to be preferred.

Price changes, ideally, perform the useful function of inducing consumers to smooth out the variations in their own demand in such a way that less fixed equipment is required to meet it. If excess capacity develops, the argument runs, prices should be lowered in order to stimulate the demand needed to make fuller use of it. Conversely, in times of capacity shortage, there is a case for raising prices sufficiently to persuade buyers to postpone their purchases. The logic of price variation, in these simple terms, is both straightforward and appealing; but there are a variety of circumstances, of importance in many markets, which deprive it of much force.

It is worth noting, in the first place, that consumers' ability to adapt to price changes will largely depend upon whether these can be foreseen. If it is known, for example, that train fares are lower midweek, then people can plan to travel then. But the ebb and flow in the demand for many commodities may be all but unpredictable and the resultant price changes, being unforeseen, may produce only limited adaptation. A firm's purchases of materials and components, for example, may be tied closely to production programmes which are difficult to modify once embarked upon. Plans for the construction of power stations, for example, are unlikely to [364] be modified in response to a fall in the price of switchgear, whereas they would seriously be disrupted if inadequate productive capacity were to create a bottleneck in the supply of such equipment. This may be the extreme case, but it seems likely that purchasers in general, whether industrial or domestic, would normally be prepared to pay at least some premium for the reasonable assurance of being able to satisfy their requirements, as and when they might arise, at roughly predictable prices.

Now the provision of a reliable supply, at roughly predictable prices, will normally put producers to the cost of carrying stocks or a margin of excess capacity, or both. Much will depend, of course, on the techniques of manufacture characteristic of each product, which will often permit output to be increased, at least temporarily, above the level for which the fixed equipment was designed. In other industries, it will not be practicable to cater for a fluctuating demand without fairly generous capacity provision, the function of which, from society's point of view, is to provide the same flexibility or room for manoeuvre that financial liquidity gives to individuals.

I have argued that short-run price competition will cause prices to fluctuate and to fall towards marginal cost when capacity exceeds demand. Yet a margin of normally unused capacity, it now appears, is a precondition, in some cases, for a reliably available supply. Here then we are faced with a fundamental dilemma. Short-run price competition, reliability of supply, and positive profits are three things which it may sometimes be impossible to combine. If, for example, we seek to combine short-run price competition, giving flexible prices, and reliable supply, provided by a margin of normally unused capacity, then prices will normally be below full costs, thus producing a negative return on the capital invested. If, on the other hand, we are to have both short-run price competition and positive profitability, then it may be necessary either to avoid excess capacity, which causes prices to fall below costs, or to have periodic scarcity severe enough to permit very high prices to be charged. In these circumstances we will have either mounting imports or else bottlenecks, lengthening order books and the dislocation of purchasers' plans. Finally, if we wish to combine both positive profits and reliability of supply, then it may be necessary, by avoiding short-run price competition, to prevent prices falling below full costs when capacity exceeds demand.

**The penalty for over-investment**
Firms may frequently be obliged to carry a margin of excess capacity, I have suggested, as a condition for avoiding recurrent and disruptive scarcities. But there are two other reasons for believing that the [365] maintenance of a continuous balance between capacity and demand will be virtually impossible. Excess capacity, in the first place, may arise through accident; given that demands are difficult to predict and that the investment plans of competing firms are imperfectly co-ordinated, only a miracle could ensure that the total productive capacity installed in an industry was always exactly appropriate to requirements. Even if prices remain stable in the face of short-term demand fluctuations, firms that over-invest will pay a corresponding penalty in terms of higher costs and lower profits. But where short-run price competition causes excess capacity to result in a fall in prices the penalty will be increased out of all proportion to the loss which the over-investment represents to society as a whole; the fall in price represents a windfall transfer to purchasers and may prevent the suppliers from recouping – in the limit – any part of their fixed expenses. The private sector of the economy is commonly exhorted to maintain a high and steady level of investment in the face of temporary set-backs;

short-run price competition, by greatly magnifying the penalty for over-investment, makes this much more difficult to do.

Excess capacity may arise also from the fact that the minimum efficient scale for an addition to capacity may, as in parts of the steel industry, be very large. When short-run price competition is practised, the installation of a large unit of additional capacity, before demand has risen sufficiently to ensure its full utilization, will cause prices to fall below full costs. In these circumstances, the alternatives may be to postpone investment, thus causing a temporary scarcity, or to install a smaller unit of capacity, thus forgoing economies of scale. It does not follow that the public interest will be best served, on all occasions, by investment in the large-scale plant, but, if such investment can be made to pay in the absence of short-run price competition, then one can normally presume that it ought to be undertaken.

### The choice to be made
Let me now endeavour to pull together the various threads of the argument. Normal profitability, excess capacity, and short-run price competition, I suggested, cannot always be reconciled. Of these the first cannot be sacrificed, for no one would suggest that private enterprise can run indefinitely at a loss. Periodic excess capacity may, in some industries, be the price we have to pay for a reliable supply; it may also be the result of scarcely avoidable errors of foresight or of the large size of the minimum efficient addition to capacity. Finally, short-run price competition may be preventable only if firms are allowed to exchange information about prices. It is apparent, therefore, that we have to make a choice. I do not propose that we should at all costs seek to stop short-run price competition. In [366] some industries, peak demands can be met without the need for a margin of normally unused capacity, merely by making more intensive use, over short periods, of equipment designed for a smaller load; the minimum efficient scale of an addition to plant is by no means always large and it may sometimes be possible, by limited price changes, to induce buyers to postpone or to bring forward their purchases. In these circumstances, firms will not need and may not wish to avoid short-run price competition. The situation is quite different, however, where inflexible production processes, employing much specialized fixed equipment and trained personnel, are found in conjunction with a demand that is both fluctuating and unresponsive to changes in price.

These considerations, by themselves, would lead us to conclude that there are certain market conditions, by no means rare in practice, in which inter-firm information agreements would be in the public interest. Such agreements, I suggested earlier, would not prevent companies from engaging in long-run price competition if they were minded to do so. There is in fact plenty of evidence of such competition in industries where prices are 'open' either naturally or by virtue of a system of information exchange; the automobile industry is a good case in point. But when entry into an industry is difficult, it is possible for established producers, wishing to live and let live, to abjure all price competition with the result that efficiency may suffer and returns be kept abnormally high. This situation may develop, of course, in industries in which prices are naturally open, but there may be others in which information agreements will make it much easier for firms to give effect to their desire not to compete at all in terms of price. Some people may argue that these agreements should then be swept away, on the grounds that it is better to put up with the damage done by short-run price competition rather than have no price competition at all. What we do here is a matter for judgement in the light of the circumstances of each case. My own view is that it would frequently be desirable to allow firms to operate a price information agreement subject to periodic official scrutiny designed to detect and prevent any abuse.

## Swings and roundabouts

The public supervision of prices and profits is a rather difficult and costly procedure making heavy demands on the services of accountants, civil servants, lawyers, and the like. One might think, therefore, that it would be applied sparingly to those industries where the suspension of competition gave firms a degree of market power that invited abuse. What is remarkable, therefore, is that governments, while seeking to outlaw restrictive agreements, are at the same time moving, in pursuit of [367] an incomes policy, in the direction of a completely general price control. The likely effects of these measures, when operated concurrently, are worth examination. In the absence of control, and for reasons other than the exercise of monopoly power, profit rates will exhibit great variation. They will vary between firms making the same product, according to differences in efficiency and in luck; and they will vary between products themselves and over the life cycle of each product, as a result of technical change, shifts in consumer demand, and many uncoordinated business decisions taken in this country and abroad. Public control, however, will be guided inevitably by some notion of a 'normal' return on capital employed, this being a rate neither higher nor lower than that required to attract capital and enterprise into the trade. By considering the level of interest rates and the profit rates earned in other countries to and from which capital could move, I do not doubt that some estimate of 'normal' profits might be made and put to good use. The danger, of course, is that this rate will in practice be equated to the average rate of profit being earned in manufacturing business as a whole and then come to be regarded as the maximum that can justifiably be earned on any product, by any firm at any time. The proscription of inter-firm agreements or arrangements, such as we have been considering in this paper, will see to it that firms are unable to limit the extent to which their profits, in the face of a temporary decline in demand, fall below this average figure. Price control, on the other hand, will see to it that profits do not rise above the average very often or by very much. Little knowledge of arithmetic is required to perceive that if we make it more difficult for profit rates to exceed the average, and easier for them to fall below it, the average itself will continuously fall. In fact, firms rely on being able to make on the swings what they lose on the roundabouts; it is by setting the profits of good times against the losses of bad, and the successful products against the failures that they are able to ride out the ups and downs of business life. To deny firms the right of such offsetting, when they operate in a world of change and uncertainty, can scarcely be the deliberate objective of government policies, but it could be their unintended effect. However conscientious and respectable our commissions, tribunals, and courts, the collective effect of their individual decisions, as these impinge over an increasingly wide field of industry, may be unfavourable to investment generally and highly unfavourable to investment of a speculative kind.

Competition is a powerful engine of economic progress, but it is mischievous to pretend that there are no other requirements for economic efficiency with which it can ever conflict. Information agreements seem to me liable to limit competition, but in a way that will frequently promote, rather than impair, the general interest. If we seek through legislation to [368] purge the economy of every conceivable restrictive arrangement, then I fear that either the authority of the laws or the efficiency of the system will suffer. It is a curious paradox that opposition to the effective working of the private enterprise sector of the economy comes, not only from its avowed opponents, but also from those who seek to force it to conform to their own mistaken conception of the ideal.

**Note**
1.  Restrictive Trading Agreements, Report of the Registrar, 1 July 1963 to 30 June 1966, Cmnd. 3188, 1967.                                                                      [369]

# [9]

## PLANNING VERSUS COMPETITION[1]

### By G. B. RICHARDSON

### I. *Scope and Method*

WHAT are the proper roles, in economic organization, of planning and of competition? In what circumstances should economic activities be fitted together deliberately through a coherent set of instructions given by a central authority? And when should this coordination be left to the spontaneous interaction of independent, de-centralized decisions? Is planning essentially an alternative to competition or can it be employed, in an indicative form, not to replace but somehow to illuminate, guide and thereby improve the operation of market forces? These questions, it need hardly be said, admit of no definite answer, objectively valid irrespective of time and place. Nevertheless, they are real questions of obvious practical importance, so that it is worth while trying to find some answers to them, however partial and provisional these may be.

I wish to make only two preliminary observations, one about scope, the other about method. The scope of this paper is very wide. But its subject is competition versus planning, not capitalism versus socialism; the questions which I raised at the outset pose themselves in countries which have no private property in the means of production but seek to decentralize decision taking. In so far as method is concerned, I seek justification in terms of what Sir Roy Harrod has called, rather grandly, the need for Continuing Conceptual Refurbishment. I try to take a fresh look at the first principles. Progress in economics does not depend only upon rigorous analysis, observation and measurement; it requires also that effort of imagination that enables us partially to escape from conventional categories of thought. Being realistic is not merely a question of testing hypotheses, important though this is; it also requires sustained and strenuous effort to consider whether our inherited stock of

---

[1] This paper was written, as its style and presentation may suggest, to be read after dinner to an informal meeting of my fellow economists at Oxford. My first intention was to modify it so as to offer a more systematic analysis more appropriate for publication, but the endeavour to do this convinced me that I had either to leave the paper much as it was or to write a very different one. The present version, if only by virtue of its lack of careful qualification, may at any rate prove provocative. Needless to say, the scope of the paper, although wide, is not as wide as the title might suggest; I suppose I might have specified my field of interest more narrowly, but it seemed better to leave it to the reader to spot all the important and relevant considerations that I have left out of account.

theoretical constructions do not distort our vision of the plain facts of economic life.

## II. *The Task of Economic Organization*

Let us begin at the beginning and ask what it is that we want competition or planning to accomplish. The answer might be that their function is to secure an efficient allocation of resources. To say this, however, although obviously correct, may be misleading. For we normally concentrate, in economic theory, on the pure logic of resource allocation and, in order to exhibit this logic clearly, we assume that both ends and means are given. Thus we assume, in the so-called theory of consumers' behaviour, that income, prices and tastes are given and concern ourselves exclusively with the logic of choice. And when we turn to the economy as a whole and seek to establish conditions for efficient allocation in Pareto's sense, we follow the same procedure; we adopt the vantage point of someone standing outside the system with full knowledge of all the relevant preferences, resources and productive techniques. This approach is justified in that it enables us to focus our attention on the pure principles of economizing; but it is important, when we turn to consider the working of economic organization, to keep well in mind the obvious fact that in reality no one is provided with a bird's-eye view. Allocative decisions are in fact taken, and in the nature of things have to be taken, on the basis of individual beliefs and opinions, usually uncertain and sometimes contradictory. It is not merely that our knowledge is probabilistic in character; the point is that it is fragmented, in the form of imperfectly consistent estimates held by different people. The function of economic organization is therefore to make the best use of this knowledge, and, in appraising the relative effectiveness of different systems, we have to think in terms not only of allocative logic but of search and discovery.

Let us suppose that a body of men land on a desert island on which, in a variety of places, buried treasure is to be found. If the men have with them a map showing the location of treasure throughout the island, then a plan of campaign can readily be drawn up. The appropriate organization is that of central planning, each man being given a particular job to do. Of course there will be problems of incentives, of distribution and so on, but the propriety of centralized decision taking can scarcely be in doubt. But let us now suppose that there is no map, or at least no one map in existence that can be presumed accurate. Each man may have bits and pieces of information that he considers relevant to the location of the treasure, but no more. There is now room for choice between alternative forms of organization. The centralized solution would be to invite the men to pool their information and opinions and endeavour therefrom to construct a map of the most likely location of the treasure; a plan of campaign could then be drawn up and jobs allocated. The purely de-centralized solution would be to allow each man to go forth and dig where he liked. Now these alternative approaches differ in two ways. Under central planning, the activities of different men will be coordinated by means of a set of integrated instructions which, ideally, will produce an optimum pattern of search —or allocation of resources—with respect to the evidence and opinion embodied in the map. Under laissez faire, on the other hand, such coordination as does take place will be the unintended result of each man taking account of what the others are doing; if, for example, men start to crowd in one corner of the island, then some will no doubt be induced to seek their fortunes in other areas where, if the evidence of treasure is less strong, the competition is weaker. Clearly, therefore, planning and competition represent alternative techniques of coordination; less obvious, perhaps, is that they differ also in the way in which they make use of knowledge. Under central planning, evidence and opinion will be consolidated in order to construct the map on which the programme of search is to be based. Under laissez faire, however, each and every opinion will affect the pattern of search provided that whoever holds it is in possession of a pick and shovel. Now it does not seem to me possible, unless the circumstances are further specified, to say whether the consolidation of knowledge will improve the pattern of search; it is easy to see that something will be gained, as bits of the jigsaw are fitted together, but easy to see also that something may be lost if heterodox opinions are sacrificed in the name of consistency, and new findings, if they appear to threaten the presumptions of the plan, are quietly put aside. All that one can say at this stage is that the relative merits of planning and competition are not solely a matter of the way in which they coordinate inter-related activities; they depend also on whether, in a particular set of circumstances, it is desirable to endeavour to weld a variety of estimates and opinions into some kind of coherent whole.

I hope that the relevance of this naive analogy is reasonably clear. In normative economics, when considering how best to adapt means to ends, we assume that we have knowledge of the available resources, opportunities and objectives in order to concentrate on the logic of the problem. In positive economics, on the other hand, when we come to consider how particular systems would work, this assumption has to be abandoned. Maps are not provided; economic organization has to find some way of constructing maps or of doing without them. In a centrally planned system, the authorities take steps to prepare a map; after discussions with the subordinate bodies in the hierarchy, with the various industrial commissions or their equivalents, they specify a feasible and desired future composition of output and then proceed to give appropriate instructions designed to ensure that it is produced. Consistency is thereby produced not necessarily, of course, with resources, technical possibilities and needs as they objectively exist, but with one central agreed or imposed conception of what these are. In practice, of course, planning systems will differ as to the detail in which the future pattern of output is set down, but the essence of the matter is that resources are allocated according to some central view of objectives and opportunities built up through some organized consolidation of the information in the hands of the central and subordinate bodies.

In competitive systems, firms do what they like in pursuit of profit and a large part of economic analysis is devoted to discussing whether this will cause the right things to be produced in the right amounts. The price mechanism is supposed to do the trick; if too much of a good is produced, the price will sink below costs; if too little, it will remain above them; in either event the profit motive, combined with free mobility and competition, should bring the required adjustment. For the flawless operation of this mechanism—subject to qualifications about externalities, etc.—most economists put forward an institutional blue-print, perfect competition, while acknowledging with regret that scale economies may make it impossible to secure its full realization in practice. Now I have maintained elsewhere that perfect competition, even if realizable, could never do what is claimed of it.[2] The essence of the matter can be put quite briefly, but there is no room here for the full supporting argument. Under perfect competition, it would be quite impossible for any firm to know how much of a good to produce. According to the usual story, entrepreneurs are guided by prices; each of them sets an output that equates the price of the good he sells to its marginal cost. Now it is clear that current prices cannot be the appropriate signals; they reflect the appropriateness of past output decisions but are not directly relevant to decisions about what to produce for the future. Presumably, therefore, firms are supposed to equate marginal costs to future prices. But how then is a producer able to predict future prices, depending as they do both on the demands of consumers and on the supply plans of all his competitors? This the textbooks do not tell us; the most we are likely to be told is that producers are assumed to know what the relevant future prices are. But a little reflection suffices to show that even this is not enough to ensure that firms know what

[2] See my *Information and Investment* (London, 1960), chs. 1 and 2. The same matter is dealt with, though less fully, in my article 'Equilibrium, Expectations and Information', *Economic Journal*, vol. LXIX (1959), pp. 223–37.

to do and that, as a result of their actions, the equilibrium configuration of output is obtained. For let us imagine that the system is out of equilibrium but that the true equilibrium prices are somehow announced to all producers as from on high. How would the possession of this information enable the individual firm to know which goods to produce, or cease producing, and in what quantities? If the future price of a good were known to be greater than the current cost of making it, then a profit opportunity may be said to exist; but if there is an un-limited number of firms equally able and ready to respond to the opportunity no individual firm will know whether to do so. A profit opportunity which is available equally for everyone is in fact available to no one at all.

My own view, therefore, is that there would be no tendency under conditions of perfect competition for the equilibrium associated with it ever to be attained. My fear is that the brief argumentation just pro-vided will not persuade anyone who has not already accepted this view now to accept it. In any case a large number of economists—perhaps even an increasing number—continue to maintain (even although un-able to prove) that perfect competition would produce the outputs and prices associated with its so-called equilibrium position. But it is particularly interesting to note that the founding fathers of the doctrine —or at least Walras and Edgeworth—had their doubts; they were aware of the informational deficiencies of perfect competition and sought to offer some remedy. Both suggested hypothetical systems of recontracting designed to ensure that the plans of producers and con-sumers were welded into a consistent set. Offers to supply a particular good were made, it will be recalled, first on a provisional basis, and did not become firm commitments until, after repeated revisions, plans to buy were seen to be consistent with plans to produce and sell. We shall consider later the way in which these proposals prefigure the organized dialogues of indicative planning. The question now before us is whether such a network of forward contracts, quite apart from administrative cost and complexity, does in fact provide a theoretical answer to the problem of coordination that the price mechanism, in perfect competition, cannot by itself resolve. I maintain that it does not. The obstacle to creating a complete and consistent network of con-tracts, in the last analysis, is simply the imperfection of our knowledge. Consumers do not wish to contract for their future purchases because they cannot foretell what their future needs and opportunities will be; and producers do not generally wish to commit themselves to forward purchases of inputs because they cannot predict the productive possi-bilities that will be open to them. By supposing that the network of contracts could ever be complete and closed, we assume away that

essential imperfection of knowledge with which economic organization
has somehow to cope.

### III. *How Competitive Systems Work*

But where do we go from here? I have rejected the traditional model
of the working of a de-centralized economic system, perfect competition; the introduction of a complementary apparatus of forward
contracts, I have further argued, merely evades the problems created
by the imperfection of knowledge. But free enterprise systems, as even
their keenest critics would admit, do in fact work, at least imperfectly;
central planning might work better, but one could not maintain that
we have chaos without it. Let us therefore endeavour to set out how
the market system does work, for until this is clear we are not likely to
be able to judge how far, and in what ways, central planning can usefully supplement or replace it.

If we are to explain how the economic world goes round—at least,
the capitalist world—we have, I believe, to attend to three circumstances. First, there takes place within it a great deal of what, for want of
a better term, I shall call piecemeal planning. Secondly, much reliance
is put on the fact that aggregates are often more predictable than are,
on average, their several components. And thirdly, there have evolved
market structures and codes of business behaviour which facilitate
foresight and thereby permit enterprise planning. We shall now deal
with each of these circumstances in turn.

a) *Piecemeal Planning*

Walras taught us, in his general equilibrium analysis, that all economic activities are inter-dependent; but, although this inter-dependence
is universal, some activities are more inter-dependent than others.
Consider the relationship between intermediate and final output.
General purpose inputs, such as steel and fork-lift trucks, will normally
be bought on a market; the individual user will not choose to place
contracts much in advance of his future requirements, and the individual seller will hope to secure some stability and predictability in the
demand for his output by having a number of different accounts on his
books. But in the case of specific purpose inputs bought by only
one firm or very few firms, other arrangements will generally prevail.
Piecemeal planning will generally be the best means of dealing with
close complementarity, both quantitative and qualitative, between
output plans. It has to secure quantitative coordination, in the sense of
making the rate of output of a final good appropriate to the rate of output of the required inputs; thus refining capacity has to be in balance
with crude oil supplies. It has also to secure qualitative coordination
where, for example, the development of a nylon polymer has to be

hand in hand with the development of the processes used to spin it. Joint production planning and joint product development can be secured by a variety of techniques ranging from loose inter-company understanding to full vertical integration. A highly informal but highly effective form of piecemeal planning is conducted by Marks and Spencers. Although it concerns itself with the product development, the output and even the investment decisions of its suppliers, yet its relationship with them is based merely on mutual trust and goodwill. The operations of a major international oil company provide an example of extensive and highly developed piecemeal planning through vertical integration. The plain fact is that so-called market economies do not rely entirely on market mechanisms; their structure permits, and has in fact been adapted to permit, a great deal of piecemeal planning. It is in terms of the need for such planning, rather than in terms of conventional scale economies, that much industrial morphology has to be interpreted.

b) *The Law of Large Numbers*

But, if planning is all around us, it is far from complete. A great bulk of output, final and intermediate, is, as we say, for the market. Producers of intermediate goods commonly deal with a large number of buyers and the producers of consumer goods almost always do. In such cases, refuge from uncertainty is sought not in planning but in what has been called the unstrict law of large numbers. Brick manufacturers do not try to forecast the demand for bricks by adding up the several demands that the many builders and contractors with which they deal say are likely to put upon them. They study the trends in aggregates. They rely in the cancelling out of random elements to which the demands of individual customers are subject. Of course, we should not rush to the conclusion that for a firm of given size the larger the number of its independent accounts the better. In the first place, the gain from grouping does not rise in proportion to the number of accounts grouped but—if sampling theory can be followed in this context—to the square root of their number. And, secondly, the firm's forecasts will generally be part synthetic, part analytical; they will supplement the projection of aggregate trends with particular information about the likely demands of particular customers or groups of customers and the larger the number of accounts the greater the cost of acquiring this information is likely to be.

In her critique of French planning Mrs. Lutz[3] puts great stress on this unstrict law of large numbers and refers to a German school of writers who make it the corner-stone of their account of how foresight and coordination is made possible in market economies. Certainly the

[3] Vera Lutz, *Central Planning for the Market Economy* (London, 1969).

principle seems to me important, but I do not think that it can bear the full weight of explanation. It is certainly true that the aggregation of the component demands for a particular product makes for pre-dictability, but if this is to result in predictability in the demand for the output of particular firms, then the structure of the markets in which they are operating has to be appropriate. Here, it seems to me, is the third essential requirement for the working of de-centralized systems; market structure and business behaviour must be such as permit firms to plan current output and investment decisions; they must facilitate enterprise planning. Perhaps this too, like much else I have said, may seem obvious and certainly ought to be. In fact, however, the point is almost completely ignored in almost all the literature, and I have had very little success in drawing attention to it.

c) *Market Structures*

Let us suppose that we are asked not to explain how markets work but to design them. We may imagine that we have been invited to advise the government of an East European economy, currently organized by detailed central direction, on how best to introduce some de-centralized decision taking. Let us suppose that we are concerned with an industry (producing a homogeneous commodity) in which enterprises are to be given freedom of decision with respect both to current output and to investment. We are asked to design an appropri-ate market structure and prescribe the rules to which the enterprises are to be made subject. Those who really believed in this theory of perfect competition might recommend along these lines; set up as many independent enterprises as the relevant scale economies permit, give them equal access to finance, instruct them to seek maximum profits and forbid them to limit the competition in any way. If this recipe were adopted, its proponents would urge, we would get as close as possible to the ideal self-regulating system with prices constantly varying to ensure the optimal adjustment of supply to demand. Were these recommendations to be accepted, then the enterprise managers would, I fear, be in despair. Even if they could form a capable estimate of the likely total demand for the product, they would have no idea how much they each and individually ought to plan to produce. We must hope, therefore, that these recommendations would be rejected.

But what then ought we to recommend? We could of course suggest that the authorities divide up the market between the several enter-prises according to geographical area or some stated percentage share. This, at any rate, unlike the previous recommendation, could give to each enterprise something they could usefully try to predict; and the success or failure of their individual predictions would be made mani-fest. But most of the merits of decentralization would be lost; neither costs nor profits would be subject to competitive pressures, and it would be absurd not to arrange for the accidental surpluses that might develop in some part of the market to be used to offset scarcities in others. Let us then consider a further set of recommendations which, for ease of exposition, I shall put in somewhat simple-minded form. Let the price of the homogeneous commodity be fixed on the basis of some estimate of normal unit costs. Allot customers between the several enterprises in such a way that each of them has a regular supplier from whom he is normally obliged to buy. But lay it down that, should a buyer find his regular supplier unable to meet his full demands, then he will be transferred, in some pre-arranged fashion to an enterprise with additional supply available.

How would these arrangements work? First we note that each supplier has now something he can aim at. His first job is to predict the demand from his regular clientele and plan to meet it. He can do this without the fear that, if other suppliers over-produce, he will no longer have a profitable outlet for his goods. Secondly, we should note that each supplier has a strong incentive not to underestimate his regular demand, for, if he does so, he will lose custom on a quasi-permanent basis to those who have the capacity to meet demands in excess of those from their regular customers. Thirdly, suppliers have an incentive not to overestimate demand, for, if they do so, they themselves will bear the losses occasioned by excess capacity. And finally, suppliers have an incentive to consider whether their rivals are likely to have underestimated demand, for, if this is so, there is an opportunity to wrest custom from them.

A market of this type, it seems to me, would have clear advantages over the perfectly competitive, flexible price type of market that often represents the textbook ideal. Not only does it facilitate foresight; it ensures that errors of forecasting are borne by those who make them. In a flexible price system, the sins of the few may be borne by the many; for over-investment, by causing a collapse of prices, will penalize all suppliers.

It is not difficult to discern the strong family resemblance between these recommended arrangements and competitive markets that actually exist in the manufacturing sector of free enterprise economies. These markets, to use the Hicksian terminology, are normally of the fix-price rather than the flexible price variety; they are so usually because of oligopoly, sometimes because of inter-firm agreements, sometimes because of governmental controls. Firms do generally have regular clienteles, either because of transport costs, or product differentiation, or goodwill or for some other reason. If they cannot meet the demand of the regular customers, they lose them. If they install too much capacity, they suffer loss, but prices do not normally fall to the level of marginal costs. Of course, there is the danger, which engages the exclusive and almost obsessional attention of many economists, that prices may be kept too high in relation to unit costs. Inter-firm rivalry or the threat of entry may, and I am inclined to believe usually do, prevent this; but, if they do not, the public authorities can intervene.

But let us return to our hypothetical East European economy. The task given to us was that of designing a framework for workable competition in the supply of a homogeneous product. But it is natural to as, whether, in this context, the gains from decentralized decision taking are really worth while. It is true that we have introduced competition in forecasting, but it is arguable that a central bureau, by collating all the available evidence, might make a better forecast than could any individual enterprise. Might it not therefore be better to maintain centralized control, fix an industry output target and give to the enterprises individual output targets derived from it? After all, it would still be possible to stimulate competition in cost reduction simply by fixing a uniform price and rewarding enterprises with the highest profits.

It seems to me that, so long as we take the case of a homogeneous product, or near homogeneous product, the argument for decentralization is not strong. I for one would not wish to denationalize the coal mines. It is when we turn to the general case of product differentiation and, more especially, of continuous product development, that the merits of competition, of decentralized forecasting and investment decisions, come into their own. So long as there is uncertainty merely with regard to the future total demand for a homogeneous product then it seems not unreasonable to pool all the individual opinions and distil some kind of average view therefrom; central planning, in other words, may be appropriate. But, where there exists uncertainty in its more general form, I can see little merit and much danger in endeavouring to agree or impose some central view about what lines of development, in product or process, ought to be pursued or about what product varieties will best meet the needs of consumers. In considering how we might design a workable market structure, I took the case of a homogeneous product, for it is in that context that the forecasting problem, created by the inter-dependence of individual producers' plans, presents itself most sharply. I wished to show how it was possible to reconcile competition with the requirements for informed output planning even in this extreme case. But our imaginary East European reformers might have been better advised not to select homogeneous product markets as the first place in which to introduce decentralized decision taking. For not only do product differentiation and development make it more important to have competition, they make it possible to dispense with the special hypothetical arrangements according to which customers were allotted among suppliers. Provided that we have short-run price stability, as indeed we generally do in manufacturing business, then firms will generally be able to proceed from estimates of the total demand for their product class to estimates of the sales which they themselves will be able to make; but they will be obliged to recognize, in this general case, that they may lose custom not only if they are unable to supply but also if they cannot offer a price product combination as attractive as that offered by rivals.[4]

I set out, in this section of the paper, to say something about the way in which market economies cope with the problem of allocating resources under conditions of imperfect competition. Of course, this summary account is quite inadequate; nothing has been said, for example, about prices, but then their role in promoting efficient allocation is well known. My aim was to make these points; first, that critical inter-dependencies both quantitative and qualitative are dealt with by private, piecemeal planning; secondly, that in the absence of such deliberate coordination enterprise planning and prediction depends very largely on what has been called the unstrict law of large numbers; thirdly, that an essential condition for this prediction and planning is the existence of market structures and codes of business behaviour different from those to which economists usually give their warmest approval; and, fourthly, that the merits of competition are strongest where products are heterogeneous and subject to constant development.

## IV. *Indicative Planning*

It is perfectly apparent, from the preceding discussion, that planning and competition are in one sense compatible; they can and do co-exist peaceably, on the basis of a division of labour, within the same economy. But I maintained at the outset, nevertheless, that planning and competition were essentially alternative ways of organizing economic activity with different roles to play. For the remainder of this paper I wish to consider whether there is a kind of planning, indicative planning, which can be adopted in conjunction with competition to coordinate the same set of economic activities. Can indicative planning be used, not to replace decentralized decision taking, but to make it better informed?

Indicative planning, as practised in France and Britain, is a pro-

---

[4] How strange it is that economists have often set up, as a paradigm of decentralized decision taking, the hypothetical system—perfect competition—in which not only the workability but also the advantages of decentralization would be most in doubt.

cedure by which the government works out, after consultation with private industry, a set of more or less disaggregated output targets for the various commodity groups within the national product. These targets are said to be consistent and usually, in some sense or other, to be agreed; they do not correspond, however, to binding obligations imposed on individual firms. What can be said in the light of the analysis of this paper, about the logic and utility of these arrangements?

In terms of our analogy of the treasure hunt, indicative planning would correspond to an arrangement which brought the men together to compose a map but then left them free to seek their fortunes as they each saw fit. On the face of it, this would not appear to be a very effective procedure, for the searchers would have neither much incentive to disclose their true opinions about the location of the treasure nor any clear indication, once the map was constructed, of what they each and individually ought to do. Nevertheless, this combination of centralized forecasting and decentralized decision has sometimes been represented as the peculiar virtue of the system; the copious French literature on the subject abounds with references to the way in which indicative planning illuminates but does not dictate enterprise decisions, often moving on to references about the reconciliation of order with freedom, harmony with diversity, organization with initiative and so on and so forth, in a manner that seems to belie the reputation of the French language for clear and precise expression.

I recall reading that the origins of indicative planning might be sought in the work of Quesnay, whose Tableau Economique represents the earliest attempt in the field; be that as it may, it seems to me that, in so far as the logic of the process is concerned, Walras is the true forerunner. The process of consultation by which a set of consistent interrelated output plans is said to be built up under indicative planning reminds us forcibly of the hypothetical system of re-contracting, which both Walras and Edgeworth said could, theoretically, provide a direct route to equilibrium. If indicative planning is taken to be such a process, then the objections made against the Walrasian conception apply here also. Given that knowledge is imperfect, admitting of both uncertainty and difference of opinion, then individual expectations and plans cannot thus be knitted together into one single consistent set. It may indeed be that the remote origins of indicative planning, based as it is on a supposed consensus, ought to be sought not in Walras, nor even in Quesnay, but in Rousseau's influential if obscure notion of the General Will.

But perhaps the analogy with re-contracting should not be pushed thus far. In the first place, the output targets in the plan are not associated with contracts to buy or to deliver; they represent some agreed expectation about what future outputs are likely to be. Secondly, the disaggregation in the plan is not carried through right down to output targets for each individual firm's product lines; the figures relate to the outputs of branches or industries usually large and highly diversified. Given these qualifications, the logic of indicative planning is less easily assailed, if only, I fear, because it becomes more difficult to discover what it is.

The target output figures set out in the plan are normally obtained by a combination of two methods. One method is to estimate the future rate of growth of the national product and proceed from there to deduce the rate of growth of the component elements. Let us call this the analytical approach. The other method is to call for estimated output figures from industries; sometimes the firms or associations approached are asked to give two estimates, one corresponding to what they themselves expect to happen, the other to what they think would be appropriate to the particular rate of growth of output postulated in the plan. Let us call this the synthetic approach.

On the face of it, one might not wish to put much faith in industry output figures reached by the analytic method, if only for the reason that this method proceeds from what is more predictable, namely aggregates, to what is less predictable, namely components thereof. In so far as the larger sub-aggregates are concerned, such as consumption, investment, government expenditure and so on, the procedure makes some sense, if only because these totals are subject to governmental policy influence. But when we come to deduce industry outputs, far less the output of particular products, the approach becomes highly questionable. One reads not uncommonly that rates of output growth for individual products could be deduced from the rate of growth of national product, provided one could calculate the appropriate income elasticities of demand. If one conceives these in terms of the relationship between changes in aggregate output and particular outputs as manifested at the end of the planning period, ex post, then of course the statement is tautologous; but if income elasticities are taken to refer to the change in the demand for an individual product consequent on a certain change in national income other things being equal, then of course the statement is not true. Income changes represent only one of the many factors which influence the demand for particular products or product groups; they often appear more important than they are simply because we are working in terms of models which abstract from the elements of changing requirements, changing products, changing processes and costs and so on.

But let us wave aside these difficulties and suppose that industry output forecasts are produced and that, for the sake of argument, each and every firm becomes convinced that they are correct. What then? I cannot believe that an accurate forecast of the output of, say, the mechanical engineering industry, in the classification featured in the British Plan of 1965, would have been of much use to an individual manufacturer of compressors, or diesel engines, or cranes, or pumps. No doubt forecasts would be somewhat more useful if they were further disaggregated, but even a forecast for cranes as such would not much help the individual manufacturer to estimate the demand for his particular type of dockyard crane, or steel-works crane, or moving overhead crane, diesel-powered crane, small electric crane and so on. And there is the further crucial point that, the more detailed the disaggregation, the less credible the analytic procedure becomes.

But forecasts, it may be said, are also synthetic. In general, moreover, they are agreed with the industries concerned. This latter claim, in my own experience, does not amount to much. The large firms or trade associations consulted are usually prepared to agree to a very wide range of industry output forecasts, not merely because they wish to please, but simply because the relationship between the likely size of the future output of their own product and the size of the so-called industry output figure is so very tenuous. The remedy then lies, it may be urged, in further and further disaggregation, down, if necessary, to the level of the outputs of each individual firm. But here we go out by the door through which we came. If indicative planning is taken to mean the knitting together of each and every output plan, then it does indeed come close to the Walrasian conception of a complete network of forward contracts. It presumes a consensus that simply does not exist, for no amount of organized dialogue, it seems to me, can hope to weld the expectations of each and every entrepreneur into a consistent plan.

If this analysis is correct, then there exists no coherent logical basis even in a closed economy for indicative planning; whether the process yields indirect benefits, such as creating confidence and inducing managements to look ahead, is a matter I do not propose to discuss. My own view is that the government should not attempt to set detailed output targets in the manner of the French and British plans, but there is good reason why it should endeavour to estimate the growth of total output and to influence the way in which it divides between investment, exports, government expenditure and the like. And I believe that the publication of its opinions and intentions on these matters will be of some use to some firms. It is evident, moreover, that governments will be much concerned with piecemeal planning; they will engage in it directly within the public sector or in partnership with the private sector and they may wish to supervise or even to stimulate the arrangements made by private firms. For many it seems natural that all the islands of piecemeal planning should gradually come together, that the sea of market relations should recede and that which was an archipelago become a continent. I believe that this is a mistaken view. My argument has been that there are sub-sets of economic activities so rigidly related that it is desirable to plan their coordination on the basis of some consensus of expectation and belief. Equally, there are wider areas within which the inter-dependence of individual activities is much looser; decentralized decision taking, coordinated through the market, is here appropriate. Rather than endeavour to impose a consensus, it is better to let individual decisions be taken on the basis of a variety of opinions as to what an uncertain future may hold in store.

*St. John's College, Oxford*

# [10]

## THE ORGANISATION OF INDUSTRY[1]

### I

I WAS once in the habit of telling pupils that firms might be envisaged as islands of planned co-ordination in a sea of market relations. This now seems to me a highly misleading account of the way in which industry is in fact organised. The underlying idea, of course, was of the existence of two ways in which economic activity could be co-ordinated, the one, conscious planning, holding sway within firms, the other, the price mechanism, operating spontaneously on the relations between firms and between firms and their customers. The theory of the firm, I argued, had as its central core an elaboration of the logic of this conscious planning; the theory of markets analysed the working of the price mechanism under a variety of alternative structural arrangements.

I imagine that this account of things might be acceptable, as a harmless first approximation, to a large number of economists. And yet there are two aspects of it that should trouble us. In the first place it raises a question, properly central to any theory of economic organisation, which it does not answer; and, secondly, it ignores the existence of a whole species of industrial activity which, on the face of it, is relevant to the manner in which co-ordination is achieved. Let us deal with each of these matters in turn.

Our simple picture of the capitalist economy was in terms of a division of labour between the firm and the market, between co-ordination that is planned and co-ordination that is spontaneous. But what then is the principle of this division? What kinds of co-ordination have to be secured through conscious direction within firms and what can be left to the working of the invisible hand? One might reasonably maintain that this was a key question—perhaps the key question—in the theory of industrial organisation, the most important matter that the Divine Maker of market economies on the first day of creation would have to decide. And yet, as I hope soon to show, it is a matter upon which our standard theories, which merely assume but do not explain a division between firm and market, throw little light.

Let me now turn to the species of industrial activity that our simple story, based as it is on a dichotomy between firm and market, leaves out of account. What I have in mind is the dense network of co-operation and affiliation by which firms are inter-related. Our theoretical firms are indeed islands, being characteristically well-defined autonomous units buying and selling at arms' length in markets. Such co-operation as takes place between them is normally studied as a manifestation of the desire to restrict competition and features in chapters about price agreements and market sharing.

[1] I am grateful to Mr. J. F. Wright, Mr. L. Hannah and Mr. J. A. Kay, each of whom gave helpful comments on a draft of this article.

But if the student closes his textbook and takes up a business history, or the financial pages of a newspaper, or a report of the Monopolies Commission, he will be presented with a very different picture.   Firm A, he may find, is a joint subsidiary of firms B and C, has technical agreements with D and E, sub-contracts work to F, is in marketing association with G—and so on. So complex and ramified are these arrangements, indeed, that the skills of a genealogist rather than an economist might often seem appropriate for their disentanglement.[1] But does all this matter?   Theories necessarily abstract and it is always easy to point to things they leave out of account.   I hope to show that the excluded phenomena in this case are of importance and that by looking at industrial reality in terms of a sharp dichotomy between firm and market we obtain a distorted view of how the system works.   Before doing so, however, I wish to dwell a little longer on the several forms that co-operation and affiliation may take; although the arrangements to be described are no doubt well known to the reader, explicit mention may never-theless help to draw attention to their variety and extent.

## II

Perhaps the simplest form of inter-firm co-operation is that of a trading relationship between two or more parties which is stable enough to make demand expectations more reliable and thereby to facilitate production planning.   The relationship may acquire its stability merely from goodwill or from more formal arrangements such as long-term contracts or share-holding.   Thus, for example, the Metal Box Company used to obtain a discount from its tin plate suppliers in return for undertaking to buy a certain proportion of its requirements from them, and the same company owned 25% of the share capital of the firm supplying it with paints and lacquers.   In the same way Imperial Tobacco owned shares in British Sidac, which made cellophane wrapping, and in Bunzl, which supplied filter tips. Occasionally shareholdings of this kind may be simply investments held for their direct financial yield, but more generally they give stability to relation-ships through which the activities of the parties are co-ordinated both quanti-

---

[1] The sceptical reader might care to look up a few cases in the reports of the Monopolies Com-mission.   The following example is found in the report on cigarette filter tips.   Cigarette Com-ponents Ltd. made filter tips for Imperial Tobacco and Gallaher using machines hired from these companies.   It has foreign subsidiaries, some wholly and some partially owned.   It was both licensee and licensor of various patents one of which was held by the Celfil Trust, registered in Liechtenstein, with regard to the ultimate control of which Cigarette Components told the Mono-polies Commission they could only surmise.   Nevertheless, this patent was of key importance in that the Celfil licensees, of which Cigarette Components was only one, were bound by price and market sharing arrangement.   Cigarette Components was itself owned by Bunzl Ltd., in which Imperial Tobacco had a small shareholding.   The raw material for the tips is cellulose acetate tow which was made by Ectona Fibres Ltd., a company in which Bunzl had a 40% interest and a subsidiary of Eastman Kodak 60%.   Agreements had been made providing that, should Bunzl lose control of Cigarette Components, then Eastman could buy out their shares in Ectona . . . etc., etc.

tatively and qualitatively. Not only is it made easier to adjust the quantity of, say, lacquer to the quantity of cans which it is used to coat but the specification and development of the lacquers can be made appropriate to the use to be made of them. And in the synthetic fibre industry likewise, linkages between firms at the various stages—polymer manufacture, yarn spinning and finishing, textile weaving—help bring about the co-ordinated development of products and processes. The habit of working with models which assume a fixed list of goods may have the unfortunate result of causing us to think of co-ordination merely in terms of the balancing of quantities of inputs and outputs and thus leave the need for qualitative co-ordination out of account.

Co-operation may frequently take place within the framework provided by sub-contracting. An indication of the importance of this arrangement is provided by the fact that about a quarter of the output of the Swedish engineering industry is made up of sub-contracted components, while for Japan the corresponding figure is about a third and in that country's automobile industry almost a half. Sub-contracting on an international basis, moreover, is said to be becoming more widespread and now a dense network of arrangements links the industries of different countries.[1] Now the fact that work has been sub-contracted does not by itself imply the existence of much co-operation between the parties to the arrangement. The plumbing work on a building contract may be sub-contracted on the basis of competitive tenders for the individual job. Frequently, however, the relationship between the parties acquires a degree of stability which is important for two reasons. It is necessary, in the first place, to induce sub-contractors to assume the risks inherent in a rather narrow specialisation in skills and equipment; and, secondly, it permits continuing co-operation between those concerned in the development of specifications, processes and designs.

Co-operation also takes place between firms that rely on each other for manufacture or marketing and its fullest manifestation is perhaps to be found in the operations of companies such as Marks and Spencer and British Home Stores. Nominally, these firms would be classified as retail chains, but in reality they are the engineers or architects of complex and extended patterns of co-ordinated activity. Not only do Marks and Spencer tell their suppliers how much they wish to buy from them, and thus promote a quantitative adjustment of supply to demand, they concern themselves equally with the specification and development of both processes and products. They decide, for example, the design of a garment, specify the cloth to be used and control the processes even to laying down the types of needles to be used in knitting and sewing. In the same way they co-operate with Ranks and Spillers in order to work out the best kind of flour for their cakes and do not neglect to specify the number of cherries and walnuts to go into them.

[1] See the *Economic Bulletin for Europe*, Vol. 21, No. 1.

Marks and Spencer have laboratories in which, for example, there is development work on uses of nylon, polyester and acrylic fibres. Yet all this orchestration of development, manufacture and marketing takes place without any shareholding by Marks and Spencer in its suppliers and without even long-term contracts.

Mention should be made, finally, of co-operative arrangements specifically contrived to pool or to transfer technology. Surely the field of technical agreements between enterprises is one of the under-developed areas of economics. These agreements are commonly based on the licensing or pooling of patents but they provide in a quite general manner for the provision or exchange of know-how through the transfer of information, drawings, tools and personnel. At the same time they are often associated with the acceptance by the parties to them of a variety of restrictions on their commercial freedom—that is to say with price agreements, market sharing and the like.

This brief description of the varieties of inter-firm co-operation purports to do no more than exemplify the phenomenon. But how is such co-operation to be defined? And how in particular are we to distinguish between co-operation on the one hand and market transactions on the other? The essence of co-operative arrangements such as those we have reviewed would seem to be the fact that the parties to them accept some degree of obligation— and therefore give some degree of assurance—with respect to their future conduct. But there is certainly room for infinite variation in the scope of such assurances and in the degree of formality with which they are expressed. The blanket manufacturer who takes a large order from Marks and Spencer commits himself by taking the appropriate investment and organisational decisions; and he does so in the expectation that this company will continue to put business in his way. In this instance, the purchasing company gives no formal assurance but its past behaviour provides suppliers with reason to expect that they can normally rely on getting further orders on acceptable terms. The qualification " normally " is, of course, important, and the supplier is aware that the continuation of orders is conditional on a sustained demand for blankets, satisfaction with the quality of his manufacture and so on. In a case such as this any formal specification of the terms and conditions of the assurance given by the supplier would scarcely be practicable and the function of goodwill and reputation is to render it unnecessary.

Where buyer and seller accept no obligation with respect to their future conduct, however loose and implicit the obligation might be, then co-operation does not take place and we can refer to a pure market transaction. Here there is no continuing association, no give and take, but an isolated act of purchase and sale such, for example, as takes place on an organised market for financial securities. The pure market transaction is therefore a limiting case, the ingredient of co-operation being very commonly present, in some degree, in the relationship between buyer and seller. Thus although

I shall have occasion to refer to co-operation and market transactions as distinct and alternative modes of co-ordinating economic activity, we must not imagine that reality exhibits a sharp line of distinction; what confronts us is a continuum passing from transactions, such as those on organised commodity markets, where the co-operative element is minimal, through intermediate areas in which there are linkages of traditional connection and goodwill, and finally to those complex and inter-locking clusters, groups and alliances which represent co-operation fully and formally developed. And just as the presence of co-operation is a matter of degree, so also is the sovereignty that any nominally independent firm is able to exercise on a *de facto* basis, for the substance of autonomy may often have been given up to a customer or a licensor. A good alliance, Bismarck affirmed, should have a horse and a rider, and, whether or not one agrees with him, there is little doubt that in the relations between firms as well as nation states, the condition is often met.

## III

It is time to revert to the main line of our argument. I had suggested that theories of the firm and of markets normally provide no explanation of the principle of the division of labour between firms and markets and of the roles within a capitalist economy of planned and spontaneous co-ordination. And I also maintained that these theories did not account for the existence of inter-firm co-operation and affiliation. It is upon the first of these two deficiencies that I now wish to concentrate.

Probably the simplest answer to the question as to the division of labour between firm and market would be to say that firms make products and market forces determine how much of each product is made. But such an answer is quite useless. If " products " are thought of as items of final expenditure such as cars or socks, then it is clear that very many different firms are concerned with the various stages of their production, not only in the sense that firms buy in components and semi-manufactures from other firms but also in that there may be a separation of manufacture and marketing (as in the case of Marks and Spencer and its suppliers) or of development and manufacture (as in the case of licensors and licencees). If, alternatively, we simply define " products " as what firms do, then the statement that firms make products is a tautology which, however convenient, cannot be the basis of any account of the division of labour between firm and market.

It is worth observing that we learn nothing about this division of labour from the formal theory of the firm. And this is perhaps not surprising as the theory, in its bare bones, is little more than an application of the logic of choice to a particular set of problems. It may be that the theory indeed makes it more difficult to answer our question in that, in order the better to exhibit this logic of choice, it is formulated on the assumption of " given production functions " which represent the maximum output obtainable from different input combinations. However useful this representation of productive possibilities, it leaves one important class of ingredients out of account. It abstracts totally from the roles of organisation, knowledge, experience and skills, and thereby makes it the more difficult to bring these back into the theoretical foreground in the way needed to construct a theory of industrial organisation. Of course I realise that production functions presume a certain level of managerial and material technology. The point is not that production is thus dependent on the state of the arts but that it has to be undertaken (as Mrs. Penrose has so very well explained)[1] by human organisations embodying specifically appropriate experience and skill. It is this circumstance that formal production theory tends to put out of focus, and justifiably, no doubt, given the character of the optimisation problems that it is designed to handle; nevertheless, it seems to me that we cannot hope to construct an adequate theory of industrial organisation and in particular to answer our question about the division of labour between firm and market, unless the elements of organisation, knowledge, experience and skills are brought back to the foreground of our vision.

It is convenient to think of industry as carrying out an indefinitely large number of *activities*, activities related to the discovery and estimation of future wants, to research, development and design, to the execution and co-ordination of processes of physical transformation, the marketing of goods and so on. And we have to recognise that these activities have to be carried out by organisations with appropriate *capabilities*, or, in other words, with appropriate knowledge, experience and skills. The capability of an organisation may depend upon command of some particular material technology, such as cellulose chemistry, electronics or civil engineering, or may derive from skills in marketing or knowledge of and reputation in a particular market. Activities which require the same capability for their undertaking I shall call *similar activities*. The notion of capability is no doubt somewhat vague, but no more so perhaps than that of, say, liquidity and, I believe, no less useful. What concerns us here is the fact that organisations will tend to specialise in activities for which their capabilities offer some comparative advantage; these activities will, in other words, generally be similar in the sense in which I have defined the term although they may nevertheless lead the firm into a variety of markets and a variety of product lines. Under capitalism, this degree of specialisation will come about through competition but it seems to me likely to be adopted under any alternative system for reasons of manifest convenience. Mrs. Penrose has provided us with excellent accounts of how companies grow in directions set by their capabilities and how these capabilities themselves slowly expand and alter.[2] Dupont, for example, moved from a basis in nitro-cellulose

[1] E. T. Penrose, *The Theory of the Growth of the Firm* (Oxford University Press, 1959).
[2] E. T. Penrose, *ibid.*

explosives to cellulose lacquers, artificial leather, plastics, rayon and cellophane and from a basis in coal tar dyestuffs into a wide range of synthetic organic chemicals, nylon and synthetic rubber.  Similarly, Marks and Spencer, having acquired marketing and organisational techniques in relation to clothing were led to apply them to foodstuffs.

There is therefore a strong tendency for the activities grouped within a firm to be similar, but this need not always be so.  In the history of any business random factors will have left an influence, and the incentive to take up a particular activity will sometimes be provided, not by the prior possession of an appropriate capability, but by the opportunity of a cheap acquisition, through a family or business connection or because of management's belief that the profitability of investment in some direction was being generally under-estimated.  There is no need to deny, moreover, that a variety of potential gains are provided by grouping activities irrespective of their character; risks can be spread, the general managerial capability of the firm can be kept fully employed and the allocation of finance can be planned from the centre.  None of this is in contradiction with the principle that it will pay most firms for most of the time to expand into areas of activity for which their particular capabilities lend them comparative advantage.  A firm's activities may also, on occasions, be more similar than they superficially appear.  If a firm acquired companies irrespective of the character of their activities we should term it conglomerate; but if the motive for the purchases were the belief that the companies were being badly managed, the hope being to restore them to health before re-selling them at a profit, the management would be exercising a particular capability.

## IV

I have argued that organisations tend to specialise in activities which, in our special sense of the term, are similar.  But the organisation of industry has also to adapt itself to the fact that activities may be *complementary*.  I shall say that activities are complementary when they represent different phases of a process of production and require in some way or another to be co-ordinated.  But it is important that this notion of complementarity be understood to describe, for instance, not only the relationship between the manufacture of cars and their components, but also the relationship of each of these to the corresponding activities of research and development and of marketing.  Now it is clear that similarity and complementarity, as I have defined them, are quite distinct; clutch linings are complementary to clutches and to cars but, in that they are best made by firms with a capability in asbestos fabrication, they are similar to drain-pipes and heat-proof suits.  Similarly, the production of porcelain insulators is complementary to that of electrical switchgear but similar to other ceramic manufacture.  And while the activity of retailing toothbrushes is complementary to their manufacture, it is similar to the activity of retailing soap. This notion of complementarity will require closer definition at a later stage, but it will be convenient first to introduce one further (and final) set of conceptual distinctions.

It is clear that complementary activities have to be co-ordinated both quantitatively and qualitatively. Polymer production has to be matched, for example, with spinning capacity, both in terms of output volume and product characteristics, and investment in heavy electrical equipment has likewise to be appropriate, in scale and type, to the planned construction of power stations. Now this co-ordination can be effected in three ways; by *direction*, by *co-operation* or through *market transactions*. Direction is employed when the activities are subject to a single control and fitted into one coherent plan. Thus where activities are to be co-ordinated by direction it is appropriate that they be *consolidated* in the sense of being undertaken jointly by one organisation. Co-ordination is achieved through co-operation when two or more independent organisations agree to match their related plans in advance. The institutional counterparts to this form of co-ordination are the complex patterns of co-operation and affiliation which theoretical formulations too often tend to ignore. And, finally, co-ordination may come about spontaneously through market transactions, without benefit of either direction or co-operation or indeed any purposeful intent, as an indirect consequence of successive interacting decisions taken in response to changing profit opportunities. Let us now make use of this somewhat crude categorisation to re-interpret the questions with which we started.

## V

What is the appropriate division of labour, we should now ask, between consolidation, co-operation and market transactions?

If we were able to assume that the scale on which an activity was undertaken did not affect its efficiency, and further that no special capabilities were ever required by the firm undertaking it, then there would be no limit to the extent to which co-ordination could be affected by direction within one organisation. If production could be set up according to " given " production functions with constant returns, no firm need ever buy from, or sell to, or co-operate with any other. Each of them would merely buy inputs, such as land and labour, and sell directly to consumers—which, indeed, is what in our model-building they are very often assumed to do. But, of course, activities do exhibit scale economies and do require specialised organisational capabilities for their undertaking, the result being that self-sufficiency of this kind is unattainable. The scope for co-ordination by direction within firms is narrowly circumscribed, in other words, by the existence of scale economies and the fact that complementary activities need not be similar. The larger the organisation the greater the number of capabilities with which one may conceive it to be endowed and the greater the number of complementary activities that can, in principle, be made subject to co-ordination through direction; but even if a national economy were to be run as a single business, it would prove expedient to trade with the rest of the world. Some co-ordination, that is to say, must be left either to co-operation or to market transactions and it is to the respective roles of each of these that our attention must now turn.

Building and brick-making are dissimilar activities and each is undertaken by large numbers of enterprises. Ideally, the output of bricks ought to be matched to the volume of complementary construction that makes use of them and it is through market transactions that we expect this to come about. Brickmakers, in taking investment and output decisions, estimate future market trends; and errors in these estimates are registered in stock movements and price changes which can lead to corrective actions. As we all know, these adjustments may work imperfectly and I have myself argued elsewhere [1] that the model which we often use to represent this type of market is unsatisfactory. But this is a matter with which we cannot now concern ourselves. What is important, for our present purposes, is to note that impersonal co-ordination through market forces is relied upon where there is reason to expect aggregate demands to be more stable (and hence predictable) than their component elements. If co-ordination were to be sought through co-operation, then individual brick-makers would seek to match their investment and output plans *ex ante* with individual builders. Broadly speaking, this does not happen, although traditional links between buyers and sellers, such as are found in most markets, do introduce an element of this kind. Individual brick manufacturers rely, for the most part, on having enough customers to ensure some cancelling out of random fluctuations in their several demands. And where sales to final consumers are concerned, this reliance on the law of large numbers becomes all but universal. Thus we rely on markets when there is no attempt to match complementary activities *ex ante* by deliberately co-ordinating the corresponding plans; salvation is then sought, not through reciprocal undertakings, but on that stability with which aggregates, by the law of large numbers, are providentially endowed.

Let us now consider the need to co-ordinate the production of cans with tin plate or lacquers, of a particular car with a particular brake and a particular brake lining, of a type of glucose with the particular beer in which it is to be used, or a cigarette with the appropriate filter tip. Here we require to match not the aggregate output of a general-purpose input with the aggregate output for which it is needed, but of particular activities which, for want of a better word, we might call *closely complementary*. The co-ordination, both quantitative and qualitative, needed in these cases requires the co-operation of those concerned; and it is for this reason that

[1] In *Information and Investment* (Oxford University Press, 1961).

the motor car companies are in intimate association with component makers, that Metal Box interests itself in its lacquer suppliers, Imperial Tobacco with Bunzl and so on.   Co-ordination in these cases has to be promoted either through the consolidation of the activities within organisations with the necessary spread of capabilities, or through close co-operation, or by means of institutional arrangements which, by virtue of limited shareholdings and other forms of affiliation, come somewhere in between.

Here then we have the prime reason for the existence of the complex networks of co-operation and association the existence of which we noted earlier.   They exist because of the need to co-ordinate closely complementary but dissimilar activities.   This co-ordination cannot be left entirely to direction within firms because the activities are dissimilar, and cannot be left to market forces in that it requires not the balancing of the aggregate supply of something with the aggregate demand for it but rather the matching, both qualitative and quantitative, of individual enterprise plans.

## VI

It is perhaps easiest to envisage co-ordination in terms of the matching, in quantity and specification, of intermediate output with final output, but I have chosen to refer to activities rather than goods in order to show that the scope is wider.   The co-operation between Marks and Spencer and its suppliers is based most obviously on a division of labour between production and marketing; but we have seen that it amounts to much more than this in that Marks and Spencer performs a variety of services in the field of product development, product specification and process control that may be beyond the capability of the supplying firms.   And one may observe that inter-firm co-operation is concerned very often with the transfer, exchange or pooling of technology.   Thus a sub-contractor commonly complements his own capabilities with assistance and advice from the firm he supplies. New products also frequently require the co-operation of firms with different capabilities, and it was for this reason that I.C.I. originally co-operated with Courtaulds in the development of nylon spinning and now co-operates with British Sidac in developing polypropylene film.

It is indeed appropriate to observe that the organisation of industry has to adapt itself to the need for co-ordination of a rather special kind, for co-ordination, that is to say, between the development of technology and its exploitation.   A full analysis of this important subject cannot be attempted here but it is relevant to consider those aspects of it that relate to our principal themes.   What then are the respective roles, in relation to this kind of co-ordination, of direction, co-operation and market transactions? Obviously there are reasons why it may be convenient to co-ordinate the activities of development and manufacture through their consolidation within a single organisation.   Manufacturing activity is technology-producing as well as technology-dependent; in the process of building aircraft or turbo-alternators difficulties are encountered and overcome and the stock of knowledge and experience is thereby increased. But there are also good reasons why a firm might not be content to seek the full exploitation of its development work through its own manufacturing activity. The company that develops a new product may itself lack sufficient capacity to manufacture it on the scale needed to meet the demand and may not have time enough to build up the required additional organisation and material facilities. It could, of course, seek to acquire appropriate capacity by buying firms that already possessed it, but this policy might prove unattractive if it entailed taking over all the other interests to which these firms were committed. The innovating firm might judge that its comparative advantage lay in developing new products and be reluctant therefore to employ its best managerial talents in increasing the output of old ones. It would be aware, moreover, that not only manufacturing but marketing capability would be needed and might properly consider that it neither possessed nor could readily acquire this, especially in foreign countries. All these considerations may lead firms to seek some indirect exploitation of a product development. And, in the case of the new process, the incentive might be even stronger in that there might be a wide variety of fields of production in which the process could be used.

The indirect exploitation of new technology could be sought, in terms of our nomenclature, either through market transactions or through co-operation with other firms. But technology is a very special commodity and the market for it a very special market. It is not always easy, in the first place, to stop knowledge becoming a free good. The required scarcity may have to be created artificially through a legal device, the patent system, which establishes exclusive rights in the use or the disposal of new knowledge. Markets may then develop in licences of right. But these are very special markets in that the commercial freedom of those operating within them is necessarily restricted. For suppose that A were to sell to B for a fixed sum a licence to make a new product, but at the same time retained the unfettered right to continue to produce and sell the product himself. In this case the long- and short-run marginal costs of production of the good would, for both parties, be below unit costs (because of the fixed cost incurred by A in the development work and by B as a lump sum paid for the licence) so that unrestrained competition would drive prices to unremunerative levels. It might at first seem that this danger could be avoided if licences were charged for as a royalty on sales, which, unlike a fixed sum, would enter into variable costs. But the licensee might still require assurance that the licensor, unburdened by this cost element, would not subsequently set a price disadvantageous to him or even license to others on more favourable terms. These dangers could be avoided if the parties were to bind themselves by price or market-sharing agreements or simply by the prudent adoption of the policy of live and let live.    But, in one way or another, it seems likely that competition would in some degree have been diminished.[1]

It would appear, therefore, on the basis of these considerations, that where the creation and exploitation of technology is co-ordinated through market transactions—transactions in licences—there will already be some measure of co-operation between the parties.    The co-operation may, of course, amount to little more than is required not to rock, or at any rate not to sink, the boat.    But there are reasons why it will generally go beyond this.

---

[1] Professor Arrow reaches a different conclusion.  The matter is considered in his article " Economic Welfare and the Allocation of Resources for Invention " published in *The Rate and Direction of Inventive Activity*, (edited by National Bureau of Economic Research, Princeton University Press, 1962).   Professor Arrow maintains that " an incentive to invent can exist even under perfect competition in the product markets though not, of course, in the ' market ' for the information containing the invention " and that " provided only that suitable royalty payments can be demanded, an inventor can profit without disturbing the competitive nature of the industry."

The issue is simplest in the case of a cost-saving invention.   Professor Arrow considers a product made under constant costs both before and after the invention and shows how the inventor can charge a royalty that makes it just worth while for firms making the product to acquire a licence. On the face of it one might then conclude that the licensor would have no need to bind himself not to reduce price below the level that provided licensees with a normal profit or to re-license for a lesser royalty, for, if he were to do either of these things, existing licensees would make losses, stop producing and therefore discontinue royalty payments.   But this conclusion is valid only under the highly special assumption of there being no fixed costs.   For firms will in general continue in production so long as price does not fall below variable costs.   Thus the licensor could find it in his interest, having sold as many licences as he could at the higher royalty, to license others at a lower royalty, or to enter the market himself.   He would thus extend the market for the product and increase his earnings provided, of course, that price were kept above variable costs and therefore high enough to induce the original (and by then no doubt aggrieved) licensees to stay in business.   It is true, of course, that *in the long run* fixed plant would wear out and firms deprived of their quasi-rents would cease producing, but the fact that an opportunity for exploitation is merely temporary does not warrant our assuming that it will not be seized.   In general the licensor would stand to gain by " cheating " the licensees in the manner described and the latter would therefore want some measure of assurance (which need not be formal) that he would not do so.   There would be a market for licences, that is to say, only if the commercial freedom of the licensor were in this way reduced.

It may be that Professor Arrow would not consider this to represent a significant restriction of competition; and indeed the important practical issue concerns the manner and degree in which the parties accept limitations on their freedom of action.   I have suggested that the licensor would be in a position, having licensed other firms, subsequently to deprive them of expected profits.   A firm will therefore seek a licence only if it believes that this will not happen, but it may consider that sufficient assurance is provided by the fact that the licensor, in his own long-run interest, will not wish to acquire the reputation for such sharp practice.   Much the same situation obtains in the context of the relationship between a large purchaser and a small supplier.   Marks and Spencer, having offered attractive enough terms to induce the blanket manufacturer to devote a large proportion of his capacity to meet its needs, might subsequently press for a price reduction that left him with a poor return.   The hapless supplier, in the short run at any rate, might have no option but to give way.   But although the purchaser could thus act, it could scarcely be in his own long-run interest to acquire the reputation for doing so.

The upshot would therefore seem to be this.   A market for licences can function only if the parties to the transactions accept some restraints, but, in certain circumstances, no more restraint might be required than enlightened self-interest could be depended upon by itself to ensure.   In practice, of course, licensing arrangements are commonly associated with much more—and often more formal—restraint of trade, the extent of which may or may not be greater than is necessary for the transfer of technology to take place.

Technology cannot always be transferred simply by selling the right to use a process.  It is rarely reducible to mere information to be passed on but consists also of experience and skills.  In terms of Professor Ryle's celebrated distinction, much of it is " knowledge how " rather than " knowledge that." Thus when one firm agrees to provide technology to another it will, in the general case, supply not only licences but also continuing technical assistance, drawings, designs and tools.  At this stage the relation between the firms becomes clearly co-operative and although, at its inception, there may be a giver and a receiver, subsequent development may lead to a more equal exchange of assistance and the pooling of patents.  Arrangements of this kind form an important part of the networks of co-operation and affiliation to which I have made such frequent reference.

## VII

This article began by referring to a vision of the economy in which firms featured as islands of planned co-ordination in a sea of market relations. The deficiencies of this representation of things will by now be clear.  Firms are not islands but are linked together in patterns of co-operation and affiliation.  Planned co-ordination does not stop at the frontiers of the individual firm but can be effected through co-operation between firms.  The dichotomy between firm and market, between directed and spontaneous co-ordination, is misleading; it ignores the institutional fact of inter-firm co-operation and assumes away the distinct method of co-ordination that this can provide.

The analysis I presented made use of the notion of activities, these being understood to denote not only manufacturing processes but to relate equally to research, development and marketing.  We noted that activities had to be undertaken by organisations with appropriate capabilities.  Activities that made demands on the same capabilities were said to be similar;  those that had to be matched, in level or specification, were said to be complementary.  Firms would find it expedient, for the most part, to concentrate on similar activities.  Where activities were both similar and complementary they could be co-ordinated by direction within an individual business.  Generally, however, this would not be the case and the activities to be co-ordinated, being dissimilar, would be the responsibility of different firms.  Co-ordination would then have to be brought about either through co-operation, firms agreeing to match their plans *ex ante*, or through the processes of adjustment set in train by the market mechanism.  And the circumstances appropriate to each of these alternatives were briefly discussed.

Let me end with two further observations.  I have sought to stress the co-operative element in business relations but by no means take the view that where there is co-operation, competition is no more. Marks and Spencer can drop a supplier; a sub-contractor can seek another principal; technical agreements have a stated term and the conditions on which they may be re-negotiated will depend on how the strengths of the parties change and develop; the licensee of today may become (as the Americans have found in Japan) the competitor of tomorrow.   Firms form partners for the dance but, when the music stops, they can change them.   In these circumstances competition is still at work even if it has changed its mode of operation.

Theories of industrial organisation, it seems to me, should not try to do too much.   Arguments designed to prove the inevitability of this or that particular form of organisation are hard to reconcile, not only with the differences between the capitalist and socialist worlds, but also with the differences that exist within each of these.   We do not find the same organisation of industry in Jugoslavia and the Soviet Union, or in the United States and Japan.   We ought to think in terms of the substitutability of industrial structures in the same way as Professor Gerschenkron has suggested in relation to the prerequisites for economic development.   It will be clear, in some situations, that co-ordination has to be accomplished by direction, by co-operation or through market transactions, but there will be many others in which the choice will be difficult but not very important.   In Great Britain, for example, the artificial textile industry is vertically integrated and the manufacturers maintain that this facilitates co-ordination of production and development.   In the United States, on the other hand, anti-trust legislation has checked vertical integration, but the same co-ordination is achieved through close co-operation between individual firms at each stage. It is important, moreover, not to draw too sharp lines of distinction between the techniques of co-ordination themselves.   Co-operation may come close to direction when one of the parties is clearly predominant; and some degree of *ex ante* matching of plans is to be found in all markets in which firms place orders in advance.   This points, however, not to the invalidity of our triple distinction but merely to the need to apply it with discretion.[1]

G. B. RICHARDSON

*St. John's College,*
   *Oxford.*

[1] In his article, " The Nature of the Firm," *Economica*, 1937, pp. 386–405, R. H. Coase explains the boundary between firm and market in terms of the relative cost, at the margin, of the kinds of co-ordination they respectively provide.   The explanation that I have provided is not inconsistent with his but might be taken as giving content to the notion of this relative cost by specifying the factors that affect it.   My own approach differs also in that I distinguish explicitly between inter-firm co-operation and market transactions as modes of co-ordination.

# [11]

# Adam Smith on Competition and Increasing Returns

## G. B. RICHARDSON*

ADAM Smith regarded competition as both a desirable and a natural state of affairs. Despite what he considered to be 'the mean rapacity, the monopolising spirit of merchants and manufacturers', he took the view that neither monopoly nor restrictive agreements would prove effective unless given state backing such as might be afforded, for example, by legal incorporation. In this connection he observes, 'In a free trade an effectual combination cannot be established but by the unanimous consent of every single trader and it cannot last longer than every single trader continues of the same mind. The majority of a corporation can enact a by-law with proper penalties which will limit competition more effectually and more durably than any voluntary combination whatever'. It would seem therefore that Smith did not wish the state to adopt an active anti-trust policy; it was necessary only that it should not support the restriction of competition save in exceptional cases, such as the granting of a patent on a new machine, a royalty to an author, or exclusive rights to merchants who 'undertake, at their own risk and expense, to establish a new trade with some remote and barbarous nation'.[1]

Smith's view of competition, in so far as public policy is concerned, can thus be stated quite succinctly. Needless to say, he is writing about the conditions of his time and it is idle to ask whether he would have approved of international commodity agreements or the co-ordination of investments in steel-making capacity. It is more rewarding to examine, as we shall now do, the theoretical arguments upon which his case for free competition is based.

Let us observe at the outset that competition features within *The Wealth of Nations* in two distinct contexts; first, in the account given of the balancing of supply and demand in particular markets, and, secondly, in

---

* Fellow of St. John's College, Oxford.
[1] It is interesting to note that Smith associates the 'wretched spirit of monopoly' chiefly with businessmen. 'Landlords, farmers and labourers', he says, 'have commonly neither inclination nor fitness to enter into combinations' but are persuaded 'by the clamour and sophistry of merchants and manufacturers' to tolerate combination between those who buy their labour or sell them goods (*The Wealth of Nations*, ed. Cannan (1930), I.x.c.25).

the explanation of structural and technological development. Smith offers us in effect both a theory of economic equilibrium and a theory of economic evolution; and in each of these competition has a key role to play. Within *The Wealth of Nations* no obvious tension exists between the two theories, partly no doubt because they are sketched out in a manner loose enough to make it difficult to establish inconsistency. Later writers, however, in striving for greater analytical rigour, developed the theory of equilibrium in terms of a model of reality that is clearly very different indeed from that implicit in Smith's theory of evolution. The question of compatibility between Smith's two lines of thought—or at any rate between the ways in which they have since been extended—thus now poses itself more sharply. Before turning to examine it, however, let us recall what Smith had to say.

We find in *The Wealth of Nations* an account of the balancing function of competitive markets that clearly anticipates our modern doctrine. The essence of it is contained in the Chapter entitled 'Of the Natural and Market Price of Commodities' which describes how actual prices tend to gravitate to their 'natural' or cost-determined levels. Competition is shown to be necessary to this process, it being pointed out that monopoly, by raising prices and reducing supply, would 'derange more or less the natural distribution of the stock of society'. Smith therefore both identifies the tendency towards equilibrium and implies (albeit imprecisely) that the allocation of resources thereby produced is optimal from society's point of view. It may therefore seem reasonable to regard later theories of competitive equilibrium as providing a formalization of Smith's vision with its several deficiencies made good. In this way, intellectual continuity seems to be preserved; what Smith could see in a glass, darkly, it took Walras, with his more refined technique, to bring fully into light. But this view of the matter seems to be mistaken. It appears plausible only so long as Smith's theory of economic evolution is left wholly out of account.[2]

Whereas Smith's theory of equilibrium is set out in Chapter VII of the first book of *The Wealth of Nations*, his view of economic evolution is expounded even earlier, in the opening three chapters. He there discusses the division of labour and what he has to say about it has become so familiar that one might expect all the implications long since to have been drawn. Perhaps therefore we need only remind ourselves that Smith is advancing here a disequilibrium theory in the sense that he views the economy as in a state of constant and internally generated change. Perpetual motion results from the fact that the division of labour is at once a cause and an effect of economic progress. In Chapter I we are told how the division of labour

---

[2] This paper was already in draft before the publication of Professor Kaldor's article 'The Irrelevance of Equilibrium Economics' in the *Economic Journal*, lxxxii (Dec. 1972) and I did not try to adapt it to take account of what he said. The arguments I put forward here are similar in important respects to those of Professor Kaldor.

increases wealth and in Chapter III how a widening of the market, which increased wealth would bring about, enables the division of labour to be carried further forward. 'That the division of labour is limited by the extent of the market—the title of this latter chapter—is a principle the full range and force of which may have been partially concealed by the fact that Smith discusses market extension in terms of transport improvement. Writing in the second half of the eighteenth century, it was natural for him to stress this aspect of the matter; but unless one recognizes that the extent of the market also depends on wealth, which is in turn created by the division of labour, the dynamic character of the interaction may not fully be realized. Yet what we have here are the essentials of a theory of self-sustaining economic growth, essentials that were to be more fully developed much later in Allyn Young's justly celebrated article entitled 'Increasing Returns and Economic Progress'.[3]

Let us recall two of Smith's observations. He points out that the division of labour, where expanding markets permit, leads to the establishment of new trades. Thus in the Highlands of Scotland, 'every farmer must be butcher, baker and brewer for his own family' whereas in towns these trades acquire separate identities (WN I.iii.2). Smith also implies that technological change is partly endogenous; it is the division of labour, by enabling men to concentrate on particular operations, that leads to improvement in machinery and technique. Smith recognized, however, that although 'many improvements have been made by the ingenuity of the maker of the machines, when to make them became the business of a particular trade', yet others were made by 'those whose trade it is not to do anything but to observe everything; and who, upon that account, are often capable of combining together the powers of the most distinct and dissimilar objects'. We are also told that speculation is itself promoted by the division of labour, it being 'sub-divided into a great number of different branches, each of which affords occupation to a particular tribe or class of philosophers' (WN I.i.9).[4]

Smith therefore provides an account of the process of innovation, sketched out in a couple of paragraphs, that is strikingly close to modern formulations. What is lacking, I suppose, is explicit analysis of innovation in terms of an investment decision in which costs are set against prospective receipts, the magnitude of which is dependent on the demand for the relevant commodity and thereby on the size of the market within which it sells. But this is a matter of presentation; what concerns us now is to note that technological progress for Smith is not an extraneous circumstance affecting economic growth but integral to his theory of economic develop-

[3] *Economic Journal*, xxxviii (Dec. 1928).
[4] Development of Smith's ideas and empirical support for them is to be found in J. Schmookler, *Invention and Economic Growth* (1966).

ment. Fundamental technical advance is not in fact needed to drive Smith's engine of economic growth: it is necessary only that the growth of output should bring into being new activities and processes which would have been introduced earlier had markets been larger and which, once introduced, bring about a further augmentation of output. Smith, however, did not choose to separate the further exploitation of technology from its improvement; for although the two things are conceptually distinct, he realized (as the inventors of 'learning by doing' have since rediscovered) that the one leads to the other.

In *The Wealth of Nations*, therefore, competition is given more to do than equate demands and supplies within the context of a given industrial structure and a given technology; the invisible hand has also to adapt both structure and technology to the fresh opportunities created by expanding markets. In our modern micro-economic theory, on the other hand, it is the equilibrating and allocative functions of competition that obtain all but exclusive attention; technical progress is made exogenous and structural evolution largely ignored. The theorist has come to attend to the things he can most easily handle and in this way our perception of reality has adapted to the development of our mental machinery. Marshall, it must be said, stands apart; unwilling to push aside the analytically inconvenient, and fully aware of Smith's two lines of thought, he reminded us that 'economic problems are imperfectly presented when they are treated as problems of statical equilibrium and not of organic growth'. Indeed he went so far as to say that the limitations of equilibrium theory 'are so constantly overlooked, especially by those who approach it from an abstract point of view, that there is a danger in throwing it into definite form at all' (*Principles of Economics* (8th ed. 1930), 461). Later economists have had fewer inhibitions.

In order to present our equilibrium analysis we now normally take a particular organization of industry as given; and that normally presumed, perfect competition, might reasonably be regarded as a denial of Smith's central principle erected into a system of political economy. For whereas for Smith the division of labour was at any point of time limited by the extent of the market, under perfect competition all the gains from the division of labour are assumed already to have been exhausted. Should the demand for a good rise then, under perfect competition, supply will increase through the entry of more firms into the industry; in the new equilibrium there will be more producers of this good and fewer of others, the structure of industry remaining otherwise unaltered. The price of the good will either stay the same or, if higher rewards have to be paid to attract additional factors, it will rise. Smith presumed, on the other hand, that a sustained increase in the demand for a good would generally permit a realization of hitherto unexploited scale economies and thereby lower its price. Thus he explicitly states that an increase in demand 'though in the beginning it may sometimes raise the price of goods, never fails to lower it in the long run. It encourages production, and thereby increases the competition of the producers, who, in order to undersell one another, have recourse to new divisions of labour and new improvements of art, which might never otherwise have been thought of' (WN V.i.e.25).

It is therefore abundantly clear that Smith had a conception of the working of the economic system very different from that implicit in the formal models employed by modern equilibrium analysis. He appears to have held that the economies of scale and specialization were never exhausted in that an extension of the market would always permit a finer division of labour and a consequent reduction in costs. In this sense, his theory of economic evolution presumes the general prevalence of increasing returns. Nowadays, on the other hand, economists employ a model—perfect competition—which postulates universally diminishing returns to scale, it being presumed that increasing returns must tend to concentration and eventual monopoly. Whether increasing returns can be reconciled with competitive conditions is, it need scarcely be said, a much discussed (and perhaps as yet unsettled) question. Let us now consider it once again in the light of Smith's account of structural evolution.

Adam Smith did not appear himself to be in the least troubled by the thought that competition and increasing returns might not be able to coexist; it was competition indeed that provided the force that drove merchants and manufacturers to seek out, develop, and exploit the inexhaustible opportunities provided by the economies of scale and specialization. It may therefore be that incompatibility between competition and increasing returns is made to appear ineluctable to the modern theorist by the nature of the model of economic reality in terms of which he habitually thinks. We typically start with a fixed list or set of products. A firm employs factors of production to make one of these products and we consider how unit costs vary with the scale of the operation. Increasing returns are said to prevail so long as the firm can increase the output of the product, given time for adjustment, with a less than proportionate increase in total cost. If we then consider a group of firms making identical products for the same market, then it is clear that, so long as any of them experiences increasing returns, competition must produce concentration and, in the end, monopoly.

Let us note first that this conclusion is altered if we relax one of the simplifications of the model and assume that firms are no longer compelled to make one specified good out of the fixed list but can differentiate their product to meet the demands of some particular group of customers. In this situation, as Chamberlin showed, an equilibrium can be reached where each producer operates under increasing returns, with marginal cost below average cost, but is nevertheless subject to competition from rivals offering

### Adam Smith on Competition and Increasing Returns      355

goods similar but not identical to his own. And the same situation is to be found where each producer has a limited regional market but is in active competition with others on its frontier. To this extent at any rate there is agreement that competition can coexist with increasing returns.

Chamberlin's theory of monopolistic competition does presume an inter-firm division of labour the extent of which is limited by the size of the market; to that extent it corresponds much more closely to Smith's vision than does the perfectly competitive model. Nevertheless, it retains a static character foreign to Smith; preferences and production possibilities are given and the equilibrium appropriate to them represents a configuration of production that will remain the same so long as they do not change. We can come closer to Smith's thinking—and closer also to economic reality—by departing more radically from the framework of assumption underlying our standard competitive models. Chamberlin in effect abandoned the assumption that final output consisted of a fixed list of goods and allowed firms by means of product differentiation to practise a horizontal division of labour. Let us now consider the implications of giving firms the freedom to practise a vertical division of labour by assuming—what is in fact the case—that the production of any one commodity is undertaken not by any one firm but by very many firms each of which specializes in a particular phase or stage of the process. It will for this purpose be convenient to regard firms as undertaking *activities* rather than making and selling pro-ducts, these activities having to do with the discovery and estimation of future wants, with research, development, and design, with the execution and co-ordination of processes of physical transformation, with the marketing of goods, and so on.[5] We must then recognize that activities have to be carried out by organizations with appropriate *capabilities*, that is to say with appropriate knowledge, experience, and skills. The capability of an organization may derive, for example, from command of some techno-logy, such as electronics, or some technique of marketing. Activities that require the same capability for their undertaking I shall call *similar* activities. Where activities represent different phases of a process of pro-duction that have in one way or another to be co-ordinated, I shall call them *complementary*. An example may make the use of these terms clearer. Clutch linings are complementary to clutches and to cars but, in that they are made by firms with a capability in asbestos fabrication, they are similar to drain-pipes and heat-proof suits.

Let us now make use of these notions to re-examine the relationship between competition and increasing returns. Whereas previously we assumed a number of competing firms to be making the same product, we must now envisage them as undertaking the same set of activities. If of

[5] The following analysis of production in terms of activities is set out more fully in my article 'The Organisation of Industry', *Economic Journal*, lxxxii (1972).

course these activities are strictly inseparable, in the sense that the firm has no option save to expand or contract the complete set, then the situation is as it was; increasing returns, if they operate, will apply to the scale of the complete set and concentration remains inevitable so long as the competitors are selling in the same market. But strict inseparability will be unusual; firms will normally be able to expand or acquire some activities and to contract or abandon others. The activities within the set, moreover, may each individually exhibit increasing returns (though in different degrees), and although complementary, they will in general not be similar. Given these conditions, firms will usually seek a selective rather than a uniform expansion, tending to specialize in a more closely similar group of activities and coming to rely, to an increasing extent, on sales to or purchases from other businesses. Whether or not increasing returns operate with respect to the activity set as a whole may therefore be irrelevant; it will not shape the developing industrial structure so long as firms can find it appropriate to expand selectively the activities in which, relative to competitors, they have a comparative advantage.

As a general rule, therefore, increasing returns would lead to specialization and interdependence rather than to straightforward concentration. But for this to happen, as Smith pointed out, the market has to be large enough. Specialization may offer significant advantages only if accompanied by investment in appropriate equipment (which may have a minimum economic scale) and given the sustained attention of a technical and managerial team. The market for a firm seeking to specialize in a particular activity will be provided by firms which originally undertook it themselves but gave it up (and therewith any attendant advantages from self-sufficiency) when an outside supplier offered a sufficient cost saving. Some of these firms may be in the same industry as the company now embarked on specialization, but others may operate in widely different fields. In examining the relationship between competition and increasing returns we first focused on a single group of competitors and the changes that would be produced within it, but these changes will interact with structural changes in industry generally so that the extent of the division of labour, as Smith said, will depend upon the size of the market as a whole.

Structural mutation of this kind is described by Smith in terms of characteristically simple examples. At one stage of a country's economic growth, the market may be large enough to support the trade of a carpenter, but only as markets further expand would this trade come to be further differentiated into those of joiner, cabinet-maker, wheelwright, ploughwright, cart-maker, and the like. That the same tendency is still at work is evidenced by the emergence of the many component makers supplying the automobile industry or by the fact that management can now turn to an increasingly wide range of consultants specializing not only in such broad fields as business organization, advertising, and market research, but also in particular technologies such as lighting, ventilation, or paper-making. But it is perhaps important to keep in mind that increasing returns *need* not produce vertical disintegration any more than they *need* produce straightforward market concentration. There may be important technical advantages in undertaking linked activities in the same place; thus the manufacture of glucose is conveniently carried out in conjunction with the wet milling of starch and paper-making in conjunction with the production of wood pulp. The consolidation of complementary activities within a single enterprise will in any case enable their co-ordination to be planned in respect of both quantities and specifications. What we must not forget are the strong forces that pull the other way, forces owing their existence both to the fact that complementary activities are in general dissimilar and to the fact that each of them may individually offer increasing returns to scale. And where these forces come to dominate, the co-ordination of complementary activities will be secured, not through administration within a firm, but through the market mechanism or by co-operation between firms. It should not be imagined, however, that this outcome need favour small-scale enterprise. Having developed a particular capability, a firm will seek to exploit it through expansion into similar activities. Thus Dupont could move from a base in nitro-cellulose explosives into cellulose lacquers, plastics, rayon, and cellophane; and Marks and Spencers, having acquired marketing and organizational techniques in relation to clothing, were led to apply them to food. In this manner, firms may become very large and concentration may rise in relation to the economy as a whole even although it remains unchanged in relation to particular markets.

I have suggested that increasing returns may lead not to market con-centration but to specialization and interdependence. But is it not the case, one might argue, that the tendency to monopoly will in the long run again reassert itself, if not in relation to complete sets of activities, then in relation to the component activities themselves? Will we not find, at the end of the road, precisely that state of monopolistic competition described by Chamberlin, the only difference being that differentiation takes place in the vertical as well as the horizontal dimension?

One answer to this question, and the most fundamental, is that the end of the road may never be reached. And this indeed is the implication of Smith's evolutionary theory. For just as one set of activities was separable into a number of components, so may each of these in turn become the field for a further division of labour. Any movement to concentration and monopoly, in respect of any one activity, may therefore be set aside in the same way as was the tendency towards monopolization of the set from which it came. Whether monopoly does in fact result is of course partly a matter of words; the smaller the degree of differentiation we make the ground for recognizing a distinct activity, the greater will be the apparent prevalence of monopoly but the keener the competition to which monopolists are subject. But monopoly power is likely to be weakened not only by the presence of substitutes and the threat of entry as ordinarily understood. Established positions are constantly under pressure not merely because of autonomous changes in taste and technique but also by virtue of the fact that at any point of time there will exist unexploited opportunities for the division of labour and the consequent regrouping of activities. For according to Smith's theory of economic development, industrial structures will be in constant need of adaptation; the very process of adaptation, by increasing productivity and therefore market size, ensures that the adaptation is no longer appropriate to the opportunities it has itself created.[6]

Increasing returns, it has been argued, may lead firms to expand selectively into similar activities rather than to push for ever larger market shares. The logic of this strategy is further strengthened, moreover, when we turn from the side of costs to that of demand. It may be easier to outflank a competitor than to take him head on, and easier to expand into new markets than painfully to edge competitors out of old ones. By the time that a firm has gained a substantial share in one market, it may be time to start looking for others; nothing stands still and there is little point in finally gaining a monopoly when demand for the product starts to turn down. With the benefit of hindsight, one may wonder whether Kreuger's famous attempt to establish a world match monopoly made much financial sense.

We have been considering whether monopoly would necessarily be produced (as our equilibrium theory might make us suppose) by increasing returns. It may be instructive, in conclusion, to ask why monopoly should not emerge in any case simply because firms choose to come together. On the face of it, they would gain from doing so. Even if the merger of all the firms in an industry was expected to leave total profits no higher than before, at least the firms would be relieved of uncertainty about the likely size of their share. And if there were any scale economies unexploited, any scope for rationalization of production or of distribution or any possibility of monopolistic exaction, then profits could be increased and everyone made better off than they would have been in competitive conditions.

---

[6] Such a theory of unending development might seem to be implied by what Smith has to say about widening markets, technical progress, and the division of labour. Nevertheless, in WN I.ix he envisages a country 'which had acquired that full complement of riches which the nature of its soil and climate, and its situation with respect to other countries, allowed it to acquire'. And in such a country 'which could therefore advance no further', 'both the wages of labour and the profits of stock would probably be very low'. It is perhaps not easy to reconcile these pessimistic prognostications with Smith's stress on the prevalence of increasing returns (at any rate in manufacturing) and with the fact that technical progress is mainly endogenous to his system. The reader seeking an explanation of these matters is recommended to consult the article by Mr. Eltis, entitled 'Adam Smith's Theory of Economic Growth', which is contained in this volume.

Certainly, therefore, there are forces that put firms together; what are the forces that keep them apart?

Adam Smith thought of competition in terms of activity rather than structure and refers, characteristically, to 'a competition' taking place between suppliers.[7] By concentrating on numbers, cross elasticities, and the like, it is easy for us to lose sight of essential characteristics of business competition, characteristics that it shares with competition in the boxing ring or the race track. Surely it is of the essence of competition that the participants hold uncertain and divergent beliefs about their chances of success; yet, despite this, theorists commonly choose to couple competition with the assumption of perfect foresight. As a result, a false assessment may be made of the circumstances upon which the preservation of competition are likely to depend. Let us suppose that a number of rival firms are aware that, should they combine, their aggregate profits would be enhanced. An appropriate sharing of these monopoly profits would therefore make it possible for each firm to be made better off than it would have been had competition continued. On the face of it combination would seem, to the outsider, to be the rational course to adopt. But it would not in fact be adopted unless each firm considered that its share of the joint profits would be greater than the profits *that it itself believed it could earn* in the competitive struggle. If the firms hold sanguine—and conflicting—views about their prospects, this condition might well not be fulfilled both because the expected monopoly profits were not high enough and because agreement might not be reached about their division. Joint profit maximization appears to be the inevitable outcome of oligopoly only when we fail to recognize that rivals will in general hold inconsistent views of their competitive chances. Vanity, pride, pugnacity, nationalism, and the spirit of adventure also work to prevent competitors from coming to terms, but the more fundamental obstacle is surely that division and uncertainty of belief which, however difficult to accommodate within our theoretical schema, is likely to prove an enduring feature of the real world.

Whether the obstacles to combination are sufficient to check the forces

---

[7] Professor Kornai, in his book *Anti-Equilibrium* (1971), 392–5, argues that genuine competition takes place within a market only in conditions of 'pressure' or 'suction', that is, approximately, of excess supply or excess demand. Given excess supply, sellers are compelled to endeavour to wrest custom from each other; given excess demand, buyers are caught up in the same kind of struggle. 'The concept of competitive equilibrium', he maintains, is therefore 'a complete paradox'.

Adam Smith, it is interesting to observe, appears to have taken the same view, in observing that: 'When the quantity of any commodity which is brought to the market falls short of the effectual demand, all those who are willing to pay the whole of the rent, wages and profit, which must be paid in order to bring it thither, cannot be supplied with the quantity they want. Rather than want it altogether, some of them will be willing to give more. A competition will immediately begin among them, and the market price will rise more or less above the natural price . . .' (WN I.vii.9). Thus Smith seems to imply that competitive activity is taking place only when the equilibrium of a market is disturbed.

working towards it will depend of course on the particular circumstances of time and place. It seems to me that governments may have a more positive part to play here than Smith, writing two centuries ago, seemed disposed to allow them; perhaps even nowadays, however, there is some substance in his view—at any rate if we think in terms of the world market as a whole—that competition is the natural state of affairs. Adam Smith was no model-builder; less than most economists does he seem to make some things clearer by bundling others out of sight. But although his focus may lack sharpness, it was unusually wide.

# [12]

# Competition, innovation and increasing returns

I shall be concerned, in this article, with the way in which competition operates when there is a high rate of innovation and when production is subject to increasing returns. These two circumstances, as one might expect, are frequently found together; a high rate of innovation, as with pharmaceuticals and software, frequently entails heavy costs of development or design, which are independent of the subsequent volume of output. These cases are important, and perhaps increasingly so; nevertheless, much of the analysis will apply also to industries where scale economies arise, not from high original or 'set-up' costs, but from other factors.

No one can reasonably doubt the pervasiveness, in industry generally, of increasing returns. Adam Smith was certainly aware of it when he said that the division of labour is limited by the extent of the market, having observed that, where the scale of an economic activity increases, it will become practicable for component processes within it to be separated out. In general, the cost savings made available by an increase in the scale of a particular economic activity do not manifest themselves uniformly in all its stages and, as a result, an increase in demand may lead, not to an increase in the size of the enterprise undertaking the activity, nor to an increase in the number of such enterprises, but to a change in industrial structure, those stages exhibiting the greatest scale economies becoming the business of specialist suppliers. Smith went so far as to make the interrelationship between the division of labour and the extent of the market the premise upon which to base what we would now call a theory of self-sustaining economic growth, of growth associated with a continuous mutation in the structure of industry; increasing output both permitting, and being promoted by, the specialization needed to realize scale economies.

It is worth observing that, for this reason, Smith's vision of the working of a market economy is quite profoundly different from that embodied in the formal models, based on universally decreasing returns to scale, that may appear to be in the line of descent. Economists, since the neo-classical development of their subject, have been inclined to regard the phenomenon of increasing returns, whatever its importance in practice, as analytically inconvenient. They saw that, if perfect competition were to be preserved, each firm must experience rising marginal costs while its output is still small relative to that of the whole industry. And, for it to be making a profit, marginal cost must be not less than average cost. Given these conditions, average cost cannot be falling with output, or, in other words, increasing returns cannot obtain.

It appeared, therefore, that if the growth of the firm was not to be checked by rising costs, it had to be checked by falling demand. A firm enjoying increasing returns could be in equilibrium, that is to say, only if it were faced by a sloping demand curve, with marginal revenue less than price. [1] Only by sacrificing the assumption of perfect competition was it possible, it seemed, for a firm experiencing increasing returns to be in profitable equilibrium.

In this connection, John Hicks (1946) famously expressed the view that 'a general abandonment of the assumption of perfect competition ... must have very destructive consequences for economic theory'. He thought it 'only possible to save something from this wreck - and it must be remembered that the threatened wreckage is that of the greater part of general equilibrium theory - if we can assume that the markets confronting most of the firms with which we shall be dealing do not differ very greatly from perfectly competitive markets'.[1] This was the course which he himself followed, and most economists, implicitly or explicitly, have done likewise.

Chamberlin (1962) chose another path, ensuring the compatibility of competition and increasing returns by allowing each firm to have a monopoly of its own product, that product however being in competition with close substitutes. He then proceeded to show that firms in this situation, given sufficient pressure from the closely competing substitutes, would, in equilibrium, earn only the normal level of profits associated with competitive markets, the difference being that price would be equal to unit cost while unit cost was still falling with output.[2]

Chamberlin certainly provided us with an account of competitive markets more realistic than that offered by the theory of perfect competition. It was, however, more in harmony with an earlier tradition. The differentiation of activity it postulates is none other than a division of labour as practised among firms, the scope for which, according to Smith, was limited only by the extent of the market. In this respect Chamberlin's model differs radically from that of perfect competition, which, by requiring many firms to be engaged on identical activities, is in effect a denial of Smith's principle. But although Chamberlin allies himself with Smith in this respect, yet he places himself within the neo-classical tradition by virtue of his commitment to traditional equilibrium analysis. So long as we focus upon the properties of static equilibria, product differentiation is required if competition is to be compatible with increasing returns. I shall hope to show that, if we consider instead the processes of change themselves, it becomes apparent that there are other circumstances able to ensure this result.

In the competitive equilibrium envisaged in models of both perfect and monopolistic competition, the marginal revenue from the sale of a product is equal to the marginal cost of its production, and its price is equal to average cost. In the perfect competition equilibrium, average cost is at a minimum, whereas in monopolistic competition it is above this level. In both cases, rates of [2] output are being equated to rates of demand, on the assumption that both will be maintained indefinitely.

That this steady state assumption is highly unrealistic need hardly be said. Many, if not most products are launched in the expectation that they will have a limited life, either because they are superseded by superior products, or simply because they go out of fashion. Durable goods, in particular, may be expected to have a particular pattern of sale, first rising as the demand for them builds up, and then, at best, falling to replacement level only. A software developer, for example, will certainly not think in terms of adjusting the rate of sales of a product to some hypothetical, constant and continuing rate of demand. He will think instead of the total quantity of sales that can be achieved before a new, superior product comes to dislodge his own; indeed, he may be already planning to bring out such a product, in order to forestall others from doing so. There will be no place in his thinking for cost and demand curves of the kind featuring in the models of competition we have been considering.

It is necessary to recognize the analytical limitations of demand and cost curves as we normally employ them. Implicit in their use is the assumption that the demand and cost conditions which they graphically represent are independent of each other, which is the case, however, only so long as the steady state is assumed, only so long, that is to say, as the postulated rates of demand can be assumed to persist indefinitely. On this assumption, the depreciation allowances that enter into costs will depend only on the physical life of the fixed equipment; although even here realism would make this itself dependent on rates of utilization. Once we allow the demand for a good to be limited in time, depreciation allowances may depend not on the physical durability of fixed equipment but on the period for which it will be required. The average cost of the product will, where this is so, depend on the total sales realized during its lifetime.

These circumstances lead us to envisage the coexistence of increasing returns with competition of a rather special kind. This may be made more readily apparent if we imagine a rather extreme and improbable situation in which one seller gains a total, but temporary, monopoly of a product. In the absence of any close substitutes, it might at first appear that the supplier would be able to earn a super-normal, mono-poly profit. But this need not be so, as it is possible for a new product to come to replace the established one after an interval sufficiently short to permit the latter to yield only a normal profit. The price of the product would then, in the event, equal its average cost, in that total sales revenue equalled total costs incurred; if we wish to imagine this outcome to have been foreseeable, we can think of the fixed costs of the product being written off through depreciation allowances that are based on a correct estimate of the duration of the demand for it. [3]

We should not think, moreover, that such an outcome could occur only by chance. If we assume free competition, this would be the outcome generally to be expected. Investment in the industry, in freely competitive conditions, should tend towards the level at which, on average, products earned only normal profits, allowing for risk. But we have to think of the tendency to normal profits as arising, in the case we are considering, not through competitive investment which increases the supply of a product to match demand for it, but through competitive investment which displaces the existing product by an improved one. We have to think of investment, not in productive capacity, but in product development. For an entrepreneur engaged in the activities needed to identify, develop and test a product able to displace the incumbent one, the expectation of profit will depend on the perception of the chances of effecting this displacement, and on how long it seems possible to hold the position gained.

It is surely desirable for us to accept, in our formal theorizing, that, in modern economies at least, by far the most important mode of competition is that based on development and innovation, whether in product or process. We concentrate too much, I believe, on monopoly revenue being obtained by the restriction of supply, and as threatened by entrants who might increase that supply. With that approach, it is natural for us to ask, for example, whether scale economies represent a barrier to entry, in that an entrant would have to produce, in order to achieve a competitive cost level, a volume of output which, if added to the industry's current output, would cause the market to be over-supplied. I do not doubt that considerations of this kind have some role to play, but it is much more common for firms to be challenged, not head on, but by those with something new to offer. It is for this reason, I suspect, that businessmen feel the world they live in to be much more competitive than economists appear to think it is, and for this reason that the industrial landscape can change so much in so short a time. David Audretsch (1995)[3] has shown just how great this change has been and how rapidly it appears to be accelerating. It took two decades for a third of the Fortune 500 to be replaced between 1950 and 1970, only one decade for a third to be replaced between 1970 and 1980 and only five years for a third to be replaced between 1980 and 1985. Equally striking has been the way in which a number of the most famous corporate giants, such as IBM, US Steel, RCA and Wang have lost, in his words, 'their aura of invincibility', while new firms have emerged and risen to prominence.

I have chosen initially to postulate a highly unrealistic and limiting form of competition (which one might think of as sequential rather than concurrent), a form of competition which operates only through innovation, one particular product being assumed to obtain a total but temporary monopoly of its product class until a new product replaces it. Only by undertaking this replacement itself could the producing firm maintain its hold on the market, and even in these [4] circumstances, the threat of competition, if strong enough, could oblige that firm to incur development expenses at a level which left it with only normal profits. I chose this case in order to show that competition, normal profits and increasing returns, could in this way all be compatible, even without assuming, as did Chamberlin, the simultaneous coexistence of a group of close substitutes. Chamberlin's competing monopolist occupies a niche in (economic) space, whereas we have been considering the possibility of occupying a niche in time. Reality exhibits something of both modes of competition, but conforms to neither. And it is worthwhile examining why.

In the special case of purely 'sequential' competition which I chose to consider, one product was imagined to enjoy a total monopoly in the market for its product class until displaced by another. This is, however, clearly unrealistic in that although a new product may be superior to an old one in all respects, the process of replacement would very rarely be immediate. We cannot legitimately proceed from the assumption that the new product is uniformly superior to the conclusion that it will be immediately, and by everyone, so perceived. Only too often analytical confusion results from implicitly assuming that what the model builder postulates to be objectively the case is believed to be the case by the economic agents within the model. What these agents do will depend on their subjective perceptions of reality, and where a new product is concerned its properties will generally become manifest only after time and trial.

The marketing of a new product will therefore take time, and, of course, money. As demand for it builds up, productive capacity will have to be enlarged. Computer software presents an interesting and limiting case in which the sales that can be realized (in this case of licences) are not subject to this capacity limitation, which is one reason, but not the only reason, why software products can sometimes very rapidly gain or lose market share. In general, however, manufactured products will gain market share only gradually, as their merits become apparent and as the capacity to produce them is built up. During this period, rival offerings will still be on the market, and their life may be prolonged somewhat by price reductions that go some way to offset their disadvantages. Meanwhile, a new product, ready to challenge the one gaining ground, will be under development.

For these reasons, and despite increasing returns, one would expect several products to be selling at the same time, and not merely because differentiation gave to each of them its own group of loyal consumers. A plurality of products could remain in competition, even if they were objectively homogeneous. The configuration obtaining would not however be an equilibrium of the kind associated with Chamberlin's monopolistic competition. In that model, as in the perfectly competitive one, several producers will continue to compete in the market place, so long as demand and cost conditions do not change. In the case that I have been discussing, a plurality of producers obtains precisely because these conditions are in constant flux. [5]

Given free competition there is likely to exist, in this case, a tendency towards what we may call a *dynamic equilibrium*, a tendency, that is to say, for the rate of investment in product development to rise or fall towards the level at which this investment yields only a normal return. The qualification *dynamic* may serve to remind us that, in the situation we are describing, competition causes the profits of firms within an industry to tend towards a normal level, albeit with a great dispersion about the mean, not by the usual adaptation of supply to demand, but through variations in the rate of innovative activity.

Dynamic equilibrium, for the reasons I have given, is consistent with the coexistence of a number of competing firms, all of them supplying, in conditions of increasing return, products for the same general market. In reality of course, a market typically supports several firms because they are differentiated as well as because of what, for want of a better term, we might call the life-cycle effect that results from continuous development. One should not imagine that the coexistence of several firms, when it depends on the latter effect, and does not therefore constitute static equilibrium of the kind associated with the theories of either perfect or monopolistic competition, is for that reason somehow necessarily impermanent. The conditions favouring this coexistence – scope for innovation, uncertainty as to the properties of new products, the time taken to market a product and to build up the capacity to produce it – are unlikely themselves to be transitory.

The perfect competition model, it has frequently been observed, offers a paradox, in that it represents markets as tending towards a condition, the static equilibrium condition, from which the very activities which, in ordinary usage, represent competition are necessarily absent. In equilibrium, producers, as well as consumers, are mere price takers, unable, *ex hypothesi*, to improve their existing products or offer new ones. Competition is seen as reaching its apotheosis, one might almost say, when it all but ceases to exist. The maintenance of a plurality of firms in dynamic equilibrium, by contrast, depends on continuously active competition in all its dimensions.

But might it not be argued that the simultaneous coexistence in this way of a number of competing, objectively homogeneous offerings, each produced under increasing returns, depends not on the intensity of competition, but on its imperfection? Without imperfect knowledge, all demand would switch to the best product within the particular market, and without imperfect mobility of resources, the supply of that product would appropriately respond. There would exist only one producer of each product variety, as in the equilibrium associated with monopolistic competition.

On the face of it, this logic may seem convincing. If everyone always knew everything, and if processes were timeless, continuing competition of the kind I have described would indeed not [6] exist, but neither of course would any economic order that we can possibly imagine. Any model based on the assumption that perfect knowledge and perfect resource mobility universally prevail is objectionable, not because it is obviously unrealistic, but because it would be impossible. An economy in which these conditions obtain obviously does not exist, and, less obviously, could not do so. Where the actions of economic agents are interdependent, it is illogical to assume that each one of them is free to do whatever he or she likes without constraint, while at the same time having perfect knowledge of what all the others will do.[4]

We must now consider whether a state of dynamic equilibrium would require there to be imperfection of a different kind, imperfection in the sense of the restraint in price competition characteristic of oligopoly. It has, after all, long been accepted that several competing goods, each being produced under increasing returns, might coexist on the market place provided the firms making them were to exercise this restraint. In the situation hypothesized, each producer assumes that his rivals would match any reduction in his price, thus denying him any increase in market share. His sales would therefore increase only in accordance with the elasticity of demand for the product as a whole, rather than the elasticity of demand for his particular offering, if measured on the assumption that the prices of the competing products remained unchanged. In these circumstances, producers might not reduce price; several firms would stay in business, despite the fact that they were each experiencing increasing returns.

Behaviour of this sort may be responsible for the survival of a number of competing firms each making the same product under increasing returns, but it is by no means a necessary condition. In any case, a firm has reasons not to avoid price reductions other than the likelihood that competitors will match them. It was noted that a firm bringing in a new product cannot expect its properties, or even its existence, to be known to everyone in the market; time will be needed to undertake effective marketing and to build up the needed reputation. And even if demand could be created instantaneously and without cost, the capacity required to meet it cannot normally be so created. In these circumstances, the firm will not expect too much from a price reduction, even if the suppliers of competing products do not retaliate. A price reduction will not be seen, in other words, as a short cut to increasing sales, an alternative to a time consuming and expensive marketing effort. The possibility of a dynamic equilibrium, with several suppliers in the market, does not depend on the kind of tacit collusion on prices associated with oligopoly.

It may be helpful, at this stage, to take stock of the argument. It is obvious, to all those who wish to see, that, in the real world, competition does coexist with increasing returns to scale. Chamberlin's theory of monopolistic competition offered product differentiation [7] as providing one explanation; each firm enjoys a monopoly in the particular variety it puts on offer, but competition from close substitutes may establish a normal rate of profit. In equilibrium, unit costs are falling with output, but so is the level of demand; the demand curve, in other words, is tangential to the average cost curve.

I have suggested that there may be coexistence for a further, different reason. In industries where there is continuous development and innovation – the difference between these, in this context, being one of degree – existing products are subject to displacement by new ones, the rate of investment in development tending, in competitive conditions, towards the level at which the life span of products is no longer than permits, on average, normal profits to be earned. The result of this process, typically, will be to leave several producers in the market, not only because they cater to different needs, but because it takes time for new products to gain ground and for old ones to be driven from the field.

In these circumstances, I believe that we are justified in talking in terms of a tendency towards a dynamic equilibrium. Product innovation generally requires investment, which will be undertaken in the hope of profit; in a regime of economic freedom, therefore, one should expect large and sustained divergences between the return on such investment to create signals and incentives which will cause them to be reduced. It goes without saying that, in real life conditions, this tendency will manifest itself in only a very approximate manner, but this is not to say that it will not manifest itself at all. Common observation shows, in a broad way, how free competition causes resources to flow in response to perceived profit opportunities, and there is no reason to regard investment in innovation or development as different in this regard from investment undertaken to increase the amount of different goods being supplied.

It may be objected, however, that the term *equilibrium* is misapplied to the state of affairs which I have sought to describe, in that it attributes stability to a state of constant flux. But for the use of this language, there is an illustrious precedent. The long-run equilibrium of an industry, as defined by Marshall (1961), is consistent with the rise and decline of firms within it, hence his famous analogy with the trees of a forest and the use he made of the concept of the 'representative firm'.[5] *Dynamic equilibrium* has obvious similarities to this state, but relates, not to the volume [8] in which a product or group of products is supplied, but to the rate at which their development proceeds.

We have to accept, in fact, that there are different kinds and levels of equilibrium. The total supply of a product may, in Marshall's account, be in equilibrium with the demand for it, while the firms within the industry, which may be expanding or contracting, are not. Similarly, the rate of investment in innovation within an industry may be in equilibrium, in the sense that the prevailing expectation of profit provides no inducement to increase or reduce it, while the plans made by firms within the industry, in respect of both the nature and the quantities of the goods they make, are frequently being revised.

It might be said that the process of competition, as I have described it, is one of permanent *disequilibrium*, the natural tendency towards monopolization of a market, which one would expect increasing returns to create, being continuously frustrated by the emergence of a new product. And if we are to regard innovation as essentially exogenous, such an account of the matter would be acceptable. I certainly do not wish to deny that it may frequently be appropriate to describe the evolution of industry in terms of reaction to random shocks. But there are surely many industries in which all firms recognize that they must continuously invest in product development in order to survive. In these industries, the displacement of existing products by new ones will not come as a surprise; the event will be consistent with the expectations held and in no way represent their disappointment. Professor Hahn (1973) has proposed a definition in saying that 'an economy is in equilibrium when it generates messages that do not cause agents to change the theories which they hold or the policies which they pursue'.[6] And if one were to accept such a definition, then my use of the term, albeit in a special dynamic context, would seem to be justified. The coexistence of competition and increasing returns could be described as a disequilibrium phenomenon only within the framework of comparative statics. If further product development were somehow suddenly impossible, then Sraffa's logic[7] would apply and this coexistence would break down. But this framework is surely inappropriate where uninterrupted product development is the normal, and universally expected, state of affairs. In that context, it seems to me that we should be concerned with the equilibrium rate of investment in development, with the tendency for the actual rate prevailing in a particular industry to vary so as to bring the expected financial yield into line with that prevailing generally.[8] [9]

It may be argued that investment in product development may not create a tendency towards a normal rate of return, as I have suggested, for the reason that incumbent firms are better able successfully to undertake it. They will be familiar with the relevant technology and their existing position in the market will make new offerings made by them more readily acceptable than those of outsiders. No doubt this is true, but such advantages are hardly the stuff of which antisocial monopolistic protection can for long be made. There is a good deal of historical experience to show that those who have become expert in doing something one way may well not be the first to observe that it could better be done some other way, and to show also that an established reputation may sap the energy and weaken the initiative of those who seek shelter behind it. We have to ask ourselves, moreover, whether any advantages of incumbency, any sluggishness in the process of competition, is to be deplored. It is certainly desirable that control over resources should move to successful from unsuccessful firms, but we should not want the process of transfer to be more rapid than the natural mobility of resources can make efficiently possible. Some academic observers would seem to believe that inter-firm competition should approximate to some ancient gladiatorial display, the resultant carnage proving how well it works. Those within industry have a livelier sense of the genuine social losses associated with closure and redundancy, and not just because their jobs are at stake.

I have been concerned with the way in which competition operates where there are increasing returns to scale and a high rate of innovation. These conditions, of course, are not universal, and the analytical framework I have sketched out does not therefore universally apply. But we should not expect competition always to work in the same way, whether in the supply of computers or of cocoa beans. I mentioned, at the outset, pharmaceuticals and software, where competition most obviously takes the form I have described. In both industries, indeed, the investment called for is overwhelmingly in development, in which we should include expensive and time-consuming testing procedures, and in marketing. There can be no question but that this investment, no less than investment in manufacturing capacity, is undertaken on the basis of expected financial return. The expectations will be highly uncertain and, in consequence, realized returns will show great variation. The spectacular returns earned from some software products come easily to mind, but it is well to remember also the many which have failed.

It may be questioned whether, given the great uncertainty associated with the return to investment in development, it makes sense to suppose that any equilibrium tendency is at work. No doubt there is wide variation in the realized profits from this investment, both within and between industries, but free competition is as likely in this activity, as in others, to prevent large differences persisting over time. Whatever the qualifications that we find it necessary to make, we accept that, in a regime of economic freedom, the pattern of output will accord, in some reasonable degree, with what people are prepared to pay for, and the processes of production, in some reasonable degree, will make efficient use of the needed scarce resources. For the same [10] reason, there is a presumption that, under the influence of the profit motive, the pattern of investment in product development will accord, if only approximately, with the value that consumers will place on different developments. And even the total value of such investment activity will be influenced, if only very loosely, by how much consumers are prepared to pay for novelty.

The reader, lamenting the looseness of this argument, may look back, with longing, to the clarity and precision of formal models. He may recall, with sympathy, Sir John Hicks's view, referred to above, that a general abandonment of perfect competition must have very destructive consequences for economic theory. But, as I have endeavoured to show elsewhere, the claims of the perfect competition model are completely spurious, as its internal logic is fatally flawed. I hope (and believe) that the argument which I have sketched above can be developed more fully and with greater rigour, but, in the end, we may have to accept Aristotle's view that 'Our discussion will be adequate if its degree of clarity fits the subject-matter, for we should not seek the same degree of exactness in all sorts of arguments alike.'[9] [11]

### Notes

1. J.R. Hicks (1946), *Value and Capital*, Second Edition, Oxford: Clarendon Press, p. 83.
2. E.H. Chamberlin (1962), *The Theory of Monopolistic Competition*, Eighth Edition, Cambridge, MA: Harvard University Press.
3. David B. Audretsch (1995), *Innovation and Industry Evolution*, Cambridge, MA: MIT Press.
4. This matter is discussed at length in Part I of my book: G.B. Richardson (1990), *Information and Investment*, Oxford: Clarendon Press.
5. Alfred Marshall (1961), *Principles of Economics* Book V, Chapter V, Ninth (Variorum) Edition, London: Macmillan, pp. 315–6. No one, it seems to me, had a better sense than did Marshall of the way in which equilibrium analysis in economics is made difficult by the element of time, or more awareness of the dangers run in this field by those who, in his language 'follow their mathematics boldly'. And, as has frequently been observed, his treatment anticipates a host of subsequent

developments. I am inclined to think that both the importance of high, fixed, development costs and the rate of product development is faster now than when he wrote the *Principles*. Perhaps it is for this reason that he does not explicitly consider equilibrium in terms of the rate of investment in innovation, but perhaps it was because he thought, as he put it, that '... such notions must be taken broadly. The attempt to make them precise over-reaches our strength.'

6. F.H. Hahn (1973), *On the Notion of Equilibrium in Economics*, Cambridge: Cambridge University Press.

7. P. Sraffa (1926), 'The laws of return under competitive conditions', *Economic Journal*.

8. In order more fully to explain the course of industrial development, the process of innovation would need to be subject to closer analysis. A familiar distinction could be made between *radical* innovation, of which the microprocessor would be an example, and *routine* innovation of the kind that I have been discussing. The former can be regarded as disequilibrating, and may give rise to abnormally high profits, whereas the latter is undertaken, by most firms most of the time, in order to earn a normal profit.

9. Aristotle's *Nicomachean Ethics*, Book 1, Chapter 3, translated by Terence Irwin (1985), Indianapolis, IN: Hackett Publishing Company.

# [13]

# Economic analysis, public policy and the software industry[1]

## Part 1 The economics of the industry

*Introductory*

That the software industry is important need scarcely be argued; its product is integral to a vast and increasing number of activities which implement the new information technology and which are already changing, and will continue to change, in ways we can now only dimly foresee, innumerable aspects of our daily lives.[2] It is a strikingly novel industry, which displays a pace of technical development and of structural mutation that can have few, if any, historical parallels. The techniques of economic analysis inevitably lag, in their development, on the changing phenomena to which they are applied, and it would not be surprising for explanations and judgements relating to the software market to take less than full account of its special characteristics. This first part of my paper offers an economic analysis of the industry; the second part deals with the policy issues, including that of intellectual property protection, upon which the existence of the market for software crucially depends.

## Costs and competition

In order to understand the working of the software industry, four key features have to be borne in mind. These features are, the zero marginal cost of using technology, the rapid rate of innovation, the existence of networks, and the role of standards. It is of course the interaction of these several circumstances which ultimately has to be considered, but I shall begin by discussing them separately.

Although there may be costs in creating knowledge, they are independent of the extent to which the knowledge is subsequently used. The costs incurred in developing a software program in particular are unaffected by the extent to which its use is licensed. In that sense the marginal cost of using the software, the cost, that is to say, of granting additional licences, is zero, or at any rate relatively small.[3] The production and distribution of diskettes, licence documents and manuals will enter into the marginal costs of the supplier when they are part of the licensing transaction, but need not do so where installation by a computer manufacturer is concerned. User support costs [5] may also be an element in the supplier's marginal costs, but development costs, which are independent of sales volume, are overwhelmingly predominant. Of course costs are incurred, indeed heavy costs, in *creating* additional demand for licences, but not in *fulfilling* that demand.

We have to accept that where the marginal cost of production is zero we are posed, or seem to be posed, with a dilemma. On the one hand, it would appear to be in the interests of consumers that the available economies of scale are fully exploited, which, in the zero marginal cost case, would suggest that one producer should cater for the whole market. There would appear to be no room for a second supplier of a particular software product, far less a third or fourth, if the first supplier can meet any level of demand, however great, without any difference in the costs incurred. On the other hand, it is in the interests of consumers that the benefit from the full exploitation of scale economies should be passed on to them in the form of lower prices, which will not dependably happen unless suppliers are subject to competitive pressure. It is also in the interests of consumers that there should be, in the development of software, a variety of approach. We need therefore to consider whether, and how, these apparently conflicting requirements are reconciled in the market for software; how is it possible, in other words, to have the advantages which monopoly would here seem to offer, while at the same time having those which only competition can provide?

We have first to note the rather obvious circumstance that competing software products need not be identical, but may offer differing features. Each product can then find its own particular market among those to whom its particular features appeal, while at the same time, the presence in the general market of users who find the products reasonably good substitutes ensures price competition between them. In this way, as in many industries, economies of scale are balanced against the demand for variety, and competition is maintained.

In the software industry, however, a further powerful factor is at work. Because of the high rate of underlying technical change, the life of a product is typically very short.[4] A firm may introduce a new product and drive hard, by means of its marketing policies, to achieve the large volume of sales that, where marginal costs are zero, makes it possible to have low prices and high returns. If successful, it may then enjoy the lion's share of a particular market. But, although it will have won a battle, it will not have won the war. Its competitors will already be planning to bring out a better competing product, and the firm itself, for the sake of its survival, will already be planning its own next move.

As we have already noted, a software product is subject to price competition through the existence of alternatives, which, at least for many users, are good, even if not perfect substitutes. But much more deadly competition is continuously provided by the stream of new and improved products [6] that take away the ground from under the feet of the established ones. No doubt it is true of most industries that firms have to run in order to stand still, but rarely do firms have to run so fast as in this one. We have only to consider how the landscape in computing changes in five years, far less ten, to appreciate how strongly the 'gale of creative destruction' blows through this particular market.

One finds, in the software industry, competition which as well as being *concurrent*, is *sequential*, in the sense that a product may dominate in a particular market sector at one time, but is always liable to be replaced, after a short interval, perhaps two years, by another. In manufacturing industry, there is not the same liability to large and rapid changes in market share, because of the time needed to install productive capacity.[5] In the software market, there is no corresponding circumstance, with the result that market shares are potentially much more volatile. I say potentially, because producers will strive to keep what they have gained, appreciating that, in a market of this kind, no position is secure. The fact that shares may not in fact change violently is not evidence for protected markets; competitive pressures are exerted by the constant threat of displacement, which established firms can ward off only through rapid and successful innovation.

There are, of course, limits to the potential volatility; a new product does not sell automatically, but only with marketing effort, and users will show some reluctance to switch to a new product from another with which they have become familiar, and in the reputation of whose maker they have come to trust.[6] Leap-frogging is also not inevitable; a firm with a lead in a particular market will strive to maintain it through continuous upgrading of the product, its experience, acquired capabilities and market connections helping it to do so. Such advantages are enjoyed by established concerns in industry generally, and firms compete in endeavouring to secure and maintain them. But there is plenty of evidence that these advantages are not normally for long decisive; where the scope for innovation is particularly high, a fresh approach may often prove successful and past success and experience can trammel as well as support. Only myopia can lead one to believe that a commanding position is unassailably and continuously secure. We all know that the future will differ from the present, but it seems to require an effort of imagination fully to appreciate the fact. The established firm, however mighty it may seem, can be brought down, or at least for a time eclipsed, by complacency, by arrogance, or simply by the fact that market opportunities or technical possibilities change in a way that favours others with different ways of thinking, more relevant experience, more appropriate market connections, or simply greater luck. This is true generally, but particularly so for an industry in which positions are so continuously [7] challenged, and in which, as past experience has shown, it is so difficult to know what the future holds in store.

We have to recognize that it is in the public interest, both that a successful product gains a large part of the market for products of that class, and, at the same time, that this tendency is neither unlimited nor irreversible. Observation confirms that this is what happens; a product may gain the predominant share of a market, but is unlikely to gain all of it; older products will typically still be in place, new ones, having gained a foothold, will be striving to tip the general market their way, and other products will have found a niche market by offering special features.[7]

The fact that one software product tends, at any one time, to have the lion's share of a particular market, is the natural outcome of increasing returns to scale and other circumstances which we shall examine below; it provides, however, no prima-facie case for presuming the existence of monopoly power, and of the detriments, such as protected inefficiency or high prices, commonly associated with the exercise of monopoly power. In the case of PC operating systems, for example, one product currently has a very large share of the market, but there are competing products, powerfully backed, seeking to displace it; and the issue is not so much which products will gain ground if circumstances remain the same, for we know that circumstances will change, and in such a way that the products competing tomorrow will not be those competing today. The past experience of the industry makes this clear; dedicated word processors, for example, gave way to the general purpose personal computer, and character-based application gave way to those that were graphically based.[8] And such paradigm shifts will certainly continue to take place in the future; the microprocessors for which the operating systems are designed are in continuous development, and computers of the future, such as PC telephones, PC-TVs and multimedia machines of whatever kinds, will be different from those of the present.

The firm winning the current race ought therefore to have its mind already on the race to come. That firm's products are liable to lose ground, not gradually as in some industries, through the gradual erosion of profit margins as a consequence of rivals' cost savings and incremental improvements, but because a new need arises which a rival has the product to meet and it does not. Competition with this *modus operandi* is of course not new;[9] what is new, and features so markedly in the software industry, is the rate at which innovation takes place. Perhaps the best [8] example of this is the growth of the Internet, particularly its World Wide Web, which doubles in size every few months. This growth has created new markets and has forced some companies substantially to change their business strategies. The fact that we cannot, in the nature of things, predict the changes that will radically transform the industry's landscape should not lead us to doubt that changes will come about; only ignorance of history, and poverty of imagination, would lead us to that conclusion. Nor should we be led to believe, when established firms do maintain their place, that the powerful influence of innovation has not been at work. Competition of the kind we are considering works as a discipline, the threat of dislodgement being ever present. Those who doubt this phenomenon should take account of the fast development of the Internet which in the space of a few years has evolved from an obscure network serving a limited number of academic sites in a few countries into a global network connecting millions of individual computers.[10] The Internet has also begun to serve as a cheap, fast and international alternative to the physical distribution of software products through traditional retail outlets. Not only do these developments mark a dramatic paradigm shift for the existing software market, they have created a market for a range of entirely new software products, such as 'Web browsers' for the Internet. Such an environment affords companies that are new or marginally important in today's software market the opportunity to capture a significant share of tomorrow's software business. Start-up companies such as Netscape, which has been remarkably successful with its Web browser, are thus on a strong footing in competing with more established companies. This constant transformation of the software industry's technological foundations provides a relentless challenge to the competitive position of every market participant.

**Systems and networks**

I have so far analysed the working of the software market without attending to one of its most important features. A software product is of no use in itself, but only when working in conjunction with other complementary products as part of a system. Thus in the simplest case of an isolated personal computer, software products must work with each other; an operating system, specifically, must work with applications, as well as with a microprocessor and other elements in a hardware platform. In the case of an extended network such as the so-called information highway, the set of related components will be much larger.[11] If these systems, large or small, are to do what we expect of them, then the component parts must be so designed as to interoperate. [9]

In what ways can this be achieved? One model would be for a whole set of related components to be made by a single firm able itself to assume responsibility for so designing them as to ensure the needed compatibility. This way of achieving a set of interoperating components may be termed *planned integration*. But although some such integration does take place in the sphere of activity we are considering, it is manifestly not how the necessary coordination is in reality generally brought about. It is instructive, nevertheless, to ask ourselves why this is so, for by identifying the disadvantages of planned integration, we shall be better able to understand the inherent economic logic of the alternative ways in which the market can bring into being the sets of interoperating products which information technology has made available for our use.

Two circumstances set limits to what can be achieved by planned integration within one firm. The first arises from the fact that the different component elements in a set, such as, for example, microprocessors, monitors, disks and software, require, although they have to interoperate, very different skills, experience and equipment in their production.[12] They require, that is to say, a variety of capabilities not all of which are likely to be possessed by one firm. The second obstacle to planned integration is simply the economies of scale that feature in the production of some of the component parts of the set. A firm able to meet the development costs of, say, all the hardware components and associated software of a computer, would have to be very large indeed; there would be room, in any economy, for very few of them, and the barrier to entry would be exceedingly high. Consumers would be limited in their choice between the complete systems of different manufacturers and not be free to select between hardware and software components as they can in fact do now.

The personal computer industry did not develop through the integration, by single manufacturers, of the related elements in a system.[13] A very large number of firms are engaged in making hardware and software components; there is some vertical integration, both IBM and Apple making both hardware and software, but within the computer industry there is a vast number of firms, of very differing size, linked in complex and changing patterns of competition and cooperation.[14] No doubt this diffuse structure owes something to historical accident, but the obstacles to extended integration noted above would, I believe, have led in any event to an industrial structure of the kind we now have. [10]

That this structure has been favourable to the development and exploitation of information technology could scarcely be denied; certainly an historical parallel to the astonishing rate of growth of the personal computer industry would be hard to find. Economic analysis is not so reliably advanced that we can very confidently prescribe optimal industrial structures, and the more modest of its practitioners will be willing to accept the success of the prevailing, but unplanned, structure as creating a presumption in its favour.

How then, with many independent firms competing and cooperating in the market place, can the compatibility, or interoperability, of their complementary products be achieved? One obvious way is through the establishment of formal standards, agreement on which may be sought through negotiation between the parties. The process is carried forward typically by small technical working groups seeking consensus, and, although governmental and inter-governmental agencies may be involved, private firms commonly provide the necessary personnel and finance.

Firms are prepared to work together in establishing compatibility standards when they perceive it to be in their interest to do so. And, where the demand for their products depends on interoperability, a motive exists to achieve standardization through agreement. But it is important to recognize that sometimes it is neither practicable nor socially desirable for compatibility to be obtained by this route. There are two circumstances which, in this context, must be given weight.

First, there is the possibility of genuine uncertainty as to the best specifications to establish in order to define, and, when need be, redefine, a compatibility standard; this consideration is important in any industry subject to rapid technical change. In these circumstances, it may be better to put up with limited compatibility rather than fix standards before it has become clear how and when to do so.

Secondly, there are situations, of great importance in the industry which concerns us, where compatibility cannot be secured merely by choosing specifications, however careful and thorough the process may be, but has to be *created* at the cost of substantial investment and the application of technical and marketing skills. Compatibility is achieved this way through the mediation of a *de facto* standard, which in this context is the name given to a product which interoperates very widely with others. It is to the adoption of these standards that we must now turn.

*The creation of* de facto *standards*
It is tempting to say that *de facto* standards, such as Novell's Netware or Microsoft's Windows, simply 'emerge' in the market. But this is to make appear as automatic a development that is sought after through the application, over a period, of substantial resources. It is true that the market is the final arbiter, but the selection it comes to make is between alternatives, in the development, testing and marketing of which their firms have invested heavily. Windows is, in this [11] respect, a good example. It is the product of extended technical development, but also of consultation with the makers of hardware and of applications software, and of elaborate, time-consuming and expensive programmes of testing, both by Microsoft and a host of independent individuals and concerns. The process of 'evangelization', by which firms are persuaded to develop applications that will fit an operating system, is a crucial part of seeking to obtain the volume of derived demand that will tip the market in its favour and make it a *de facto* standard. If all goes well, these efforts will lead to an effect of the snowballing kind I referred to earlier; hardware manufacturers will load the operating system because of the demand for applications that work with it and, as the installed base grows, so will the volume of related applications and the consequential derived demand for the operating system. If, however, momentum does not build up in this way, a great deal of money can be lost. The market provides the emerging standard with a pragmatic sanction; for those firms seeking to provide it, the risks are high and the prizes and penalties correspond.

In the working of industry as I have described it, there is every reason to expect operating systems that are *de facto* standards to be open, in the sense that the firm that created them will give freely the information about them that is needed by applications developers in order to make their products compatible. There is also every reason to expect that their use should be charged for. Without the prospect of an income from their licensing, the investment in their development, in the crucial process of evangelization and in subsequent user-support programmes, would not have been undertaken. Any argument that these systems should be costless cannot be sustained. The case for charging is the same as that made, in respect of all software designed to meet a market need, at the beginning of this paper.

## Conclusions

If the analysis that I have presented is correct, the software industry is very competitive, and this despite the fact that particular products may enjoy large market shares. The most powerful force at work to preserve competition is the high rate of innovation prevailing; this ensures that no firm is invulnerable, but has to fight to maintain its position. Market shares are made potentially more insecure by the fact that the extent to which a product can be licensed is not limited by considerations of productive capacity. The public interest, it seems to me, is promoted by the resultant balance between competition, on the one hand, and, on the other, the exploitation of unlimited scale economies. The working of the market in this context does also produce *de facto* standards and, thereby, a substantial degree of interoperability.

Questions arise as to the role, in this context, of legislation protecting intellectual property, as to whether competition could be made yet more effective by government action, and as to whether standards should be set in a manner different from that which I have described. These are the matters to which I now turn. [12]

## Part II   Public policy

### Introductory

In the first part of this paper, I sought to provide an economic analysis of the market for computer software; my aim in this part is to consider some public policy issues that arise in this context. I shall be concerned with the protection of intellectual property, with competition policy and with the establishment of industry standards, my hope being to help identify what should be on governmental agendas and what should not.

### The rationale of intellectual property protection

Software developers are paid for authorizing the use of their products, and were this use not to require authorization, unauthorized use being prohibited by law, they would have nothing to sell. The case for copyright protection, as normally put, is that it is necessary to provide an innovator with the incentive to undertake the investment, and bear the risks, of developing and marketing his product.[15] Without a 'closed period' sufficient to enable the innovator as the sole legally permitted seller of his product to recover its cost and make a profit, the essential motivation would be lacking. But this way of putting the matter, although valid, fails to make clear that intellectual property protection is necessary irrespective of whether personal gain is the incentive to invest. It may give the impression that such protection would not be necessary if the investment were undertaken in a collectivist regime or by public authorities within a mixed economy.

Such a conclusion would be false. In any economic system with claims to rationality, a way must be found of assessing whether an investment is justified, whether the resultant benefits to society are greater than their opportunity costs; whether they are greater, that is to say, than the benefits that might have been obtained had the resources been put to another purpose. Where fundamental research is concerned, and the potential benefits uncertain, diffuse and deferred, assessment is very difficult, and the investment is, in the main, paid for by public bodies without a close calculation of return. The new knowledge produced may then be made available as a free good. That fundamental research is of great importance, not least in computer science, goes without saying, but there will be, in any kind of economy, a great deal of investment in the development of new products for which there is believed to be a specific need. And where investment of this kind is [13] concerned, we have to find a way of making rational choices, of deciding whether and in what quantity resources should be applied to the development of this or that particular product for which there is believed to be a potential consumer demand.

The method of assessment generally used is, of course, that of comparing the monetary cost of the resources applied with what consumers would pay for the resultant product.[16] If the latter exceeds the former, then there is a presumption that the investment was socially worthwhile. This test, although subject to qualification, is an essential starting point, but without intellectual property protection, it could not be applied. Unlicensed copying would prevent the relevant market prices from being established.

One might imagine that, in the absence of such protection, a public authority might somehow estimate how much they think that consumers would be prepared to pay for a software product which will in fact be made available to them free, and invest on the basis of that estimate. Such a procedure would however be, at best, exceedingly hazardous, for if the product were not in fact to be sold, there could be no way of finding out whether the estimates made were right or wrong. To further allocative efficiency, a system of prices has to be introduced, and a requirement for this, where we are concerned with technology that can be easily appropriated, is having patent and copyright protection in place.

A viable software industry, we must therefore firmly conclude, is quite crucially dependent on the effective copyright or patent protection. Only the very unreflecting would take the view that the creation of these legal rights, by the state, somehow dilutes competition within an industry; the reality is that these rights are a necessary condition for the very existence of a competitive industry in which resources are applied to create knowledge or information, from the licensed use of which it is hoped that revenue can be obtained.

## Competition and barriers to entry

I sought to show, in the first part of this paper, that the computer software industry is highly competitive, despite the fact that one manufacturer's product may, for a time, enjoy the lion's share of its market. The rate of innovation was high enough to ensure, I maintained, that such a product would be continuously vulnerable to displacement. It has however been argued that, even if the possession of a large market share does not in itself afford the advantages of a monopoly, its existence within a set of complementary products necessarily does. This is the contention that I shall now consider. [14]

Put simply, the argument runs as follows: even if a system superior to say, Windows or Novell's NetWare, were to become available, consumers would be unwilling to switch to it because of all the application software on the market designed to be compatible with the established products. In order to displace these products, a complete new set of complementary products would have to become available and offer such advantages as would justify the cost of switching to them. This interlocking, it is suggested, constitutes a strong barrier to entry and provides the owners of the established systems with monopoly power.

There are a number of weaknesses in this argument. First, there is the simple point that a new product, say, an operating system, may be compatible with those applications designed for the established one.[17] Moreover, a new operating system would not have to be able to run every existing application in order to compete with an established one; provided its inherent merits were strong enough, the ability to run a sufficient number of important existing applications could carry the day.

If the new system were compatible with no existing application, then its acceptance would certainly be more difficult, but it would not be impossible. The firm introducing it would be obliged, as was the owner of the prevailing standard at an earlier stage, to induce independent software developers to write suitable applications or otherwise to do so itself. And where the life cycle of a product is as short as in this industry, entry on this basis is feasible.[18] So long as we analyse the possibilities of entry in terms of a static situation, the difficulties appear greater than in reality they are. The rate of innovation is such that the landscape is ever changing, with new opportunities continuously opening up. If established firms maintain their position, then they will have adapted their own products appropriately. No one can stand still.

As in every industry, being already established or being first in the field does offer advantages peculiar to that situation. If consumers are familiar with the product, if they are satisfied with it and with the support they have received, and if they know that it fits well with other products related to it in use, then they will display towards its vendor some limited loyalty. But the existence of reputations in the market place, and the position of a product within a network, provide no evidence of monopoly; it is, indeed, in the striving to gain, or defend, or challenge such positions [15] of advantage that competition characteristically manifests itself.[19]

We also need to reflect on the circumstances that, from society's point of view, justify new entry, or the displacement of one product by another. If a firm finds difficulty in selling, say, a new operating system, for the reason that it is incompatible with established and important applications software, then this is as it should be; there is a real cost to consumers and to society in having to replace existing application programs, and if that cost does not appear to consumers as likely to be compensated by the advantages of the new operating system, then this circumstance is in no way an unfair barrier to entry, but something that should properly enter into the calculations of a firm considering whether to offer the new system on the market.

For the reasons I have given, I do not think that a software program, which is a *de facto* standard linked to a network of complementary products, is thereby likely to have an unassailable market position. It may be maintained, however, that there at least exists the possibility that a software product, if it has become a standard, may become so strongly entrenched that undue profit is earned from licensing it. Competitors seeking to displace the standard have of course a motive for saying so, but, setting this aside, let us consider what the public policy response should be were the situation hypothesized be judged to exist.

It will not do to argue that such standards should be brought 'into the public domain': unless the public, through some official agency with appropriate capabilities, is prepared to meet the cost of maintaining and developing these standards, they will have to be privately owned. It would, of course, be possible to restrict the profits being earned on the product, either by curtailing the life of the associated intellectual property protection, or by controlling licensing charges. But whether such an approach would, on balance, further the public interest, is another matter. In an industry so fluid, where risks are great, where prospects of spectacular success are balanced by prospects of sudden massive failure, the notion of 'undue profits' is difficult to define and to apply. The analogy with public utility regulation is scarcely close, as the industries concerned, compared with [16] the software industry, are strikingly sedate.[20]

### The threat of leverage

Yet another detriment, or at any rate danger, is sometimes identified as a possible indirect consequence of the possession by an operating system, or other key program, of a large share of a particular market. A firm, it is pointed out, may be able to exploit a monopoly in one market in order to obtain a monopoly in another, a practice referred to sometimes as leverage. In the computer software industry, it has been suggested, a firm might use a monopoly in an operating system in order to oblige customers to license its own applications programs, which were compatible with that system, rather than those of competitors, which were not. No firm does in fact have a full monopoly in the market for operating systems, in the sense that computer users are obliged to buy its product. It may however be maintained that the possession of a large share of the market may be enough to permit a degree of leverage to be exerted. A firm might be able, it has been suggested, so to develop an operating system that certain applications software programs, in competition with its own, will not work with this system. A weaker form of the accusation is that such a firm could seek, not wholly to disable applications software competing with its own, but merely to put such applications at a disadvantage by giving their potential developers less timely information about the interfaces with which they must be compatible.

Whether any particular firm does or does not behave in this way is first of all a matter of fact, and it is fair to start by noting that, although this behaviour has been alleged, regulatory investigation does not so far appear to have provided confirmation.[21] General reasoning, moreover, leads us not to be surprised at this outcome. We took note earlier of the importance, in establishing a *de facto* standard, of the process of 'evangelization', and it is hard to believe that a firm, having invested heavily in inducing and assisting independent software vendors to develop applications for its operating system, would then seek to disable or disadvantage these applications. Of course it would be *possible* for the firm so to behave, but the breach of faith implicit in such behaviour could scarcely assist any future evangelizing efforts. To the extent, moreover, that a firm were to limit the variety of competing applications with which its operating system would be compatible, the greater would be the vulnerability of that system to displacement by an alternative product. [17]

Although it might be unwise for a firm to seek the kind of leverage in question, this does not prove that it would not do so. As economic analysis, in the nature of things, cannot rule out the possibility of such conduct, one cannot rule out the possible need for regulatory supervision. It seems to me wrong, however, to urge that the development of operating systems and application software should be disjoined, in order to exclude any possibility of abuse in question. The public interest could only suffer if a firm, having acquired a capability in the development and marketing of one kind of software, were prohibited from making the most of it through extending its range into another, particularly as the risks of displacement to which any particular product is exposed provide a cogent reason for some diversification. Forcibly to separate the development of the two related products would be to deny the public a benefit in order to claim to prevent an abuse for the existence of which there is no presumption and against which, in any case, there would be better remedies. It would be damaging, moreover, and rather absurd, to insist that, say, an operating system had to be compatible with a wide variety of applications, even where this necessarily involved depriving it of important advantages. Although it would be wrong to say that abuses in this area could never exist, I am inclined to think that the general interest will at present best be served, in the great majority of circumstances, by allowing the firm supplying a software product to determine the features affecting its compatibility on the basis of its own commercial interests.

### Specifications and standards

The emergence within the industry of software programs that have become *de facto* standards, which are proprietary, and for the licensed use of which users have to pay, is sometimes said to be against the public interest. Such key interfaces within the system, the argument runs, should be available to all without charge. Let specifications that ensure compatibility be laid down, it has been suggested, each developer of the interface software being then free to devise his own implementation of them. In this way, the argument continues, we can get the best of all worlds, achieving universal compatibility while maintaining competition between the different implementations.[22]

Within the context that concerns us here, this hope is illusory. An operating system, or its associated applications programs, is not to be compared with, let us say, the electrical plugs and sockets, for which compatibility can be secured by simple specifications. An elaborate process of consultation and development is needed to obtain widespread compatibility, and we know that, as new and improved versions of the standard are developed, the process has to be continuous. [18]

Who then would undertake and pay for the work of devising specifications, adherence to which is presumed to ensure compatibility and to which, say, all operating systems would have to conform? Who would undertake and pay for the periodic changes in the specifications that underlying technical changes, say in the microprocessor, would make necessary? How, and on whose authority, could the specifications be imposed? And if somehow adherence to the specifications could initially be obtained, what is to prevent developments in the various implementations that would, in effect, start a drift from the standard? A developer might bring in a new product which met the specifications, and was therefore (let us assume) compatible with existing applications, but which offered functionality which made feasible new applications that would work with this particular implementation but none of the others. Is such a developer to be prevented from making this innovation? For what reason, and on what authority? These considerations lead one to believe that, while scope for agreed standardization will certainly exist, some key interfaces will have to continue to be owned, and their use to be paid for.

*Private enterprise, the information highway and the future*
The progress made in software development owes much to fundamental work done by government agencies and in the universities. But it has also been furthered by the undertaking, by many firms large and small, of many speculative and risky investments, and, in consequence, by the spectacular success of some firms and the demise of many.[23] A variety of approaches have been followed, and competition has selected between them. In the nature of things, it would be difficult to mount, within the public sector of an economy, such a plurality of differing approaches, such a massive experimentation. If a government investment fails, the general public, or the party in opposition, is likely to attach blame and call for explanation; because of this, risky investments may be avoided, there being a natural reluctance simultaneously to adopt differing approaches, not all of which can prove successful. There is a good deal of evidence that the course of the development of the software and related industries has rarely been predicted correctly in the past, either by governments or by firms, and there is no reason to believe that future development will be any more predictable.[24] In these circumstances, there is much to be said for an economic system that permits a good deal of trial and error, leaving it to the market to select the products, firms, and strategies that are successful.

There is a further circumstance which favours private enterprise in this sphere of economic activity. The industry is characterized by much structural mutation; firms both compete and collaborate, they enter into changing alliances, sometimes across traditional industrial boundaries, they take other firms over, they lose staff who set up new firms, they flourish, and they fail. Such [19] continuous restructuring is the response called for by the pace of technical change and the need to relate activities which are complementary, with respect, say, to the development of an information highway, but which have been undertaken within previously distinct industries, such as communications, computers, publishing and television. And such permanent metamorphosis, particularly on an international scale, is a condition State enterprises are very much less likely to be able to manage.

As regards the future of the information highway, it seems to me that, although we have a reasonably good general idea of the potentialities of interactive systems of communication, no one can say with confidence exactly how they will be realized. Given this uncertainty, there is a strong case for a regime of commercial freedom. It is argued in a Commission of the European Communities (CEC) White Paper (COM (93) 700 final, Brussels, 5 December 1993, p. 66)[25] that we need 'the establishment of a coherent and concerted approach to strategic alliances, the uncontrolled development of which could result in the creation of oligopolistic situations prejudicial to competition at world levels'. It is recommended that the effect of the alliances be assessed 'simultaneously and in a concerted manner by the competent authorities'. One is bound to wonder, and worry, about what the authors had in mind. Worldwide alliances already exist, and will certainly further develop; they are essential to realize the potential of the information super-highway, which will require firms from different industries and in different countries to become engaged. There will also be competition between these alliances, and this competition (although no doubt intense) will be oligopolistic, for the reason that scale economies rule out the possibility of there being room for a large number of such groupings in the market place. In what way, and for what reason, are the 'competent authorities' to assess the alliances?

Perhaps the purpose of the assessment would be to decide which of the alliances were to receive public support and which were not. Or perhaps the authorities would endeavour to bring into existence groupings different from those that would have formed otherwise. It is in either case hard to envisage these aims being realized in any informed and rational manner; civil servants depend for information and opinion about the costs, technology and future prospects of particular industries very much upon what they are told by the firms within them; by people, that is, with interests at stake. It is not possible to make strategic judgements, however, by reasoning from first principles, but only on the basis of limited and unreliable information and opinion of this kind. Even if it were possible in principle, therefore, for public authorities to determine an optimal pattern of alliances, and an optimal strategy for future developments in this area, they are unlikely in practice to be able to identify it. The reality is that no one knows for sure how the potentialities [20] of interactive communication will precisely be realized, and society in these circumstances is likely to be best served by there being some variety of approach, the resources being committed by firms that stand to lose or gain from the outcome.

I do not maintain that there is no role for government, or intergovernmental, action in this sphere. The very existence of the industry depends on a legal construction, copyright, which only governments can design and regulate. Nor do I wish to suggest that there will be no scope at any time or in any circumstances for governmental initiatives in setting standards. I believe, however, that governments should, in this matter, be pragmatic. Intervention can do more harm than good unless informed by an understanding of how free competitive enterprise operates in the software industry and an appreciation of its essential appropriateness to the circumstances prevailing. [21]

## Notes

1.   Author's note: Microsoft assisted me in the preparation of this paper with financial support, under its ongoing programme to support academic research in the areas of information technology and public policy, and by enabling me to visit its headquarters in Redmond, USA, where members of its staff helped me to acquire relevant factual information. The opinions expressed in the paper are my own. My thinking in the subject has been influenced partly by specialized academic literature on the software industry, but to a greater extent by ideas that I have developed (and written about) myself over the years. I have been influenced also by my previous experience as a Member of the UK Monopolies and Mergers Commission, as Economic Adviser to the UK Atomic Energy Authority and as Chief Executive of Oxford University Press.

2.   The development of the software industry is the subject of many articles in periodicals and newspapers (such as the *Economist* and *Financial Times*) which I have found useful. Indirectly relevant is the very extensive literature of standardization. The historical development of the industry is well dealt with by Langlois, R. N. (1992), 'External economies and economic progress; the case of the microcomputer industry', *Business History Review*, **66** (1), 1–50. Additional references that the reader may find illuminating are referred to in the notes below; I should like to express my appreciation to Ms Kirsten Bindemann, who kindly compiled them.

3.   Smith, G. V. and R. L. Parr (1993), *Intellectual Property: Licensing and Joint Venture Profit Strategies*, New York: John Wiley and Sons.

4.   McClellan, S. T. (1984), *The Coming Computer Shakeout*, New York: John Wiley and Sons.

5.   This idea is developed in my own DRUID Working Paper no. 96-10, 'Competition, innovation and increasing returns' (July 1996).

6.   Some of the practicalities involved in marketing computer software, given in particular the legal context, are discussed in detail in Davidson, D. M. and Davidson, J. A. (1987), *Advanced Legal Systems for Buying and Selling Computers and Software*, New York: John Wiley and Sons.

7.   The analysis presented in this paper derives in part from my own academic work on the process of competition. This is set out most fully in Richardson, G. B. (1990), *Information and Investment*, Oxford: Clarendon Press, p. 67, p. 228.

8.   Dvorak, J. (1994), *Dvorak Predicts: An Insider's Look at the Computer Industry*, Berkeley, CA: McGraw-Hill. This book deals with the current state of competition within the software industry rather than with the general principles that are here my concern.

9.   Idem.

10.   According to a study by International Data Corp. at the end of 1995 there were between 8 and 10 million individual users of the World Wide Web. By the end of 1996 the number is expected to grow to 30 million. By the year 2000, that number may go as high as 200 million. Stets, D., 'Computer expert warns of Internet reaching overload', *The Atlanta Journal and Constitution* (14 Jan. 1996).

11.   A compendious survey of the law on computer software is provided by Kutten, L. J. (1995), *Computer Software*, Callaghan, IL: Clark Boardman; and also in Scott, M. D. (1992), *Scott on Computer Law* (2nd edition), New Jersey: Prentice Hall Law and Business.

12.   This point, crucial in this context, is developed more fully in an article which I wrote to identify the circumstances in which the coordination of economic activity can take place simply through market transactions between firms, as distinct from the circumstances in which it requires cooperative arrangements between firms and the circumstances in which it is best brought about by direction within a firm. Richardson, G. B. (1992), 'The organisation of industry', *Economic Journal*, September, 883–96.

13.   On integration see also e.g. Porter, M. E. (1980), *Competitive Strategy: Techniques for Industries and Competitors*, London and New York: Macmillan Publishers.

14.   See Porter, M. E., op. cit.

15.   The Business Software Alliance (BSA) and the Software Publishers Association (SPA) state that the software industry loses approximately 50% of its potential profit to pirates. Cited in Dvorak, J. (1994), *Dvorak Predicts: An Insider's Look at the Computer Industry*, Berkeley, CA: McGraw Hill, p. 4. See also Davidson, D. M. and Davidson, J. A. (1989), *Advanced Legal Systems for Buying and Selling Computers and Software*, New York: John Wiley and Sons.

16.   The basis of this proposition is to be found in the literature on efficient resource allocation; see Richardson, G. B. (1964), *Economic Theory*, London: Hutchinson and Co., ch. 2.

17.   This will, of course, not be a matter of pure chance. Any firm seeking to create a market for a new product has a very strong commercial incentive to offer such compatibility. Where compatibility

fails to exist, moreover, the opportunity is created for specialist firms to develop, where feasible, software products which bridge the gap.

18. Porter, M. E. (1990), *Competitive Strategy, Techniques for Industries and Competitors*, London and New York: Macmillan Publishers.

19. The reputation, experience and connections of an established firm afford it a comparative advantage over potential entrants, but this does not constitute a barrier the existence of which is contrary to the public interest. Firms invest in the acquisition of these intangible assets in the expectation of deriving a return from them. All this should be very well known, and was dealt with at length by one of the greatest of economists, Alfred Marshall. See Marshall, Alfred (1890), *Principles of Economics*, Chapter 11, London: Macmillan. It is interesting to reflect on his observation on p. 287 of this chapter, that 'the very conditions of an industry which enable a new firm to attain quickly command over new economies of production, render that firm liable to be supplanted quickly by still younger firms with yet newer methods.'

20. Recent activities of the European Telecommunications Standards Institute (ETSI) provide a dramatic illustration of the public difficulties presented by the appropriation of intellectual property rights through the standard-setting process. In 1993, ETSI's general assembly approved an 'Intellectual Property Rights Undertaking', which would have required members to license their patented technologies under 'reasonable and non-discriminatory' conditions, if these were used to implement an ETSI technical standard, unless the rights owner objected within 180 days. A major confrontation ensued that pitted various industrial sectors against one another and threatened a major trade dispute. In 1994, ETSI's membership overwhelmingly voted to annul the policy.

21. Scott, M. D. (1992), *Scott on Computer Law* (2nd edition), New Jersey: Prentice Law and Business.

22. For a presentation of the argument that there should be no intellectual property protection for standard interfaces in the information society, see 'Barrier free interfaces and the European information infrastructure', submitted to the European Committee for Interoperable Systems (ECIS) to the European Parliament hearing on the Global Information Society (February 1995).

23. McClellan, S. T. (1984), *The Coming Computer Industry Shakeout*, New York: John Wiley and Sons.

24. Which is not to say that predictions will not be made, for example those found in Dvorak, op. cit.

25. 'Growth, competitiveness and employment – the challenges and ways forward into the 21st century.'

# Name index

# Economists of the Twentieth Century

Monetarism and Macroeconomic
Policy
*Thomas Mayer*

Studies in Fiscal Federalism
*Wallace E. Oates*

The World Economy in Perspective
Essays in International Trade and European
Integration
*Herbert Giersch*

Towards a New Economics
Critical Essays on Ecology, Distribution and
Other Themes
*Kenneth E. Boulding*

Studies in Positive and Normative
Economics
*Martin J. Bailey*

The Collected Essays of Richard E.
Quandt (2 volumes)
*Richard E. Quandt*

International Trade Theory and Policy
Selected Essays of W. Max Corden
*W. Max Corden*

Organization and Technology in Capitalist
Development
*William Lazonick*

Studies in Human Capital
Collected Essays of Jacob Mincer, Volume 1
*Jacob Mincer*

Studies in Labor Supply
Collected Essays of Jacob Mincer, Volume 2
*Jacob Mincer*

Macroeconomics and Economic Policy
The Selected Essays of Assar Lindbeck
Volume I
*Assar Lindbeck*

The Welfare State
The Selected Essays of Assar Lindbeck
Volume II
*Assar Lindbeck*

Classical Economics, Public Expenditure
and Growth
*Walter Eltis*

Money, Interest Rates and Inflation
*Frederic S. Mishkin*

The Public Choice Approach to Politics
*Dennis C. Mueller*

The Liberal Economic Order
Volume I Essays on International Economics
Volume II Money, Cycles and Related Themes
*Gottfried Haberler*
Edited by Anthony Y.C. Koo

Economic Growth and Business Cycles
Prices and the Process of Cyclical Development
*Paolo Sylos Labini*

International Adjustment, Money and
Trade
Theory and Measurement for Economic Policy
Volume I
*Herbert G. Grubel*

International Capital and Service Flows
Theory and Measurement for Economic Policy
Volume II
*Herbert G. Grubel*

Unintended Effects of Government
Policies
Theory and Measurement for Economic Policy
Volume III
*Herbert G. Grubel*

The Economics of Competitive Enterprise
Selected Essays of P.W.S. Andrews
*Edited by Frederic S. Lee
and Peter E. Earl*

The Repressed Economy
Causes, Consequences, Reform
*Deepak Lal*

Economic Theory and Market Socialism
Selected Essays of Oskar Lange
*Edited by Tadeusz Kowalik*

Trade, Development and Political
Economy
Selected Essays of Ronald Findlay
*Ronald Findlay*

General Equilibrium Theory
The Collected Essays of Takashi Negishi
Volume I
*Takashi Negishi*

The History of Economics
The Collected Essays of Takashi Negishi
Volume II
*Takashi Negishi*

Studies in Econometric Theory
The Collected Essays of Takeshi Amemiya
*Takeshi Amemiya*

Economics and Social Justice
Essays on Power, Labor and Institutional Change
*David M. Gordon*
*Edited by Thomas E. Weisskopf and Samuel Bowles*

Practicing Econometrics
Essays in Method and Application
*Zvi Griliches*

Economics Against the Grain
Volume One
Microeconomics, Industrial Organization and Related Themes
*Julian L. Simon*

Economics Against the Grain
Volume Two
Population Economics, Natural Resources and Related Themes
*Julian L. Simon*

Advances in Econometric Theory
The Selected Works of Halbert White
*Halbert White*

The Economics of Imperfect Knowledge
Collected Papers of G.B. Richardson
*G.B. Richardson*

Economic Performance and the Theory of the Firm
The Selected Papers of David J. Teece
Volume One
*David J. Teece*

Strategy, Technology and Public Policy
The Selected Papers of David J. Teece
Volume Two
*David J. Teece*

The Keynesian Revolution, Then and Now
The Selected Essays of Robert Eisner
Volume One
*Robert Eisner*

Investment, National Income and Economic Policy
The Selected Essays of Robert Eisner
Volume Two
*Robert Eisner*